Intellectual and Cultural Property

This book focuses on the fraught relationship between cultural heritage and intellectual property, in their common concern with the creative arts.

The competing discourses in international legal instruments around copyright and intangible cultural heritage are the most obvious manifestation of this troubled encounter. However, this characterization of the relationship between intellectual and cultural property is in itself problematic, not least because it reflects a fossilized concept of heritage, divided between things that are fixed and moveable, tangible and intangible. Instead the book maintains that heritage should be conceived as part of a dynamic and mutually constitutive process of community formation. It argues, therefore, for a critically important distinction between the fundamentally different concepts of not only intellectual and cultural heritage/property, but also of the market and the community. For while copyright as a private property right locates all relationships in the context of the market, the context of cultural heritage relationships is the community, of which the market forms a part but does not – and, indeed, should not – control the whole. The concept of cultural property/heritage, then, is a way of resisting the reduction of everything to its value in the market, a way of resisting the commodification, and creeping propertization, of everything. And, as such, the book proposes an alternative basis for expressing and controlling value according to the norms and identity of a community, and not according to the market value of private property rights.

An important and original intervention, this book will appeal to academics and practitioners in both intellectual property and the arts, as well as legal and cultural theorists with interests in this area.

Fiona Macmillan is Professor of Law at Birkbeck, University of London, and Visiting Professor of Law at the University of Roma Tre and the University of Technology, Sydney. During the period of researching and writing this book she was also a Visiting Professor of Law at the University of Gothenburg.

Intellectual and Cultural Property

Between Market and Community

Fiona Macmillan

Routledge
Taylor & Francis Group
LONDON AND NEW YORK

First published 2021
by Routledge
2 Park Square, Milton Park, Abingdon, Oxon OX14 4RN

and by Routledge
605 Third Avenue, New York, NY 10017

First issued in paperback 2022

Routledge is an imprint of the Taylor & Francis Group, an informa business

Publisher's Note
The publisher has gone to great lengths to ensure the quality of this reprint but points out that some imperfections in the original copies may be apparent.

British Library Cataloguing-in-Publication Data
A catalogue record for this book is available from the British Library

Library of Congress Cataloging-in-Publication Data
A catalog record has been requested for this book

ISBN: 978-0-367-62087-5 (pbk)
ISBN: 978-1-138-38806-2 (hbk)
ISBN: 978-0-429-42584-4 (ebk)

DOI: 10.4324/9780429425844

Typeset in Galliard
by codeMantra

For my parents, James Macmillan and
Lois Marjorie Macmillan

And for the youngest members of my family, Jahna, Taylar, Jayalaani and Bennelong, Gumbaynggirr people and citizens of a Western post-colonial state, in the hope of a better world to come.

Contents

Preface xi
List of abbreviations xiii

1 Copyright and cultural production **1**
1 Introduction 1
1.1 The Fall of Icarus and the burden of genius 1
1.2 Structure of the book 4
1.3 A brief note on terminology 6
2 The long history of copyright and its consequences 7
2.1 Regulating the "creative arts" 7
2.2 Printers' privileges, market regulation and aesthetic theory 8
3 Copyright in international law 12
4 The politics of copyright 16
5 The political economy of copyright: critical approaches 22
5.1 The property paradigm 22
5.2 The market paradigm and investment rights 24
5.3 Labour 27
5.4 The state, politics and geo-politics 31
5.5 Creativity and innovation 35
5.6 The non-propertized space of cultural production 37

2 Hyperreality and the non-propertized domain of intellectual space **40**
1 Introduction: imagining intellectual space 40
2 Intellectual space, intellectual property and the non-propertized zone 43
3 The power of property in intellectual space 48
4 Cultural property/heritage in intellectual space 51
5 While we're talking about the Romans … 57

3 Heritage, law and community **60**
1 Introduction: the UNESCO regime in geo-political context 60
2 The concept of cultural heritage 66
2.1 The UNESCO regime 66
2.2 An overarching concept? 69
2.3 Identity, community, property 70
3 Intangible cultural heritage 72
3.1 Defining intangible cultural heritage 72
3.2 Intangible cultural heritage and community 75
3.3 Intangible cultural heritage and intellectual property 79
4 Cultural property and decolonization 83
4.1 Claims of developing countries and Indigenous Peoples 84
4.2 Tangibility, intangibility and the privatization of cultural heritage 87
4.3 Public v private claims to cultural heritage 88
5 Asking too much of heritage? 90

4 Community and cultural property **92**
1 Introduction: critical heritage studies v the authorized heritage discourse 92
2 Recognizing community 94
3 Community and law 102
4 Community and copyright law 104
5 The complex reality 108

5 The monumental occidental tragedy **112**
1 Introduction: the West v the rest 112
2 Tangibility, intangibility and digitization 114
2.1 Re-representation and co-constitution 118
2.2 Access and use 120
2.3 Intellectual property (again) 121
3 Immoveability and monumentality 123
4 Moving targets 127
4.1 Origin and community (again) 128
4.2 Decontextualization 132
4.3 Conservation and destruction 136
5 Authenticity 140
6 Nature and culture 150
7 Being flattened by the capitalist steamroller 157

6 **Explorations in the cultural landscape – arts festivals** 159
1 Introduction: here, there and everywhere 159
2 Definitions: being together in no man's land 160
3 Saturated by copyright? 162
3.1 Performance and text 166
3.2 Ephemeral performances 167
3.3 Interactive works 167
3.4 Things that are not copyright works 168
4 The festival space: cultural production and community 170
5 Law in the festival space 172
6 Re-appropriating the space of community 174

7 **Living between market and community** 177
1 The dynamic duo 177
2 Copyright, creativity and the commons 181
3 Cultural rights 184
4 Heritage or property? 187
5 Embedding the market in community 196
5.1 Rethinking copyright 199
5.2 Radicalizing cultural (heritage/)property 202
6 A last (short) word on heritage as a cosmopolitan ideal 208

Index 211

Preface

This book is the product of at least 25 years of often disorganized thought about the relationship between intellectual property and cultural production. It is impossible for me to thank all the people who have had a role in helping me to develop what I hope are now better organized and further elaborated arguments. However, there are some whose contribution has been fundamental.

During the writing of this book, I have been part of academic communities that have sustained me in a variety of ways that are essential to the scholarly process. For this support, I thank my colleagues in the School of Law at Birkbeck, in the Department of Law at the University of Roma Tre, in the Department of Law at the University of Gothenburg, in the Faculty of Law at the University of Technology, Sydney, and in the interdisciplinary community of the International Society for the History and Theory of Intellectual Property (ISHTIP, www.ishtip.org).

Colin Perrin has been, as always, the most generous and princely of publishers. I am grateful for his irreplaceable help in giving order to the ideas and arguments in this book and – not for the first time – for his Zen-like patience.

I owe particular debts of gratitude to Kathy Bowrey and to Rosemary Coombe, with whom I seem to have been discussing the ideas presented in the book forever (or, at least in Kathy's case, since about 1996). Those discussions, and their work, have been essential to the elaboration of the book's arguments.

For expanding my disciplinary and interdisciplinary horizons (and for other non-metaphorical adventures, including a terrifying walk in a very dark forest), I thank Helle Porsdam, Eva Hemmungs Wirtén, Lucky Belder and Valdimar Hafstein, with whom I collaborated on the three-year HERA (Humanities in the European Research Area) "Cultivate" project, *Copyrighting Creativity: Creative Values, Cultural Heritage Institutions and Systems of Intellectual Property*. Chapter 6 is based on the research I carried out as part of this project.

My special thanks go to my own close community of scholars, many of whose work is cited, all of whom have offered important insights on our common areas of interest that have found their way into this book: Donatella Alessandrini, José Bellido, Merima Bruncevic, Henrique Carvalho, Emilios Christodoulidis, Jannice Käll, Teresa Numerico and Joey Slaughter. It is not just that they have sustained me with their intellectual generosity. It is also that that they have provided me with the affection that I argue in this book is essential to the production of a liberatory concept of community.

Chapter 1, which I wrote some time ago, starts with the re-telling of story by Saki. By a strange twist of fate, the story begins in Northern Italy, and specifically in Bergamo, which has recently suffered a catastrophic outbreak of the Covid-19 Coronavirus. This book was finished during the period of national and international lockdown. Never has community seemed more important to me. And never has it seemed more pressing that markets are embedded in, and play their role as part of, community. I hope that the book will be some sort of contribution to a necessary re-thinking of the world.

Fiona Macmillan
Rome, April 2020

List of abbreviations

CCD	UNESCO Convention on the Protection and Promotion of the Diversity of Cultural Expressions
CDPA	Copyright, Designs and Patents Act 1988 (UK)
CICH	UNESCO Convention for the Safeguarding of the Intangible Cultural Heritage
DRIPs	United Nations Declaration on the Rights of Indigenous Peoples
GLAM	Galleries, Libraries, Archives, Museums
ICOMOS	International Council on Monuments and Sites
TRIPs AGREEMENT	WTO Agreement on Trade-Related Aspects of Intellectual Property Rights
UN	United Nations
UNESCO	United Nations Educational, Scientific and Cultural Organisation
UNIDROIT	International Institute for the Unification of Private Law (*Institut international pour l'unification du droit privé*)
WHC	UNESCO Convention Concerning the Protection of the World Cultural and Natural Heritage
WIPO	World Intellectual Property Organization
WIPO IGC	WIPO Intergovernmental Committee on Intellectual Property and Genetic Resources, Traditional Knowledge and Folklore
WTO	World Trade Organization

Chapter 1

Copyright and cultural production

1 Introduction

1.1 The Fall of Icarus and the burden of genius

In Saki's *The Background*, the unfortunate Henri Deplis, a Luxembourger by birth and a commercial traveller by profession, receives a legacy from a distant relative.[1] Finding himself "in a small town of Northern Italy", he decides to "patronize local art" by getting a tattoo from one Andreas Pincini, who "was, perhaps, the most brilliant master of tattoo craft that Italy had ever known".[2] In return for the agreed price of 600 francs, Pincini covers Deplis' back with a tattoo of the Fall of Icarus. Deplis is disappointed by the design as he

> had suspected Icarus of being a fortress taken by Wallenstein in the Thirty Years' War, but he was more than satisfied with the execution of the work, which was proclaimed by all who had the privilege of seeing it as Pincini's masterpiece.[3]

And, as it turns out, also the tattoo artist's final work as he dies before Deplis has paid him. At this point, any lingering disappointment on the part of Deplis gives way to a new series of problems. He is unable to pay the agreed price to Pincini's widow, who cancels the sale to Deplis of the "work of art" and presents it instead to the municipality of Bergamo. Deplis slips away to Rome but, as Saki tells us:

> [H]e bore on his back the burden of the dead man's genius. On presenting himself one day in the steaming corridor of a vapour bath, he was at once hustled back into his clothes by the proprietor, who was a North Italian, and who emphatically refused to allow the celebrated Fall of Icarus to be

1 Saki (H H Munro), "The Background" in *The Chronicles of Clovis* (London & New York: John Lane, 1912), 60–66.
2 Saki, n 1 above, at 61.
3 Saki, n 1 above, at 61.

> publicly on view without the permission of the municipality of Bergamo. Public interest and official vigilance increased as the matter became more widely known, and Deplis was unable to take a simple dip in the sea or river on the hottest afternoon unless clothed up to the collar-bone in a substantial bathing garment. Later on the authorities of Bergamo conceived the idea that salt water might be injurious to the masterpiece, and a perpetual injunction was obtained which debarred the muchly harassed commercial traveller from sea bathing under any circumstances. Altogether, he was fervently thankful when his firm of employers found him a new range of activities in the neighbourhood of Bordeaux. His thankfulness, however, ceased abruptly at the Franco-Italian frontier. An imposing array of official force barred his departure, and he was sternly reminded of the stringent law which forbids the exportation of Italian works of art.[4]

A diplomatic fracas was followed by a controversy over the provenance of the work, followed in its turn by another over Pincini's private life: "The whole of Italy and Germany were drawn into the dispute, and the rest of Europe was soon involved in the quarrel".[5] Clearly traumatized, our man Deplis "drifted into the ranks of Italian anarchists" until finally one day "in the heat of debate" a fellow anarchist spilt a "corrosive liquid" on his back completely obliterating Pincini's last work.[6] The fellow anarchist receives a prison sentence "for defacing a national art treasure" and Deplis is deported.[7] His final fate is to wander "the quieter streets of Paris, especially in the neighbourhood of the Ministry of the Fine Arts" where he "nurses the illusion that he is one of the lost arms of the Venus De Milo, and hopes that the French government may be persuaded to buy him".[8]

Many of the themes of this book are reflected in this ironic and slightly macabre story. Perhaps most obviously, the story examines the implications of the idea that the function of "genius" in converting the surface on which it is inscribed into property might also give rise to competing claims. In this story, not only has Deplis' interest in his own body been subsumed in that created by Pincini's work of art, but also he finds his right over his body to be circumscribed by a sort of public interest in the work that he carries on his back. His body has not only been turned into someone else's private property, but also into a site of contested state heritage. The mixing of the human body with the work of art echoes Locke's famous notion of the mixing of labour and found items, but this is not just about the relationship between labour and the production of capital.[9] Not

4 Saki, n 1 above, at 62–63.
5 Saki, n 1 above, at 65.
6 Saki, n 1 above, at 65.
7 Saki, n 1 above, at 66.
8 Saki, n 1 above, at 66.
9 John Locke, *Second Treatise of Government* (London: Awnsham & Churchill, 1690), ch 5.

only was this labour a work of genius, it was also a work of national genius. These two claims set the work, now irretrievably mixed with the body of Deplis, off on two different trajectories. On the one hand, Deplis' back has become the private property of Pincini and then his unhappy widow. On the other, the cultural significance of Pincini's genius makes Deplis' back a site of contestation involving Bergamo, Italy, Germany, France "and the rest of Europe". In the story, Saki dilutes the possible conflict between these two trajectories, the property claim and the heritage claim, by the transfer of the property in the work (and body of Deplis) to the city of Bergamo. However, he leaves in play the heritage claim, contested between different levels of community represented by local, national and supranational entities. Saki seems to have his tongue firmly in his cheek here too: perhaps the fact that Deplis is liberated by an anarchist is intended to remind us of the contestability – if not more – of all these political structures as forms of community.

One of the special charms of Saki's story, at least for me, is the character of the heritage that has subsumed the body of the unfortunate Deplis. Not something old and dusty on a museum shelf or a picturesque ruin (of the sort imagined by Deplis prior to the execution of the commission), rather the idea of heritage in this story is something that is absolutely contemporary, vaguely outside the mainstream of artistic production and perhaps also outside a certain type of cultural respectability.[10] The story thus puts into question – ironically, of course – certain received notions of what might be cultural heritage/property. At the same time, it absolutely confirms others. In particular, it is the very tangible nature of the disputed work (and body) that gives force to this story, even though what we might call the intangible nature of Deplis' distress is increasingly present. However, Saki's piss-take of both intellectual property and cultural heritage does not just remind us of the tangibility/intangibility distinction that permeates regulation in these areas. It also invokes a range of other Cartesian dualisms that are critical to the way in which the concepts of intellectual property and cultural heritage have played out in Western law and politics. The story questions the division between what is movable and what is immovable. Of course, the tattoo could be moved from its site (Deplis' back) but the consequences would not be reasonable or pretty – either for Deplis or for Pincini's work of art. Deplis, himself, can move within limits but only by carrying the burden of genius he bears upon his back. The Western obsession with conservation (good) as the opposite of destruction (bad) is played out as he suffers a variety of privations in the name of the former. And, even the discourse of authentic versus fake rears its

10 The fact that tattoos have become part of the social mainstream now should not be allowed to obscure the fact that even in more recent times, authorized representatives of the establishment would likely have had difficulty in understanding a tattoo as an artistic work: see, e.g , Lawton LJ in *Merchandising Corp v Harpbond* [1983] FSR 32; cf. L Bently & B Sherman, *Intellectual Property Law* (Oxford: Oxford University Press, 5th edition, 2018), ch 3, section 5.

head: Deplis' tragedy is to pass, after a "political" intervention, from being the site of an authentic work of genius to a needy fake. On top of all of this, the story cocks an obvious snook at the nature-culture distinction.

There are, of course, things that are not in Saki's story that are important to the narrative of this book. It says little (or nothing) about the geo-political role of Western capitalist relations in shaping approaches to the regulation of cultural production, and nothing about the associated effects of the long and continuing post-colonial period. Still, by asking us to think about the limits to the framework of Western thought, it creates a nice little jumping off point.

1.2 Structure of the book

Developing the theme of the pervasiveness and significance of private property rights over what is considered to be creative labour, this book commences with an examination of the way in which Western cultural production has been saturated by intellectual property rights. Of particular importance in this respect is copyright. Starting from the relationship of authorization and constitution that will be argued exists between copyright and currently accepted concepts of the "arts", this first chapter critiques copyright's claim to stimulate and protect artistic creativity by locating this claim within its historical, political, economic and legal contexts. The chapter seeks to establish the proposition that intellectual property rights locate meaning and value within a market context. Chapter 2 engages with and critiques the frequent assertion that intellectual property's system of private rights over cultural production is, or could be, adequately balanced by the notion of the public domain (or commons) in intellectual space. The chapter argues that while being a place of potential political significance, in the sense that it might offer a bulwark against the creeping propertization of everything, the value of the public domain/cultural commons has proved illusory. Not only has it been so seriously under-imagined that its political potential has not been realized, there is also concern that it, or the rhetoric that sustains it, is potentially damaging to other rights, including the right to enjoy and control cultural heritage as a community right.[11] The central argument of the chapter is that concepts of the public domain or the commons are not capable of defending the interests of community in cultural production.

The book turns to a direct engagement with concepts of cultural heritage in Chapter 3, which investigates the way in which the highly contingent political nature of this concept is reflected in the trajectory of international law that governs it. In particular, the chapter focusses on the way in which the relevant international law instruments fail to understand adequately the relationship between heritage and community. This mutually constitutive relationship is the starting point for the analysis in Chapter 4, which considers cultural heritage through

11 See, e.g., K Bowrey & J Anderson, "The Politics of Global Information Sharing: Whose Cultural Agendas Are Being Advanced?" (2009) 18 *Social and Legal Studies* 479–504.

the lens of critical heritage studies. The chapter aims to develop a theoretical concept of cultural property/heritage that frees itself from Western tropes based on the Cartesian dualisms of nature and culture, tangible and intangible, moveable and immoveable. Instead, the chapter proposes a concept of heritage as

> a constitutive social process that on the one hand is about regulating and legitimizing, and on the other hand is about working out, contesting and challenging a range of cultural and social identities, sense of place, collective memories, values and meanings that prevail in the present and can be passed on to the future.[12]

The chapter interrogates the concept of community and then, picking up on the discussion from the previous chapter, it develops an argument about the recognition of community by law.

Chapter 5 takes forward this theoretical analysis by investigating the Western obsessions with the nature/culture distinction, tangibility, immovability, monumentality, conservation and authenticity that have dominated thinking about cultural property/heritage. The chapter considers the way in which this has deepened the misperception of a fundamental difference between the West, Indigenous Peoples and other communities in the global South that have campaigned for protection of their intangible cultural property/heritage, sometimes claiming it as a form of intellectual property.[13] The problematic relationship between cultural heritage/property and intellectual property is also the subject of the case study of arts festivals in Chapter 6. The chapter has two important points of departure. First, it treats heritage as a process, and second, it seeks to demonstrate that this idea of heritage is not confined to Indigenous Peoples and other communities of the global South but is also a part of life in the Western world. Proceeding from the claim that as a public site, as a rupture in time and space, and as an exception to the regular conduct of life, arts festivals are a particular and illustrative expression of community, this chapter investigates the way in which arts festivals expose and mediate the relationship between community and cultural production. The chapter explores the scope and significance of the

12 L Smith, *Uses of Heritage* (London & New York: Routledge, 2006), at 82.

13 My use of the expression, "the global South", conforms to that of Boaventura de Sousa Santos:

> I do not envisage the South as a geographical place, but rather as a metaphor for the knowledges born in the struggles of the oppressed and excluded against the systemic injustices caused by capitalism, colonialism and patriarchy, with many of those who make up the epistemological South leading their lives in the geographical South:

B de Sousa Santos, "The New Thesis Eleven", *Critical Legal Thinking: Law and the Political*, 20 January 2018, http://criticallegalthinking.com/2018/01/20/new-thesis-eleven/, accessed 01/02/2018. The same obviously applies, with the necessary modifications, to my use of "the West".

conflict between the public and communal values of arts festivals as forms of cultural heritage and the private intellectual property rights that permeate the festival environment.

And, of course, the final chapter seeks to draw all this together, picking up various loose threads strewn throughout the book. It is dedicated to two themes: rethinking intellectual property and radicalizing cultural heritage/property. It will, finally, seek to resolve that which is much more than just a semantic problem and which is embedded in the irresolution conveyed by the forward slash in the expression "cultural heritage/property". And it will return to the concept of the market in order to consider if and how the market can be embedded in community in such a way that it forms part of the constitutive process of community rather than supplanting it. The chapter is not uncritical of the idea of community and the extent of its liberatory potential. Nevertheless, it defends its preference for a dominant frame of reference for practices of cultural production that privilege the identity, solidarity and mutual obligations of community over the deadweight of private property rights, often exercised not even by other members of the community but by the media and entertainment corporations who have commodified so much contemporary cultural output. The final argument of the book is for a new concept of cultural heritage/property that is capable of providing a political and legal counterweight to the power of the intellectual property system and, consequently, offering resistance to the processes of capitalist accumulation that dominate the current era of total market thinking.[14]

1.3 A brief note on terminology

For the purpose of making the argument that I want to make in this book, I have found myself constrained to use a number of terms and expressions that contain questionable conceptual value judgements or that seem to beg some of the very questions that I am seeking to prise open in this account. Some of these will already be evident at this preliminary stage. The expression cultural heritage strikes me as problematic, although there are problems with the use of the expression cultural property that also need to be resolved. I intend to hedge my bets on this one until the last chapter, hoping that it will not drive the reader to distraction. As I have also indicated earlier, I am using a number of apparently geographical expressions to describe concepts that are, in reality, geo-political even though I am aware that they are unable to capture the complexity of global geo-politics. The global South as a geo-political concept is counter-posed, confusingly I know, to both the West and the North. In general, I refer to the West in order to draw direct attention to the colonial period and its consequences. The North is used more sparingly and usually in the context of the current inequitable distribution of global power,

14 See E Christodoulidis, "The European Court of Justice and 'Total Market Thinking'" (2013) 14 *German Law Journal* 2005–2020.

without intending to exclude the colonial period as a significant precursor to this inequality. I have no good explanation for the absence of the East in this scheme of things, except to say that east of the particular geo-political spot where I am writing this book might take me into the linguistic territory of the first, second and third worlds. In the interests of avoiding total confusion, I intend to avoid these expressions if I can.[15] I do, however, use the expression "developing countries" from time to time. As much as I dislike it, it has proved a convenient shorthand for referring to states that – nearly always for reasons connected to their colonial past and post-colonial present – fall short of Western ideas about the most effective structures for accumulating capital and thus "improving" their standards of living.

Other expressions that I do not like much, but have used in the absence of anything that might better serve the purpose, include "the arts", "the creative arts" and "creativity". While I have signalled my unease with these expressions, I have mostly chosen to avoid lengthy discourses on their shortcomings. Of course, the failure to come up with better expressions signifies the limits of my intellectual horizons. However, in this respect, I am in substantial – and often good – company.

2 The long history of copyright and its consequences

2.1 *Regulating the "creative arts"*

The idea that systems of intellectual property and cultural heritage/property form two different frames of reference for the regulation of creativity in what is often referred to as the arts or the creative arts is at the heart of this book. The claim of the regime of cultural heritage over the arts will be investigated in later chapters; however, it does not seem particularly controversial to assert at this point that concepts of cultural heritage are strongly associated with the creative arts.[16] The focus of this chapter, however, is the claim of the intellectual property regime over the arts, which largely implicates the chapter in a consideration of the role of copyright.[17] The comment on copyright's history contained in this section will be used to open up an enquiry into the implications of the relationship of constitution and authorization that exists between copyright and those practices that are accepted as constituting the creative arts. Of course, it stands

15 *Cf* the use of the expression "third world" by commentators from the South, as Chimni suggests, in a spirit of resistance: B S Chimni, "Third World Approaches to International Law: A Manifesto" in A Anghie, B S Chimni, K Mickelson & O Okafor (eds), *The Third World and International Order: Law, Politics and Globalization* (The Hague: Martinus Nijhoff, 2003).

16 E Hobsbawm, *Fractured Times: Culture and Society in the Twentieth Century* (London: Little, Brown, 2013), ch 12.

17 Even if, from time to time, other intellectual property rights also make their presence felt: see, e.g., M Blakeney, "Contemporary Art and Patents" (2019) 9 *Queen Mary Journal of Intellectual Property* 244–261.

to reason that if the cultural heritage regime is also concerned with the same subject matter, then the relationship of constitution and authorization examined here must also impact on that regime.

2.2 *Printers' privileges, market regulation and aesthetic theory*

The historical association between the subject matter of copyright and the concept of the arts is somewhat ambiguous. There seems to be some general acceptance that copyright was born out of the device of printers' privileges, most probably originating in fifteenth-century Venice and then subsequently adopted with local variations by a range of other European sovereign states and principalities.[18] Under the Venetian system, which was designed to stimulate foreign trade rather than to engage in aesthetic debates about forms of creative output, the important distinction drawn between various possible forms of the arts was whether they were reproducible through the new(ish) technique of printing or not. Consequently, nothing in the law turned on the general distinction between, for example, written works and images. Considerations of local market stability and foreign trade value were paramount in obtaining a printing privilege.[19] In this sense, the origins of the intellectual property system lie in market regulation and not in a particular aesthetic theory. Nevertheless, there is some evidence that in framing their arguments for privileges, the petitioners came to reflect the then predominant discourse or paradigm of creativity, which was based in theories of rhetoric. The rhetorical paradigm of creativity, which continues to retain considerable purchase in some quarters, focussed upon the labour or creativity of the artist in gathering together and arranging "ideas" into a particular and distinctive end product.[20]

Despite the tortuous and twisting path from the Venetian system to the modern systems of copyright protection, this early history resonates through modern

18 See J Stapleton, *Art, Intellectual Property & the Knowledge Economy* (Doctoral Thesis, Goldsmiths College, University of London, 2002), http://www.jaimestapleton.info/download.htm, ch 2. Other states included France (see E Armstrong, *Before Copyright: The French Book Privilege System 1498–1526* [Cambridge: Cambridge University Press, 1990, republished 2002]) and the Papal States (see J C Ginsburg, "Proto-Property in Literary and Artistic Works: Sixteenth Century Papal Printing Privileges" (2013) 36 *Columbia Journal of Law and the Arts* 345–458).

19 Stapleton, n 18 above. This is in partial contrast to the grant of Papal printing privileges, which appear to have been motivated partly by market considerations and partly by the desire to diffuse Counter-Reformation doctrine: Ginsburg, n 18 above, at 347, 358 and 367.

20 Between the Medieval and the Renaissance periods, an important alteration had taken place in relation to the origins of the "ideas", which resulted in an emphasis on the creator's contribution to the ensuing artistic work: Stapleton, n 18 above, at 70–71, citing E Panofsky, *Idea: A Concept in Art Theory* (London: Harper & Row, 1968, trans J J S Peake), at 35–40 & 51; U Eco, *Art & Beauty in the Middle Ages* (London: Yale University Press, 1986). See also Armstrong, n 18 above, at 78–91; Ginsburg, n 18 above, at 367.

copyright protection of the "arts" in a number of ways. The result has been the evolution of a system of protection that is, at least, idiosyncratic. In some respects, this reflects the general uncertainty that pervades the relationship between copyright law and creativity in the arts. Among the myriad consequences of this uncertain historical association, three stand out. The first is that creativity is protected under copyright law only where its product falls within one of the listed categories of "copyright work". The list of protected works is a result of a process by which, at certain points in its history, copyright law reacted to developments in the creative arts by drawing them into its scheme of protection.[21] Even though this suggests that there has been a relatively dynamic relationship between copyright and its possible objects of protection, it seems that copyright's scheme of protection has now become relatively rigid. This has various implications for the relationship between copyright and the creative arts. One of these arises as a result of the fact that to the extent that any concept holds the list of copyright-protected works together, however loosely, it is one derived from the rhetorical discourse of the Renaissance period. In the hands of modern copyright law, this is reduced to a focus on the production of the discrete "work" by a recognizable creator (or creators). Another implication of the reduction of copyright works to a closed list is that, while copyright recognizes that more than one of its protected subject matters can exist simultaneously in one creative work, there is no evidence that it applies to hybrid works that cross the boundaries between the different categories of protected works. The difficulty that copyright has in dealing with such "trans-boundary" works is accentuated by the fact that the idea or type of creativity that is protected by copyright varies amongst the different categories of copyright works. For example, while a case might be made that the creativity in the look of the final copyright product is protected in relation to dance works (considered to be dramatic works in some copyright regimes) and in relation to "artistic works" (meaning some types of works of visual art), this does not seem to be true, at least in some jurisdictions, with respect to films.[22] (And, it should be added here that the situation is made neither clearer nor more coherent by the fact that films are not regarded by copyright law as works of visual art.)[23] Further complications arise as a result of the growth in the twentieth century of forms of artistic practice based in the discourse of semiotics.[24] These artistic practices, which focus on the process rather than just the product, have posed a particular problem for the protected

21 Bently & Sherman, n 10 above, ch 2, section 4.

22 On dance works, e.g., the UK Copyright Designs and Patents Act 1988, ss 1(1)(a) & 3. On artistic works generally see, e.g., the list in the UK Copyright, Designs and Patents Act 1988, s 4. On the UK approach to the protection of works of visual art, see further F Macmillan, "Is Copyright Blind to the Visual?" (2008) 7 *Visual Communication* 97–118. On film, see *Norowzian v Arks Ltd (No 1)* [1998] FSR 394; *Norowzian v Arks Ltd (No 2)* [2000] FSR 363.

23 See Macmillan, n 22 above.

24 See further Stapleton, n 18 above, ch 3.

subject matter of copyright, perhaps especially with respect to the definition of "artistic works" (works of visual art). Consequently, impermanent works, or works that interact with their environment, often do not benefit from copyright protection.[25] Similarly, creativity in the technical process of film-making does not seem to be recognized by copyright law.[26]

The second consequence of the long relationship between copyright and the creative arts also arises from the impact of rhetorical discourse and is evident in the way in which copyright searches for a balance between protecting creativity and permitting its use in further creative works. One of the important methods – perhaps the most important method – used by copyright law to achieve this balance is the so-called idea/expression dichotomy. This fundamental dichotomy is a key concept not only in copyright law but also in rhetorical aesthetic theory, which distinguished between the idea and its realization in the artwork. The application of this concept in order to achieve a balance between the rights of owners and users of copyright works, while at the same time protecting the public interest in ensuring that creativity is not stifled by the excessive exercise of ownership rights, has been particularly problematic. The growth of artistic practices and traditions derived from semiotics that focus precisely on this creative tension between idea and expression (for example, forms of appropriation in which a work is relocated and re-contextualized in a new work) has not made this troublesome dichotomy easier to apply.[27] These difficulties in application have, of course, had an impact on the way in which copyright law engages with its environment. In particular, it seems likely that the conceptual difficulties involved in the application of the idea/expression dichotomy tend to bolster the power of the owners of copyright works in relation to those who wish to use those works. This cramps creativity, limits free speech and causes distortions in the copyright system.[28]

25 See, e.g., *Merchandising v Harpbond* [1983] FSR 32, concerning the make-up on pop musician Adam Ant's face; *Creation Records Ltd v News Group Newspapers Ltd* [1997] EMLR 445, concerning the assemblage of various objects along with the members of the British band, Oasis, in a swimming pool.

26 This is, at least, consistent with the fact that creativity in the look of the final film product is similarly ignored: see n 22 above.

27 See, e.g., J Kwong, "Fixation and Originality in Copyright Law and the Challenges Posed by Postmodern Art" (2014) 19 *Media & Arts Law Review* 29–46.

28 As I have argued in other places: see, e.g., F Macmillan, "Legal Policy and the Limits of Literary Copyright" in P Parrinder & W Chernaik (eds), *Textual Monopolies: Literary Copyright and the Public Domain* (London: London University Press, 1997); F Macmillan, "Copyright and Corporate Power" in R Towse (ed), *Copyright and the Cultural Industries* (Cheltenham: Edward Elgar Publishing, 2002); F Macmillan, "Commodification and Cultural Ownership" in J Griffiths & U Suthersanen (eds), *Copyright and Free Speech: Comparative and International Analyses* (Oxford: Oxford University Press, 2005); F Macmillan, "Public Interest and the Public Domain in an Era of Corporate Dominance" in B Andersen (ed), *Intellectual Property Rights: Innovation, Governance and the Institutional Environment* (Cheltenham: Edward Elgar, 2006);

Third, more as a consequence of copyright's origins in market regulation than its embrace of rhetorical aesthetics, it might be argued with some plausibility that copyright's focus is the protection, not of primary creative works, but of derivative or entrepreneurial works.[29] That is, of works in a tradable or commercially exploitable form. Thus, the authors of primary creative works, such as literary, dramatic, musical and artistic works, arguably derive less economic benefit from the copyright system than the "authors" of sound recordings, films (which are in a strange hybrid category), broadcasts and published editions (or books, as normal people would say).[30] This is consistent with the proposition that a primary function of copyright law is communicative.[31] Yet, it reinforces the confusion about copyright's concept of protected creativity, as well as leaving the question of what copyright law might be attempting to achieve in relation to the primary creative works in something of a state of limbo. A connected issue is that some works seem to raise different issues in copyright law because, unlike other primary creative works, their connection to particular forms of entrepreneurial copyright work is less clear. This issue is closely, if not intimately, related to questions of materiality in the sense that dematerialized works of primary creativity, notably various forms of literary work and musical work, have an obvious connection with entrepreneurial works. This is not the case for some types of dramatic works and some works of visual art.

Over time, there has been an intense and particular engagement between copyright and the creative arts. The relationship has sometimes been dynamic and even flexible, but it has mainly tended towards a certain rigidity and stasis. As I have already suggested, the engagement between copyright and the creative arts suggests a relationship based on a degree of mutual constitution and authorization. Depending on its intensity and on the degree of its mutual exclusivity, this relationship might be responsible for undermining roles that the creative arts could play in other spheres, in particular the public and political spheres.[32]

F Macmillan, "What Might Hans Christian Andersen Say about Copyright Today?" in H Porsdam (ed), *Copyright and Other Fairytales: The Commodification of Creativity* (Cheltenham: Edward Elgar, 2006); Macmillan, n 22 above.

29 This is notwithstanding the fact that printing privileges were granted both to printers and to authors. On the system of Papal privileges in this respect, see Ginsburg, n 18 above.

30 See R Towse, *Creativity, Incentive and Reward: An Economic Analysis of Copyright and Culture in the Information Age* (Cheltenham: Edward Elgar, 2001), esp chs 6 and 8, in which it is argued that copyright generates little income for most creative artists. Nevertheless, Towse suggests that copyright is valuable to creative artists for reasons of status and control of their work.

31 For a discussion of this proposition, see W van Caenegem, "Copyright, Communication and New Technologies" (1995) 23 *Federal Law Review* 322-347; N W Netanel, "Copyright and a Democratic Civil Society" (1996) 106 *Yale Law Journal* 283-387.

32 See, e.g., C Douzinas, *Philosophy and Resistance in the Crisis* (Cambridge & Malden, MA: Polity, 2013), at 163–165, on the relationship between politics, the arts and Habermas' concept of the public sphere (see J Habermas, *The Structural Transformation of the Public Sphere: An Inquiry into a Category of Bourgeois Society* [Cambridge, MA: MIT Press, 1991]).

3 Copyright in international law

As an area of academic study, copyright has always been vaguely romantic. Perhaps attracted by the two dominant justificatory discourses of copyright law, it has tended to be populated by scholars with a particular interest in the creative or cultural aspects of the subject matter with which it is concerned. Amongst those prone to be receptive to this type of thing, who would not have been seduced by the attractions of the incentive-based justification, with its promises of ever more cultural production and innovation? And, as for the natural rights theory, the life-affirming qualities of the idea of recognizing the special status of acts of cultural production and those who engage in them are more or less evident.[33] Critical engagement with copyright law has, however, exposed its uncertain and compromised relationship with a range of concepts that inform this justificatory discourse. The copyright treatments meted out around things such as authorship, creativity and cultural production – not to mention their specific instantiations in literature, drama, dance, art, music and film – have been exposed in a probing, excellent and often interdisciplinary literature that inevitably dowses overly romantic sensibilities.[34] This body of literature addresses, in varying ways and degrees, the mismatch between concepts and conditions of creativity and cultural production, on the one hand, and their mutant second life according to copyright (and other intellectual property laws), on the other. It also reflects on the consequences of copyright's legal identity as a property right and the way in which the occidental framing of the property concept impacts on creativity

33 For two excellent analyses of copyright's justifications, see W Fisher, "Theories of Intellectual Property" in S R Munzer (ed), *New Essays in the Legal and Political Theory of Property* (Cambridge: Cambridge University Press, 2001); J Waldron, "From Authors to Copiers: Individual Rights and Social Values in Intellectual Property" (1993) 68 *Chicago-Kent Law Review* 841–887.

34 There is a large literature here, of which an indicative list might include the following: R J Coombe, *The Cultural Life of Intellectual Properties: Authorship, Appropriation and the Law* (Durham, NC: Duke University Press, 1998); C J Craig, *Copyright, Communication and Culture: Towards a Relational Theory of Copyright Law* (Cheltenham: Edward Elgar, 2011); J Gaines, *Contested Culture: The Image, the Voice and the Law* (Chapel Hill, NC & London: University of North Carolina Press, 1991); E Hemmungs Wirtén, *No Trespassing: Authorship, Intellectual Property Rights, and the Boundaries of Globalization* (Toronto: University of Toronto Press, 2004); D McClean & K Schubert (eds), *Dear Images: Art, Copyright and Culture* (London: ICA, 2002); N W Netanel, *Copyright's Paradox* (Oxford & New York: Oxford University Press, 2008); P Parrinder & W Chernaik (eds), *Textual Monopolies: Literary Copyright and the Public Domain* (London: University of London Press, 1997); M Rose, *Authors and Owners: The Invention of Copyright* (Boston, MA: Harvard University Press, 1993); D Saunders, *Authorship and Copyright* (London: Routledge, 1992); B Sherman & A Strowel (eds), *Of Authors and Origins: Essays on Copyright Law* (Oxford: Clarendon, 1994); M Sunder, *From Goods to a Good Life: Intellectual Property and Global Justice* (New Haven, CT: Yale University Press, 2012); M Woodmansee & P Jaszi (eds), *The Construction of Authorship: Textual Appropriation in Law and Literature* (Durham, NC: Duke University Press, 1994).

and cultural production globally. However, it was perhaps the emergence of a literature on the political economy of copyright that did most to expose its ugly underbelly and the way in which the romantic discourse of copyright has been corrupted by its engagement with the capitalist system.[35] The ensuing debate between copyright maximalists and copyright minimalists (and even abolitionists) has been played out on an international legal turf that is substantially imbricated with the values of this system.[36]

More than 20 years after the birth of the World Trade Organization (WTO) and its (in)famous Agreement on the Trade-Related Aspects of Intellectual Property Rights (TRIPs Agreement), it's easy to forget that international law in the area of intellectual property was once the exclusive preserve of the World Intellectual Property Organization (WIPO), a United Nations instrumentality. The relocation of intellectual property law within the WTO system was, amongst other things, an acknowledgement of the ever-increasing significance of intellectual property rights in international trade and investment. This was not something reflected in the relevant international legal instruments prior to the WTO. Reflecting the then strong influence of the civil law concept of authors' rights, the foundational Berne Convention for the Protection of Literary and Artistic Works (1886) makes copyright sound like something enjoyed only by individual (human) creators; and although the Rome Convention for the Protection of Performers, Producers of Phonograms and Broadcasting Organizations (1961) protects corporations investing in the creation or distribution of copyright works, the habit of referring to them as enjoying "related rights" created some rhetorical distance from the heartland of copyright. Nevertheless, the evidence of the widespread ownership, trade and investment in copyright interests by the multinational media and entertainment corporations was there for anyone who wanted to see it.

Building on the broad and substantial base provided by the exclusive property rights conferred on them by their copyright portfolios, taking advantage of the horizontal integration of their business interests across a wide range of diverse cultural outputs and organizing themselves internationally through a corporate group structure, a small number of multinational corporate interests came to dominate the global market for the creation and distribution of certain forms of cultural production.[37] As I have argued extensively elsewhere, this dominance, which is particularly marked in (but not limited to) the music and film industries, has produced a range of undesirable cultural and political effects.[38] These effects

35 In particular, R V Bettig, *Copyrighting Culture: The Political Economy of Intellectual Property* (Boulder, CO: Westview, 1996).

36 For an abolitionist argument, see, e.g., J Smiers, *Arts under Pressure: Protecting Cultural Diversity in the Age of Globalization* (New York: Zed Books, 2003).

37 See esp Bettig, n 35 above.

38 E.g., F Macmillan, "The Cruel ©: Copyright and Film" (2002) 24 *European Intellectual Property Review* 483–492; F Macmillan, "How the Movie Moguls Learned to Stop Worrying and Love the New Technology" in L Moran, I Christie, E Loizidou & E Sandon (eds), *Law's Moving*

include things like the global homogenization of cultural output, the creation of a monological corporate culture, the repression of acts of resistance against such a culture, the silencing of alternative discourses and a general constriction of creativity and innovation. My argument has never been that this is some type of global conspiracy (although it might be), but rather that these are simply the effects of a system of property rights that privileges the investment in certain forms of creativity over other non-market values inherent in those creative forms. Certain aspects of copyright law have been particularly significant in this context. The fact that copyright conveys rivalrous private property rights is clearly of central importance, but the methods by which these rights can be obtained and their scope are also critical to understanding copyright's relationship to investment and capital accumulation. For instance, as is discussed at greater length below, not only do the corporate commodifiers in the media and entertainment industries obtain copyright interests by assignment from the authors who, according to copyright law, are the first owners of copyright, but they are also granted ownership rights in some forms of cultural products from the outset as if they were authors.[39] And then, the scope of the copyright interest is broad, while the various exceptions and defences to its exercise seem to be subject to continuing contraction.

Many people who clung to, or were convinced by, the romantic conception of copyright law only seemed to notice this state of affairs after the immense power of these corporations was put to the task of reshaping international law to reflect their interests.[40] It was almost as if the announcement of the relocation of the "trade-related" aspects of intellectual property law, including *even* copyright, into the newly created WTO regime, revealed an aspect of the life of intellectual property that had previously been concealed. This is not to say, however, that this relocation did not have significant legal and political effects. Since the arrival of the TRIPs Agreement, intellectual property law has been explicitly configured as being about "rights" in relation to "trade". For those who would want to see copyright bolstering the fundamental role of cultural productivity as having a value in its own right, rather than a purely instrumental role, some comfort might be taken from the fact that the reference to "trade-related aspects" suggests that there may be some other aspects. But it is cold comfort. Not only is the TRIPs Agreement the dominant normative instrument of international intellectual property law, its location within the suite of WTO agreements means that it is an integral part of a powerful system of international economic law-making.[41]

Image: Law and Film (London: Glasshouse, 2004); Macmillan, "Commodification and Cultural Ownership", n 28 above; Macmillan, "Public Interest and the Public Domain", n 28 above.

39 See Section 5.2.

40 S K Sell, *Private Power, Public Law: The Globalization of Intellectual Property Rights* (Cambridge: Cambridge University Press, 2003), esp chs 5 and 6.

41 See further D Kennedy, "The International Style in Postwar Law and Policy: John Jackson and the Field of International Economic Law" (1995) 10 *American University Journal of International Law and Policy* 671–716; Macmillan (2004), n 38 above.

These two aspects of the TRIPs Agreement are, of course, intrinsically related. The systemic power and concomitant strong enforcement procedures of the WTO are a large part of the reason that the TRIPs Agreement has acquired the ability to define the parameters of intellectual property law discourse. Consequently, the TRIPs Agreement has provided an authoritative consolidation and normalization of the pre-existing real life of intellectual property law generally and copyright law specifically. And that real life is not only as a self-declared "trade-related" right, but even more as an investment right.[42]

The copyright provisions of the TRIPs Agreement are, more or less, the same as those that were already laid down in the Berne Convention.[43] This means that there are not enormous differences between the legal framework of international copyright law before and after TRIPs. Yet, as is well-known, context is everything. The reification of intellectual property rights as trade rights, capable of enforcement through a system of trade retaliation, emphasizes certain aspects of the international copyright landscape at the expense of others. This perception is reinforced by two further factors. The first is that the TRIPs Agreement has shown itself to be a useful uniform basis upon which to negotiate bilateral investment treaties, which may strengthen the oligopolistic nature of the market for cultural goods and services.[44] This gives further weight to the aforementioned suggestion that the TRIPs Agreement might be even better characterized as an investment agreement than as a trade agreement. The second factor reinforcing the nature of the change in the international copyright landscape was that the interpretation and enforcement of international copyright law was vouchsafed to trade law experts. The early example of the WTO panel in *US – Section 110(5) of US Copyright Act* is perhaps worth mentioning as an illustration of the new life of copyright law in the hands of those who know little about its old life.[45] This case considered the so-called three-step test for the validity of national copyright

42 F Macmillan, "Looking Back to Look Forward: Is There a Future for Human Rights in the WTO?" (2005) 6 *International Trade Law and Regulation* 163–180; F Macmillan, "The World Trade Organization and the Turbulent Legacy of International Economic Law-making in the Long Twentieth Century" in J Faundez & C Tan (eds), *International Law, Economic Globalization and Developing Countries* (Cheltenham: Edward Elgar, 2010); F Macmillan, "Copyright Policy and the Right to Science and Culture – Report 2015 (A/HRC/28/57/)" in H Porsdam & L Belder (eds), *Negotiating Cultural Rights: Issues at Stake, Challenges and Recommendations* (Farnham: Ashgate, 2017).

43 TRIPs Agreement, Art 9.1, incorporates the Berne Convention, Arts 1–21, except Article 6*bis* (moral rights) by reference. TRIPs Agreement, Arts 10–14 add some further obligations. In particular, Arts 11 and 14.4 broaden the exclusive rights of the copyright holder by the addition of rental rights in relation to computer programmes, films and phonograms. However, neither of these provisions are unique in international copyright law: see WIPO Copyright Treaty 1996, Art 7; WIPO Performances and Phonograms Treaty 1996, Arts 9 and 13.

44 See P Drahos, "BITS and BIPs: Bilateralism in Intellectual Property" (2001) 4 *Journal of World Intellectual Property* 791–808.

45 *US – Section 110(5) of US Copyright Act*, WT/DS/160/R, 15/6/2000 (hereafter *US Copyright*).

exceptions in Article 13 of the TRIPs Agreement.[46] The exceptions, the scope of which has progressively diminished, are the key to establishing some sort of balance between the exercise of the rivalrous private property right of the copyright owner and important objectives, such as the promotion and diffusion of cultural creativity and innovation. This dispute offered the opportunity for the WTO panel to reflect on the legitimate policy purposes of national exceptions to the rights of the copyright holder, which might be thought to include, for example, the need to balance the interests of copyright owners and users in certain cases. This opportunity was not seized by the panel. Not only did the panel ignore Article 7 of the TRIPs Agreement itself, which speaks about intellectual property rights being used in a manner which is "conducive to social and economic welfare, and to a balance of rights and obligations", it also overlooked the whole concept of copyright as a balance between rights and obligations.[47] The loss of any discourse about balance in copyright law obviously enlarges copyright's potential as a tool of cultural domination and homogenization.

4 The politics of copyright

Despite this unashamedly negative account of the relocation of international copyright law into the regime of international economic law, it must be conceded that it has had an important and positive political effect. This is because it was a key moment in raising awareness about the real nature of intellectual property rights, including copyright. While this owes something to the punitive effects of the TRIPs Agreement regime (and the WTO) on the global South, it has also generated a serious inquisition into the general nature and effects of intellectual property rights. So far as copyright is concerned, the consequent period of prolonged debate often goes under the description of the "copyright wars".[48] Not

46 TRIPs Agreement, Article 13 provides:

> Members shall confine limitations and exceptions to exclusive rights to certain special cases which do not conflict with a normal exploitation of the work and do not unreasonably prejudice the legitimate interests of the right holder.

For a critique of this provision in the light of the Berne Convention, Art 10, see T Aplin & L A F Bently, "Displacing the Dominance of the Three Step Test: The Role of Global Mandatory Fair Use" in W L Ng, H Sun & S Balganesh (eds), *Comparative Aspects of Limitations and Exceptions in Copyright Law* (Cambridge: Cambridge University Press, 2018); L A F Bently & T Aplin, "Whatever Became of Global Mandatory Fair Use? A Case Study in Dysfunctional Pluralism" in S Frankel (ed), *Is Intellectual Property Pluralism Functional?* (Cheltenham: Edward Elgar, 2018).

47 For a longer exposition of this decision, see F Macmillan, "Development, Cultural Self-Determination and the World Trade Organization" in A Perry-Kessaris (ed), *Law in the Pursuit of Development: Principles into Practice* (London: Routledge/Cavendish, 2010).

48 Which are one part of the greater conflict over intellectual property: see, e.g., A Johns, *Piracy: The Intellectual Property Wars from Gutenberg to Gates* (Chicago, IL: University of Chicago

unlike other multi-party conflicts, the copyright wars offer a rich array of strategic positions. I hope, however, it is not too simplistic to say that these positions might be captured under four, not necessarily discrete, banners.[49] These are copyright as a fundamental property right; copyright as a fundamental personal and/or cultural right; copyright as a means to encourage cultural innovation and diffusion of that innovation; and copyright as a self-defeating restriction on creativity, innovation, free speech and participation in cultural life. The brief sketch of these strategic positions in this section is intended to provide a basis for the further consideration of the political economy of copyright in the next section.

An important characteristic of this debate/war is a degree of confusion between reality and normativity; that is, about what the law is (or does) and what it should be (or do). Of course, this is intrinsic to all legal debates, but trying to prise apart these strands in this context has its analytic uses. This is well illustrated by what is generally known as the maximalist position in copyright debates; that is, the position that posits copyright as a fundamental property right. That copyright is a property right is an accurate (probably) statement of its legal nature, the significance of which is explored in the next section. However, the claim that it is fundamental has a certain normative ring to it. While this position is generally located theoretically in a highly questionable reading of Chapter 5 of Locke's *Second Treatise*, sometimes accompanied by a Kantian natural rights discourse, more recent support for it is often derived from human rights instruments, notably Article 15(1)(c) of the UN Charter on Economic Social and Cultural Rights.[50] In a number of ways, the claim that copyright (or any other intellectual property right) is a human right is intellectually unjustifiable and dangerous, particularly so when accompanied by a discourse that claims

Press, 2010); P Decherney, *Hollywood's Copyright Wars: From Edison to the Internet* (New York & Chichester: Columbia University Press, 2012); P Baldwin, *The Copyright Wars: Three Centuries of Transatlantic Battle* (Princeton, NJ: Princeton University Press, 2014).

49 As the discussion below indicates, there is some overlap here with the four theories of intellectual property proposed in Fisher's well-known account: Fisher, n 33 above, but my account is somewhat different.

50 Locke, n 9 above. For its dependence on Lockean arguments, Fisher describes a version of this argument as labour theory, subjecting it to a pungent critique: see Fisher, n 33 above, at 184–189. So far as the role of Kantian discourse is concerned, much tends to be made here of the argument in J G Fichte, "Proof of the Unlawfulness of Reprinting: A Rationale and a Parable" in *Berlinische Monatschrift* (1793), 443–482 (trans M Woodmansee & reprinted in L Bently & M Kretschmer (eds), *Primary Sources on Copyright 1450–1900*, www.copyrighthistory.org, accessed 09/09/2018), which purports to rely on the argument in I Kant, "On the Wrongfulness of Unauthorised Publication of Books" in *Berlinische Monatschrift* (1785) & republished in M J Gregor (ed), *Immanuel Kant: Practical Philosophy* (Cambridge: Cambridge University Press, 1996, trans M J Gregor). For convincing critiques of Fichte's argument, see A Barron, "Kant, Copyright and Communicative Freedom" (2012) 31 *Law & Philosophy* 1–48; F Kawohl, "Commentary on Fichte: Proof of the Unlawfulness of Reprinting (1793)" in Bently & Kretschmer, *ibid.*, accessed 09/09/2018.

a human right to private property.[51] The baselessness of the argument that the grant of private property rights over intellectual output is mandated by Article 15(1)(c) of the UN Charter on Economic Social and Cultural Rights is fairly evident from its text, which recognizes the rights of authors to have their "moral and material interests" protected, but says nothing about the grant of private property rights in order to achieve this end. This was recently acknowledged in a report issued by the Special Rapporteur in the field of cultural rights, even if the same report left the idea that there is a human right to private property untouched.[52]

Looking at the content of copyright law generally, the evidence for the argument that copyright is a fundamental property right is weak, even if it is clear that it is a property right. (As noted earlier, the normative work here is done by the word "fundamental", which is central to the claims of the maximalist position.) The interesting irony (or, at least, so it seems to me) of this strategic position is that it tends to be advanced with particular passion, not by the authors of primary creative works, but by those who own intellectual property rights by virtue of having invested in the production and/or distribution of such works.[53] There is an interesting coherence here with Slobodian's argument that those who assert a fundamental right to property are usually concerned with capital mobility, that is not "the right to own and stay, but ... the right to sell and leave".[54] Under these circumstances, it is perhaps no surprise, as Boyle notes, that "this ideology cloaks itself in the rhetoric of free markets", but at the same time its fundamentalist nature makes it immune to arguments that more rights do not necessarily stimulate innovation or cultural production.[55] For maximalists, it is simply an article of faith.

A fundamental rights claim is also at work in the second strategic position identified earlier, although its political impact is entirely different. The claim, which covers a broad range of sub-positions, that copyright is a fundamental personal, cultural and/or political right is generally based on the Kantian concept of natural rights. Prised apart from the Lockean property rights discourse, this position has much more going for it in a normative sense. At its most general, it also seems coherent with Article 15(1)(c) of the UN Charter on Economic Social and Cultural Rights and with Article 27(2) of the Universal Declaration on Human Rights, on which the former provision is based. The idea that a person is entitled

51 Such as the Charter of Fundamental Rights of the European Union, Article 17(2). See further Macmillan (2005), n 42 above; Macmillan (2010), n 42 above; Macmillan (2017), n 42 above.

52 Report of the Special Rapporteur in the field of cultural rights, F Shaheed, *Copyright Policy and the Right to Science and Culture*, UN Doc. A/HRC/28/57, 24 December 2014, paras 26–29.

53 On maximalism, see further J Boyle, *The Public Domain: Enclosing the Commons of the Mind* (New Haven & London: Yale University Press, 2008), at 198–199 & 228–229.

54 Q Slobodian, *Globalists: The End of Empire and the Birth of Neoliberalism* (Cambridge, MA: Harvard University Press, 2018), at 145.

55 Note 53 above, at 198; see also *ibid.*, at 228–229.

to the "moral and material" benefits of their intellectual creation is intuitively pleasing and, assuming that the moral interest includes the right to control the use of one's work, it also chimes nicely with empirical research demonstrating that it is this aspect of copyright that is particularly important to authors even in the absence of material benefits.[56] This strategic position has generated some compelling work on the nature of the copyright interest, including Drassinower's argument that copyright is essentially a personal right against forced speech.[57] This argument forms a part of some of the most interesting theoretical literature in copyright, which posits that copyright's role as a fundamental cultural and political right turns, or should turn, on its relationship with speech rights.[58] Elements of such an argument can also be found in the report of the Special Rapporteur in the field of cultural rights.[59] Generally, these accounts advance the importance of a strong public domain or intellectual commons, which should be defended by copyright law itself. There is a danger of overstatement here, but perhaps it is not entirely incorrect to describe this position as tending towards copyright minimalism and thus having a completely different direction of travel to the first strategic position. Normatively, the arguments underpinning this second strategic position have considerable appeal although the claim that they reflect the reality of copyright law is open to debate.[60]

The borders of the second strategic position often seem to cross over into the territory of the third, which is that copyright is instrumental to achieving cultural production, innovation, diffusion of cultural works, development and (even) participatory community.[61] This is strange because theoretically the arguments of the second and third positions are quite different.[62] However, in an intellectual environment that has not always been notable for the quality of its theoretical engagement, there has been a tendency to roll these two cautiously pro-copyright positions together. As Waldron notes, this is a consequence of a type of inductive reasoning that "moves from encouragement to incentive to

56 Towse, n 30 above, esp chs 6 and 8, in which it is argued that copyright generates little income for most creative artists, but is nevertheless valuable to creative artists for reasons of status and control of their work.

57 A Drassinower, *What's Wrong with Copying?* (Cambridge, MA & London: Harvard University Press, 2015).

58 For a temporal arc of some of the foundational scholarship in this respect, see N W Netanel, "Copyright and a Democratic Civil Society" (1996) 106 *Yale Law Journal* 283–387; Griffiths & Suthersanen (eds), n 28 above; Netanel, n 34 above; Craig, n 34 above; Barron, n 50 above; Drassinower, n 57 above. See also Fisher, n 33 above, at 189–194.

59 Note 52 above, esp paras 49–51.

60 See, e.g., Drassinower, n 57 above; F Macmillan, "Finding the Inherent Dignity of Copyright: On Drassinower's *What's Wrong with Copying?*" (2016) 28(3) *Intellectual Property Journal*, https://www.abe.pl/en/journal/29708/intellectual-property-journal, accessed 30/06/2020.

61 On intellectual property as a tool of development and participatory community, see, e.g., Sunder, n 34 above.

62 As is well demonstrated by Drassinower, see n 57 above.

benefit to reward to desert, so that something which starts off as a matter of desirable social policy ends up entrenched in an image of moral entitlement".[63] Both these arguments, that copyright is fundamental for, or instrumental to, cultural production, rely on the same normative assumptions that cultural production and circulation are societal goods.[64] As a result of this common concern with creativity, the porous borders between these two strategic positions have also been used to create compelling arguments about the importance of balance and the maintenance of the public domain.[65] While the incentive argument probably comes closest to reflecting the shape of copyright law in, at least, most common law jurisdictions, many of its scholarly advocates have significant concerns about increasing imbalances and inequities in the law's trajectory.[66] These imbalances and inequities begin with the relationship between creativity and copyright's concept of the author. And then they re-appear all over the copyright landscape between copyright owners and users of copyright works, and between the actual authors of copyright works and those who invest in their production and distribution. The imbalance between authors and investors is a consequence of the fact that the grant of copyright is used as an incentive for both, but that one of these groups is more powerful and much better organized to influence the development of copyright law.[67] The argument for such a generous incentive for distribution is located in historical circumstances that made it "an expensive, capital intensive exercise".[68] This argument is no longer compelling (assuming that it ever was), but it has had profound effects of the trajectory of copyright law.

All this means that, while being generally pro-copyright positions, both the second and third strategic positions are also open in varying degrees to the criticisms of copyright advanced under the banner of the fourth anti-copyright (in its current form) strategic position. The fourth position shares the same normative assumption about the importance of cultural production and diffusion as the second and third positions, but (obviously) a radically different idea about

63 Waldron, n 33 above, at 851.

64 There is, even in critical copyright scholarship, little critique of these assumptions: see L Liang, "Beyond Representation: The Figure of the Pirate" in M Biagioli, P Jaszi & M Woodmandsee (eds), *Making and Unmaking Intellectual Property: Creative Production in Legal and Cultural Perspective* (Chicago, IL & London: University of Chicago Press, 2011), at 175–176, citing J H Mason, *The Value of Creativity: The Origins and Emergence of a Modern Belief* (Aldershot: Ashgate, 2003). However, there are works that put claims about the social and personal importance of cultural production under more sustained consideration; see, e.g., Sunder, n 34 above.

65 See esp Boyle, n 53 above.

66 E.g., the English Statute of Anne 1710 describes itself as "An Act for the Encouragement of Learning" and in the US, the incentive approach is constitutionally mandated: US Constitution, Art 1, s 8, which refers to promoting "the progress of science and useful arts". See also Fisher, n 33 above, at 173–176.

67 Report of the Special Rapporteur, n 52 above, paras 38–43; Macmillan (2017), n 42 above; Boyle, n 53 above, esp 196–198.

68 Boyle, n 53 above, at 198.

the role of copyright in achieving these ends.[69] Things are particularly messy here when it comes to the digital environment where many of the assumptions about the relationship between the grant of rights, creativity, cultural production and distribution have been subjected to critical probing.[70] Again, there is some theoretical misfiring and occasional target errors. For instance, amongst those rallying to this fourth anti-copyright position, there is a tendency to be extremely critical of any argument based on natural or fundamental rights. This seems to be a consequence of a failure to distinguish between the claim that copyright is a fundamental property right (the first strategic position in this account) and the claim that it is a fundamental personal, cultural and/or political right (the second strategic position).[71] Those adhering to the latter of these two positions are sensitive to the negative effects of copyright on cultural innovation, production and diffusion, which are closely associated with the fact that it is a private property right operating in an oligopolistic global market for cultural products.[72] There is also, of course, considerable crossover between the instrumental argument that copyright is necessary to encourage cultural production and diffusion and that which posits copyright, in its current manifestation, as a threat to those very values. An important point of distinction, however, is that those who argue in favour of copyright for its capacity to stimulate cultural production and diffusion are favourably disposed to the concept of copyright as a rivalrous private right. They celebrate the instrumental (not fundamental) value of the property right – even if it is often accepted that more limitations on its exercise are needed precisely because of its capacity to defeat the very policy aims that it claims to support. On the spectrum from the third to the fourth strategic position, there are also those who acknowledge the value of copyright as an incentive to creativity but are either unsure or unconvinced that its incentivizing capacity justifies its costs.[73] The anti-copyright crew, the fourth strategic position, is a broad church (of non-believers) and embraces a variety of positions on the protection of authors' rights. What unites it, however, and differentiates it from the third strategic position is its rejection of the idea that authors' rights should be legally realized as alienable private property rights. This, of course, means that there is at least some degree of coherence between the second and fourth strategic positions.

69 Essentially, as Liang observes, this is a disagreement about the meaning of the modernist concept of creativity: see Liang, n 64 above, at 169.

70 See, e.g., Boyle, n 53 above, at 185ff. At the same time, a potent critique of the "free culture" movement lies precisely in its tendency to make totalizing claims about copyright as if this was its only context: see L J Murray, S T Piper & K Robertson, *Putting Intellectual Property in Its Place: Rights Discourses, Creative Labor, and the Everyday* (Oxford & New York: Oxford University Press, 2014), esp ch 2.

71 As Boyle, n 53 above, at 193, says: "In fact, all the mottos of free software development have their counterparts in the theory of democracy and open society".

72 See, e.g., Barron, n 50 above; Craig, n 34 above; Drassinower, n 57 above; Netanel, n 34 above.

73 See Fisher, n 33 above, 181.

5 The political economy of copyright: critical approaches

The essence of the argument in this book is that the political economy of intellectual property is determined by its legal characterization as a private property right. Yet, its intrinsic nature as a property right is the subject of some theoretical scepticism. Most of this turns on the difficulty of understanding property as an intangible that implicates tangible objects.[74] These theoretical difficulties have not, however, had a substantial impact on the life of at least some intellectual property rights in the marketplace where their contested character as property does not seem to have restrained their life as bearers of investment rights. Yet only to understand the life of intellectual property at this level of abstraction would be to vastly underrate its complexities and complicities. A critical political economy of copyright needs to consider its use by the media and entertainment industries, but it cannot neglect its entanglement with politics and state power at both the national and international levels. Any engagement with its capacity to concentrate capital in the form of investment rights must also consider the nature of its relationship with labour. If we talk about copyright as a property right, then not only should we understand it as a means of promoting capital mobility, but also as a means of making a living from one's (cultural) labour and controlling the use of one's intellectual output. At the same time, the invocation of copyright in the context of the so-called creative industries should raise some questions about its effect on values like creativity, attached or detached from industry. And the question of copyright's relationship with creativity not only raises issues about its public role as the keeper of authorized creativity, but also about its impact on the spaces, tangible and intangible, in which we all live. These are all large issues, in the sense of their importance and in the sense of the quantity of scholarship that pertains to them. They are also issues to which this work will return, in various ways, in subsequent chapters. Accordingly, the following comments are intended to provide a basis for the argument that intellectual property rights generally, and copyright specifically, are market rights that have substantial impacts on economic, social, political and cultural lives.

5.1 The property paradigm

The idea of intellectual property as property, tautological as that may sound, has been the subject of a great deal of theoretical attention.[75] As has already been indicated earlier, it has also – much less attractively – stoked the fires of the

74 See, e.g., the essays collected in H R Howe & J Griffiths (eds), *Concepts of Property in Intellectual Property Law* (Cambridge: Cambridge University Press, 2013); J Bellido, "Book Review: *Concepts of Property in Intellectual Property Law*" (2014) 2 *Birkbeck Law Review* 147–156.

75 See the excellent survey of some of this literature in Bellido, n 74 above.

intellectual property fundamentalism that, in the context of copyright, is often referred to as the maximalist position. The various discourses around the idea of copyright as a property right have never really managed to overcome their Lockean origins in, not just tangible property, but also tangible real property. In understanding the political economy of copyright law, this is not insignificant. Not only does it allow us to establish orienteering points for copyright's engagement with the objects of its regulation, it also tells us how it is linked to law's inherently imperialist project. "The law", Edelman observes, "is terrified of an empty space. The land invites me to ownership. It thirsts for a master".[76] The implications for the space in question are clear. As Boyle succinctly notes (in the context of intellectual property), the legal relations of property distribute power in that space: "When you set up the property rules in some new space, you determine much about the history that follows. Property rules have a huge effect on power relationships and bargaining positions".[77]

Of course, when this idea is applied to the realm of copyright, it poses serious questions about over what it is that copyright gives mastery. What exactly is the empty space in question here? To give any kind of answer to this question, we need first to pay attention to the interplay of the intangible and the tangible in copyright's sphere of operations. This constant movement, which has given so much grist to the mills of intellectual property theorists, is critical to an understanding of the impact of the property paradigm on the political economy of copyright. If copyright moves through a variety of spaces, an analysis of its political economy has to be flexible enough to follow. The question of how property rights distribute power in any given space depends, in the first instance, on identifying that very space. This is a particularly tricky enterprise because, despite its utility as a starting point, it is not enough here simply to distinguish between tangible and intangible (or intellectual) spaces. In both of these categories, we must also distinguish between private and non-privatized spaces, and various gradations of one or the other. In the conceptually nebulous space of the intangible, functional spaces also seem to be important. In both tangible and intangible spaces, it may sometimes matter to draw a distinction between national spaces and supranational spaces. And, on top of all of this, it is necessary to take into account the overlapping and interlocking nature of all these spaces. The discussion that fills the remainder of this chapter makes some observations on the political economy of copyright in the space of investment markets, the space of labour, the local and geo-political space of the state, and the space of creativity.

76 B Edelman, *Ownership of the Image: Elements for a Marxist Theory of Law* (London & Boston, MA: Routledge, 1979), at 42.

77 Boyle, n 53 above, at 56. See also C Butler, "Critical Legal Studies and the Politics of Space" (2009)18 *Social & Legal Studies* 313–332; K Bowrey & N Graham, "The Placelessness of Property, Intellectual Property and Cultural Heritage Law in the Australian Legal Landscape: Engaging Cultural Landscapes" in C Antons & W Logan (eds), *Intellectual Property, Cultural Property and Intangible Cultural Heritage* (London & New York: Routledge, 2018).

The focus is both on the function of copyright's proprietary interests in these spaces, the ways in which they are distributed and the ways in which they are enforced. As will become evident, copyright as a proprietary right impinges on both tangible and intangible spaces.

5.2 The market paradigm and investment rights

If it is not too banal to say it, it is perhaps worth recalling the obvious point that the idea of the market is as old as humanity itself.[78] The exploitation of legally recognized property rights in the context of market trading, or what commentators such as Polanyi and Braudel describe as the market economy, if not quite that old, is at the same time hardly a novelty.[79] We live, however, in a period where the market has become detached from its social and political roots.[80] Now, instead of being embedded in social and political relations, the critical characteristic of our neoliberal world, as Slobodian argues, is the legal "encasement" of the market in order to protect it from political interference.[81] A consequence of this legal project of encasement has been the production of what has been described as "total market thinking".[82] Everything becomes subject to the logic of the market and value can only be expressed through the market, which means that it can only be expressed in the form of a commodity. Cultural and creative works are as much subject to this logic as anything else. And when we talk about the commodification of artistic works, then the relevant instrument of commodification is almost always copyright because it is copyright that turns the relevant creative forms into private property. Consequently, it is in the context of the market that copyright locates relationships; and it is in the market that it expresses and controls the meaning of value.

There are, of course, many different markets in which copyright might play a role. As has already been noted, the corporate dominance of the markets for media and entertainment products produces both cultural and political effects. This global corporate dominance is also associated with copyright's function as an investment right in the system of flexible capital accumulation. For multinational media and entertainment corporations, copyright operates, like a corporate

78 What Braudel described as "material life": F Braudel, *The Wheels of Commerce* (New York: Harper & Row, 1982), at 21–22; Arrighi, following Braudel, *ibid.*, as "an extremely elementary and mostly self-sufficient economy": G Arrighi, *The Long Twentieth Century: Money, Power and the Origins of Our Times* (London & New York: Verso, 1994, reprinted 2002), at 10.

79 K Polanyi, *The Great Transformation: The Political and Economic Origins of Our Time* (Boston, MA: Beacon Press, 1944, reprinted 2001); Braudel, n 78 above.

80 A phenomenon that Polanyi demonstrates predates the current triumph of neoliberal thought: Polyani, n 79 above.

81 Slobodian, n 54 above.

82 E Christodoulidis, n 14 above, citing A Supiot, *L'esprit de Philadelphie. La justice sociale face au marché total* (Paris: Seuil, 2010).

share, as an intangible value-bearing right.[83] The continual process of merger and acquisition in the media and entertainment sector, which has led to a high degree of concentration in the global markets for media and entertainment products, bears witness to the financialized role of intellectual property rights.[84] The main assets of these corporations are their intellectual property portfolios, comprised by copyright interests in content, patent rights over content-carrying technology and, of course, the value of their trade names. The objective of the continual process of merger and acquisition in this sector is to gain access to these assets and, in particular, to unite property rights over content with property rights over content-carrying technology.[85] It is for this reason that some of the most strident voices amongst copyright maximalists, arguing for copyright as an (untrammelled) private property right, come from representatives of this sector.

The life of copyright as a financialized corporate asset depends upon the way in which the property rights granted by copyright are distributed; and the way in which the property rights granted by copyright are distributed is a central factor in the production of corporate dominance in the media and entertainment sector. It is well understood that corporate actors acquire substantial interests in copyright by assignment from the original authors of creative works as a condition of their investment in the reproduction and distribution of these works.[86] But this is only one part of the story. Not only do the corporate commodifiers in the media and entertainment industries obtain copyright interests by assignment from the authors of copyright-protected works who, according to copyright law, are the first owners of copyright, but they are also granted ownership rights in some forms of cultural product from the outset as if they were authors. That is, not because they have taken some form of assignment or licence from a human being in circumstances of uneven (or not) bargaining power, but because they have been granted copyright by operation of law from the outset as if they were authors. Music production companies, not the musicians, own *from the outset* the exclusive rights over the sound recording that will become the commercially distributed product; in many jurisdictions, film production companies own, or own jointly with the director, *from the outset* copyright in the film; broadcasting corporations own copyright in their broadcasts *from the outset*; publishers own the copyright in the appearance of the pages of works they publish (whether printed or electronic) *from the outset.*[87] All these rights are owned by the corporations before we even start talking about other rights they may acquire by contractual transfer from human authors under circumstances possibly affected by unequal bargaining power.

83 See Bettig, n 35 above.

84 Bettig, n 35 above; Macmillan (2005), n 28 above.

85 Macmillan (2005), n 28 above.

86 See, e.g., Report of the Special Rapporteur, n 52 above, paras 38ff.

87 And it is in the context of film that we see the total fusion of the creative work with the process of capital accumulation: see Edelman, n 76 above, ch 3. As I have argued elsewhere, film is born commodified: Macmillan (2002), n 38 above.

As Edelman observes in the context of the cinema industry, all this happens because it is demanded by the relations of production.[88] Not to understand the significance of this distribution of property rights is to fundamentally underrate the centrality of corporate systems of distribution in the accumulation of capital in copyrights as liquid assets. It also perhaps results in some myopia about the extent of the influence that corporate interests have over the shape of the markets in which copyright operates, and the control that they accordingly exercise over the direction of copyright law.[89] Perhaps Braudel would have recognized this international space of capital accumulation as part of what he described as "the zone of the anti-market, where the great predators roam and the law of the jungle operates" – the place he described as "the real home of capitalism".[90]

None of this is to say that copyright is not valuable to individuals working in the areas of creative production to which it applies. Copyright not only allows individuals to gain an economic benefit over their creative labour, but also confers control on them – although that control is considerably diminished if copyright does not remain in the hands of the original creator. The types of socially embedded markets that one might have in mind in the context of the exercise of property rights by the (real) author of a work obviously do things other than create value for transnational corporate interests. As Murray, Piper and Robertson show, markets can form parts of communities where the focus is on what they call "lived value" rather than financialized measures of value.[91] The problem is that, while copyright may have a role in creating value in socially embedded markets, the international intellectual property law system, which defines ownership and controls the use of many forms of contemporary cultural production, identifies value through a system of total market thinking. Its creation of an extensive system of private property rights over cultural products is designed to make those products into liquid investments. The result is that copyright law, the primary function of which is to protect investment and the accumulation of capital, sustains a system of control of cultural output in the hands of a concentrated group of multinational corporate agglomerations.[92] This echoes through the spaces inhabited by copyright.

88 Edelman, n 76 above, ch 3.

89 See also Boyle, n 53 above, at 198; P K Yu, "How Copyright May Affect Pop Music without Our Knowing It" (2014) 83 *University of Missouri-Kansas City Law Review* 363–401, esp at 394–397, where he discusses the pressure to characterize music downloads as a hybrid transaction, neither sale nor licence, thus allowing the production companies as rights holders to control subsequent use (as if it were a licence) and pay lower royalties to artists (as if it were a sale); Report of the Special Rapporteur, n 52 above, para 19; Macmillan (2005), n 42 above; Macmillan (2010), n 42 above; Macmillan (2017), n 42 above.

90 Braudel, n 78 above, at 229–230.

91 Murray, Piper & Robertson, n 70 above, at 10.

92 See also Macmillan (2005), n 42 above; Macmillan (2010), n 42 above; Macmillan (2017), n 42 above.

5.3 Labour

As long as copyright is primarily an investment right, it remains a potent instrument for – and, in fact, an ideal example of – the replication of the labour/capital division, where the labour of the author (or authors) is separated from the capital in the property. Despite the constant invocation of Locke's labour theory as a justification for the granting of intellectual property rights, it is notable that the labourer, as a worker, is pretty well absent from copyright law (and the rest of intellectual property law). Copyright's conception of the author of a work is, in many instances, only very tenuously connected with the labour that goes into its production. As argued earlier, the very concept of "author" has been redefined by copyright law in order to build the interests of capital into the heart and soul of the copyright interest. On top of this, copyright's distinction between author and owner effectively severs whatever labour is recognized in its concept of the author from the capital represented by the property right over the protected copyright work. This author/owner distinction means that granting copyright is not the same thing as ensuring that even those recognized by copyright law as the creators of copyright works are able to enjoy economic rights in relation to them. It is the case that in some jurisdictions, the authors recognized as such by copyright law enjoy the so-called moral rights. But, as Edelman notes, the right of economic exploitation always takes precedence over these rights: "The moral right disappears at the very moment it can impede production".[93] Generally, copyright's fixation on the owner, rather than the author, marginalizes the author/worker/labourer from the outset. There is no place in this picture for the labour theory of value.[94] Instead, the figure of the owner (not the author) is the incarnation of capital, and the means by which copyright enables its accumulation. And this is, of course, how the copyright model has produced a system for the commodification of creativity and the privatization of culture, in which the media and entertainment corporations are the major winners.

It seems unlikely that Locke would have appreciated the extension of his theory to intangibles. Unlike tangibles, intangibles are both non-rivalrous and non-wasteable. They are non-rivalrous in the sense that there are no limits on the number of people that can use a piece of intangible property at the same time; and they are non-wasteable because they are not degraded by use. These are exactly the two characteristics that make it clear that Locke's argument does not apply to intangibles. This is because the main concern of Chapter 5 of the

93 Edelman, n 76 above, at 62.

94 Cf. "A different tradition, of the *material* constitution, invites us to begin with the thought that those who produce value in a society also determine its disposal, and that *to act on the contradiction* – as will emerge here in the fraught articulation of social rights and capitalist interests – is to act against the usurpation of value and the denial of a speaking position to the producers of value": E Christodoulidis, "Social Rights Constitutionalism: An Antagonistic Endorsement" (2017) 44 *Journal of Law and Society* 123–149, at 126.

Second Treatise of Government is the responsible – or what we might now call sustainable – use of land.[95] However, Locke would perhaps have had little problem with copyright's concept of the author and its author/owner distinction. When intellectual property scholars quote the famous passage from Locke about mixing one's labour with what is found in the state of nature and thereby gaining a property right over the result, nobody ever seems to comment on the part where Locke goes on to explain:

> Thus when my horse bites off some grass, my servant cuts turf, or I dig up ore, in any place where I have a right to these in common with others, the grass or turf or ore becomes my property, without anyone's giving it to me or consenting to my having it. My labour in removing it out of the common state it was in has established me as its owner.[96]

One could easily draw an analogy here between Locke's servant (and his horse) and the actual author or maker of a copyright work. Locke would have been scandalized by the idea of his servant gaining property rights. The labour of the servant and the horse are simply a means for the economically most powerful figure in the equation to assert a private property right.

It is important to emphasize that the problem is not just that copyright law embraces a distinction between authors and owners that tends to militate against the interests of authors. More than this, as has been argued earlier, it is characterized by a confusion between these two concepts that means that the interests of so-called "authors" cannot easily be identified or generalized.[97] The actual worker/labourer has pretty well disappeared under the joint burden of not only the author/owner distinction, but also the loss of any real concept of "author" in the copyright system. The difficulty (or unreality) of identifying the maker of a work interrupts the connection between labour and the consequent property right. The effect, as already mentioned, is to produce a net separation between labour and capital. This is as true in the analogue world as it is in the digital realm. An excellent example of its operation in the former is provided by Robertson's study of art studio practices.[98] As this study shows, the star system in high end art studios means that the name of the author-artist functions like a brand and, in this capacity, provides a guarantee of authenticity. Copyright's author function hides the unacknowledged use of the labour of others:

> [I]n the art world, authorship in general, and single authorship in particular, is central. This privileging is not uncontroversial ... Paradoxically, one of the

95 Locke, n 9 above. And see Fisher, 33 n above, at 184–189.
96 Note 9 above.
97 See Section 5.2.
98 Murray, Piper & Robertson, n 70 above, ch 8.

> outcomes of postmodern efforts to undermine authorship and individual "genius" ... has been a much wider acceptance of art as consisting solely of the idea of the work, untouched by the labor of making it.[99]

The central trope of the author-as-individual-genius-as-copyright-owner is alive and well in that part of the art world studied by Robertson:

> [B]ecause the image of a studio full of people producing work does not jive with the image of the individual artist genius, such practices are often erased or rendered invisible. Like consumer products arriving seemingly untouched in the store, art works are often presented so as to hide the labor of their making ... [T]o put labor front and center would be to unravel the premise that the idea makes the art not the work.[100]

These observations share a common ground with conclusions that were drawn by Edelman many years earlier in relation to the always-already commodified cultural product of the film.[101] He notes that the common copyright provision that places the producer in the role of author of the work means that "[c]apital assumes the mask of the subject, it is animated, it speaks and it signs contracts".[102] He continues:

> The *determinant influence of capital* becomes, for the law, the *creative influence*; *financial direction* becomes *creative direction*; the *authors* become *proletarians* who are paid for the job which accomplishes a "task" work and not a creative activity, halfway between the man and the machine, and who can be shown the door if they do not give satisfaction. Capital takes on the face of Art but retains the necessary methods of capital: the methods of buyers of labour power, the methods of slave-drivers, the methods of privileged contractors ... This is an amazing revelation. Creative activity, that is, the expression of the "personality of man", can be subject to a contract ... The *contract* is no longer a pure and simple act of will. Its functioning permits the extraordinary mutation which *turns an artist into a proletarian*.[103]

As a result, the director is reduced to the role of assistant, along with all the other assistants whose indivisible work makes up the final product, but who are also replaceable parts of capital's machine: "The thing which is *indivisible*,

99 Murray, Piper & Robertson, n 70 above, at 170.
100 Murray, Piper & Robertson, n 70 above, at 174.
101 Edelman, n 76 above, ch 3.
102 Edelman, n 76 above, at 57.
103 Edelman, n 76 above, at 58 (emphasis in the original).

that is, which constitutes the essence of the cinema work, is *capital itself*, whose representative – the producer – is the sole author".[104]

At least, however, Edelman's creative workers turned proletarians enjoy the benefit of a contract. When we turn to the digital realm, the situation looks a little different. This is because the combination of the severing of capital and labour, on the one hand, and the reality of creative practices in the digital environment, on the other, has produced the phenomena of work without payment and created a confusion between work and non-work, the fruits of which are subsequently propertized – using copyright – by a corporate interest.[105] Consequently, we might say that thanks to the strange coalition between new ways of working and old ways of appropriating the fruits of labour (through copyright), we have a situation in which we can all be a part of the new "creative and cultural economy". We can all be a part of the market – and we can all be exploited in it.[106] The acceptance of this state of affairs results in the undermining of hard won labour rights.[107] Dyer-Witheford has described this involving the creation of a cyber-proletariat.[108] Other commentators, such as Fraysse and O'Neill, have focussed on specific figures in this cyber-proletariat such as the so-called "prosumers" – users of digital products that improve them so that the owners of the intellectual property rights associated with them can reap more profits off them.[109]

Much of this exploitative activity is celebrated and promoted under the rubric of the intellectual and cultural commons. As a result of this discourse, it does not seem unlikely that those who engage in collaborative working practices in virtual space, such as prosumers participating in the so-called "sharing economy", think that they are working (or playing) in some happy version of the commons. This

104 Edelman, n 76 above, at 59 (emphasis in the original).

105 In most legal systems, work without payment deprives the worker of the status of "worker" for the purposes of labour protections: see, e.g., *Betriebsrat der Ruhrlandklinik gGmbH v Ruhrlandklinik gGmbH*, Case C-216/15, [2016] All ER (D) 125 (Nov), ECJ (5th Chamber) where nursing staff assigned to work at not-for-profit association and not having a contract of employment were considered not to be "workers" under EU law.

106 T Terranova, "Free Labour: Producing Culture for the Digital Economy" in P K Nayar (ed), *The New Media and Cybercultures Anthology* (London: Wiley-Blackwell, 2010).

107 See further R Gill & A Pratt, "Precarity and Cultural Work in the Social Factory? Immaterial Labour, Precariousness and Cultural Work" (2008) 25 *Theory, Culture and Society* 1–30; A McRobbie, "'Everyone Is creative': Artists as the Pioneers of the New Economy" in M J Leger (ed), *Culture and Contestation in the New Century* (Chicago, IL: University of Chicago Press, 2011); Murray, Piper & Robertson, n 70 above, 10–23; N Dyer-Witheford, *Cyber-Proletariat: Global Labour in the Digital Vortex* (Chicago, IL: University of Chicago Press, 2015); O Fraysse & M O'Neil (eds), *Digital Labour and Prosumer Capitalism: The US Matrix* (New York: Palgrave Macmillan, 2015).

108 Dyer-Witheford, n 107 above.

109 Fraysse & O'Neill, n 107 above. And on the relationship between on-line gaming, virtual worlds and copyright, see E Hayot & E Wesp, "Solomon's Bluff: Virtual Property and the Aesthetics of Modern Worldmaking" in P K Saint-Amour (ed), *Modernism and Copyright* (Oxford & New York: Oxford University Press, 2011).

advocacy of the commons – and the idea that it exists *in this context* – comes about because we have not factored in a phenomenon that has no precise analogue equivalent. This phenomenon is represented by the technology corporations that provide the means for participation in the digital, networked world. It is these multinationals that profit from the commons, from a space without limitations on the use of information and communicative acts, selling technology improved for free by users and defending their "rights" by control over access. As Murray, Piper and Robertson observe:

> Creative commons non-commercial licences notwithstanding, the great volume of "free" collective creativity is making a small number of people (via corporations) a great deal of money: one only has to think of YouTube to see this. Free culture discourse is impoverished in its conceptualization of the structures and workings of groups, because it understands them only within a neoliberal discourse of voluntarism.[110]

On the Internet, in the digital world, we are always between the Scylla of intellectual property content owners and the Charybdis of the technology providers. And sometimes, they even work together in order to consolidate their respective market power.[111] In the end, whatever is left in the virtual space of the techno-commons or so-called sharing economy increasingly tends to be appropriated by corporate interests of one type or another.[112]

5.4 The state, politics and geo-politics

Having been one for so many years, I know that it is common for intellectual property scholars to draw attention to the fact that intellectual property rights were among the first private law rights to be subject to harmonization through treaty making at the international level.[113] This is part of a phenomenon that has seen a great deal of national, supranational and international law-making attention focussed on intellectual property rights and their enforcement. As a result, intellectual property rights have become invasive in the cross-sections and intersections of private and public spaces, tangible and intangible spaces, and national and international spaces. Here, I try to prise out a few of the most striking (and relevant) strands of this complex tapestry. The central proposition around which the following discussion flows is the fact that intellectual property rights

110 Murray, Piper & Robertson, n 70 above, at 23.

111 See Yu, n 89 above, 398–400.

112 See further T Slee, *What's Yours Is Mine: Against the Sharing Economy* (New York: OR Books, 2016).

113 Famously, in the Paris Convention for the Protection of Industrial Property (1883) and the Berne Convention for the Protection of Literary & Artistic Works (1886).

as private property rights are subject to significant amounts of public (state and interstate) enforcement. In a certain sense, this is not all that surprising. Private forms of tangible property also rely for their enforcement on civil and criminal laws. The obsession of supranational and international law-makers with intellectual property rights and their enforcement might be explained by a similar concern for the protection of private property allied to the intangible nature of intellectual property rights and their consequent tendency to escape the boundaries imposed on their tangible cousins by state borders.

However, if the explanation for the expenditure of considerable state resources on the enforcement of private intellectual property rights like copyright lies in their familial resemblance to private property rights in tangibles, then it seems worth pausing to think more about this line of "genetic" reasoning. To accept uncritically that what applies with respect to the protection of private property rights in tangibles is appropriate with respect to private rights in intangible property is also to accept that there are no important differences between these forms of property or in the political, cultural and social consequences stemming from their protection. There are good reasons why we should not accept this proposition. The non-rivalrous and non-wasteable nature of intangible property means that its "theft" is of an entirely different order than that of tangible property. Like taking someone's physical property, using someone's intellectual property without their permission may be ethically questionable, but this is not because it deprives the owner or anyone else of its further use. Justifications for the enforcement of private property rights over intangibles cannot, therefore, depend on the need to prevent the "infringer" wrongfully depriving the "owner" of the right to use the intangible. Nor can they depend on some sort of benevolent, but misguided, response to the famous "tragedy of the commons", according to which resources held commonly are plundered, degraded and eventually exhausted.[114]

So far as the management of spaces is concerned, strange consequences flow from the idea of a property right over intangibles, perhaps because intangibles have no obvious natural limits. For example, one of the restricted rights in copyright (things that only the owner can do or authorize) is the performance of the copyright work in public. Usually, particularly in the current neoliberal period, when we talk about resistance to power and domination by expanding the "public", we mean expanding the private-property-free zone (the commons), but expanding the definition of the public in the context of the performance of copyright works means expanding the scope of the copyright interest to generate returns for the owner. What really seems to be happening here is that

114 See Christodoulidis, n 94 above, at 130–131, commenting on G Hardin, "The Tragedy of the Commons" (1968) 162 *Science* 1243, at 1244. See further, e.g., E Ostrom, *Governing the Commons: The Evolution of Institutions or Collective Action* (Cambridge & New York: Cambridge University Press, 1990), esp ch 1.

the so-called public spaces, into which copyright works are being performed, are being privatized by the very action of their performance. Long before the expression "neoliberalism" had entered the lexicon of political contestation, the copyright-collecting societies acting on behalf of copyright owners had already pulled off the impressive trick of using an intangible property right to regulate both tangible and intangible spaces: privatizing it by calling it public.[115] It is difficult to see how this would not have had an effect on the dilution of the boundary between public and private spaces (both tangible and intangible).

The role of intellectual property rights in controlling the boundary between private and public spaces has a political significance that tends to be obscured by their legal character as private property rights. In particular, the role of intellectual property in the exercise of state power, especially at the geo-political level, has received limited attention. This is strange bearing in mind the well-acknowledged origins if the intellectual property system, especially patents and copyright, in state attempts to gain control over innovative practices and new technologies.[116] Perhaps the explanation for this blind spot about intellectual property's political significance partly lies in the current neoliberal tendency to think of the economic as not being political, and so not to see the relationship between state power and capital accumulation.[117] In the context of this book, however, it is worth thinking about the way in which the power of the intellectual property system has been harnessed not only to the economic interests of multinational corporate actors, but also to the interests of that community that imagines itself as the Western nation state.[118] Johns traces the way in which enforcement practices have, at the same time, penetrated into apparently private domains, such as people's homes, and also "outward, across the world".[119] Starting from at least the time of the industrial revolution, a key strategy of the imperial powers in the colonial period and of the global North in the current period has been the use of intellectual property rights as one of the means of gaining access to the resources of the formerly colonized global South.[120] This enterprise has required the coordination of private and public resources on a massive scale. As Johns observes:

> By the mid-1980s major trade associations had divisions dedicated to coordinating antipiracy measures in Asia, Africa, Europe and the Americas.

115 J Bellido & F Macmillan, "Copyright after Collectivisation" (2016) 3 *Intellectual Property Quarterly* 231–246.

116 Johns, n 48 above, at 204–205; see Section 2.2.

117 "Blind spot" understates the significance of this: see Arrighi, n 78 above.

118 See B Anderson, *Imagined Communities: Reflections on the Origin and Spread of Nationalism* (London& New York: Verso, 1983, reprinted 2006).

119 Johns, n 48 above, at 207.

120 F Macmillan, "Critical Law and Development" in E Christodoulidis, R Dukes & M Goldoni (eds), *Research Handbook on Critical Legal Theory* (Cheltenham: Edward Elgar, 2019).

> The Joint Anti-Piracy Intelligence Group, founded in 1984, became an intellectual property counterpart to Interpol … [208] Such bodies have consolidated, becoming permanent players alongside governments, the United Nations, and indeed Interpol itself in a vast administrative and juridical machinery devoted to antipiracy actions. … In short, the policing of intellectual property has become a huge hybrid enterprise, in which the interests of states, private corporations, multinationals, and world bodies like the United Nations are intertwined. Its strategies and tactics, as well as its institutional character, have roots extending back to the origins of capitalism in the early modern period.[121]

The technology focus of patent law that might make it a more obvious weapon of choice in this search for political and economic dominance should not be allowed to obscure the important role that copyright policy has played in state strategies. If we were to measure the interests of nation states by the resources that have been allocated, respectively, to patent and copyright enforcement internationally, it would be clear that copyright is also highly significant to them.[122] Halbert has shown the way in which copyright policy has been explicitly aligned to the US state interests.[123] From the export of national cultural tropes and the imposition of cultural hegemony, via the embedding of global political dogma and the repression of the political claims of Indigenous Peoples, to the (alleged) relationship between piracy and national security, national copyright policy has had a significant role to play. What goes for the US also goes in varying degrees for the rest of the global North. The obsession of these states with intellectual property enforcement, increasingly dependent on invasive technologies, exposes the role of intellectual property in the maintenance of the global dominance of not only a handful of multinational corporations, but also of the small collection of elite states in which those corporations have made their homes. With their capacity to invade the sort of space that is not encompassed in the physical space that makes up the sovereign territory of modern nation states, intellectual property rights have been a potent method for the imposition of Western law globally. They have re-ordered every political and legal system in which they find themselves in order to dominate property relations within that system and so to import Western legal ordering. And with this re-ordering, they have also imported the ideology and practice of Western capitalist accumulation, along with Western ideas about the meaning and significance of concepts like creativity and innovation.

121 Johns, n 48 above, at 207–208. And see also Sell, n 40 above, on the coalition of interests that resulted in the US pressure for the WTO TRIPs Agreement.

122 See further Sell, n 40 above.

123 D J Halbert, *The State of Copyright: The Complex Relationships of Cultural Creation in a Globalized World* (Oxford & New York: Routledge, 2014).

5.5 Creativity and innovation

No critical political economy of copyright would be complete without making reference to its relationship – alleged and actual – to creativity and innovation. If the literature on the geo-political impact of copyright as a property right is perhaps thinner than it should be, then we might say that we are faced with the opposite problem when it comes to its impact on creativity and innovation. This, of course, is because the justificatory discourse of copyright is replete with references to totalizing concepts of this type. And, as already noted earlier, much of the strategic skirmishing around copyright has focussed on the question of its relationship to these intuitively attractive concepts. However that relationship is understood, and whether it is fundamental or instrumental, the saturating presence of this discourse provides a good basis for the claim that copyright acts as a "system … of cultural value" and "an archive of creativity".[124] But the tricky questions here are what kind of cultural value and what type of creativity? Since property rights always involve the drawing of boundaries, how do the no-trespassing lines drawn by copyright impact on our understanding of cultural value and on our creative and innovative practices? And what happens in the no-man's land of what has been variously called the commons, the cultural commons or the public domain? In this final section of this chapter, I make some introductory comments on these questions in order to set the scene for a more detailed consideration of the non-propertized domain of intellectual space in Chapter 2.

Creativity and cultural innovation may be intuitively attractive concepts but the question of what they actually are is a culturally contested one. To the extent that copyright has some relationship with them, it is clear that we are talking about Western concepts of creativity and innovation. This is evident from the origins of copyright, from the shape of the law, and from its current uses and enforcement practices. The lists of works that are protected by copyright reflect Western discourses of creativity.[125] The importance of the rhetorical paradigm of creativity in early concepts of intellectual property has already been noted.[126] Subsequently, as copyright law developed as a distinct branch of intellectual property law, it seems to have been the case that one of the markers of the social acceptance of a practice as part of the creative arts in occidental society was the fact that it came to be protected as a copyright work.[127] So, two things that are clear about the system of cultural value that comprises the copyright regime are that it is essentially occidental and that it contains what might be called a "high

124 J Gibson, "An Aristocracy of Authors" (2019) 9 *Queen Mary Journal of Intellectual Property* 1–2, at 1.
125 See Section 2.2.
126 See Section 2.2.
127 Bently & B Sherman, n 10, ch 2.

culture" bias.[128] The fact that the geo-political projection of copyright that has been promoted by Western capitalist states has imposed this regime on the rest of the world does not alter the fundamentally Western bias that characterizes copyright as a system of cultural value. But the impact of Western traditions and values goes deeper than just to the question of what categories of works are protected. It also has a profound effect on how those categories are understood and how their boundaries are policed.[129] That this policing also expresses itself through the prism of class and race should come as no surprise in light of the foregoing.[130]

Profoundly intertwined with all this, the Western tradition of creativity, as it is embedded in copyright's system of cultural value, has been deeply influenced by the nature of copyright as a property right and its relationship to capital accumulation. What is understood as being creative has undergone profound changes as a result of what Edelman describes as "a *necessity* of industry".[131] Focussing on the history of the process by which photography and film-making came to be regarded by copyright law as creative (rather than technical) acts, Edelman describes the way in which law initially resisted the idea that the production of such works amounted to creative acts, but inevitably capitulated:

> The time of resistance was not *economically neutral*. It was the time of craft production. The fact that industry takes the techniques of cinema and photography into account produces a radical reversal. Photographer and film-maker must become creators, or the industry will lose the benefit of legal protection.[132]

But the impact of the needs of capital goes beyond a cultural redefinition of the concept of creativity realized through the legal device of copyright as property right. We have already seen in the aforementioned discussion how the needs of capital separated the concept of the author from that of creativity with the result that, according to copyright law, authors may also be persons who invest

128 See also Murray, Piper & Roberston, n 70 above, at 153.

129 For some thought-provoking material on this point, see, e.g., Robertson's study of art production in the Chinese village of Dafen in and its reflections on the concept of "originality": Murray, Piper & Roberston, n 70 above, ch 8; see also the comments in Murray, Piper and Robertson on "appropriation as an art practice with a single history", which disregards the long Western practice of appropriating non-Western art: *ibid.*, at 32. See further, ch 5, section 5.

130 See, e.g., Boyle, n 53 above, ch 6; K J Greene, "Copyright, Culture & Black Music: A Legacy of Unequal Protection" (1999) 21 *Hastings Communications & Entertainment Law Journal* 339–392; A Vats, *The Color of Creatorship: Intellectual Property, Race and the Making of Americans* (Stanford, CA: Stanford University Press, 2020).

131 Edelman, n 76 above, at 51.

132 Edelman, n 76 above, at 44.

in production and/or distribution of copyright works.[133] Effectively, therefore, so far as the question of the copyright and creativity relationship is concerned, capital dictates two important moves. The first is the redefinition of the concept of authorial creativity to satisfy the "necessity of industry" by the grant of property rights to an extended class of works; and the second is the severing of the redefined concept of creativity from the concept of authorship in order to permit investors in production and distribution to be awarded property rights as if they were authors. The distribution of rights in this way shows, in the end, the fundamental disassociation of the system from the type of creativity that might be suggested by its putative focus on things like literary, dramatic, musical and artistic works. It also creates fundamental costs on the relationship of the system to creativity and cultural innovation.[134] If we accept that commodification of creativity already creates a burden on future creativity by limiting the use of works subject to copyright, then we should be even more concerned about the fact that the form that commodification takes in the current copyright system has, at best, only a contingent relationship to the idea of creativity that underpins much of copyright's justificatory discourse.[135]

5.6 The non-propertized space of cultural production

It is sometimes suggested that the grant of property rights and their enthusiastic enforcement stimulates creativity and cultural innovation. Perhaps under the influence of one of the justificatory discourses of the patent system, the idea is that the existence of clear no-trespassing lines will stimulate innovation by driving competitors to find new ways of doing things that avoid impinging on existing property rights. Apart from the fact that this argument conjures up an image of the wasteful expenditure of resources re-inventing the already-propertized wheel (for the sole purpose of acquiring a new property right), applied to the field of copyright, it misunderstands the nature of cultural production in a number of significant ways.[136] Here, I focus on two that are of particular relevance to my argument. The first misunderstanding focusses on the importance of clear boundary lines, and the concern that a lack of clarity will chill creativity. While it is not clear how one might investigate this claim, an intuitive response to it is that it vastly over-estimates the impact that law has on creative activity. The idea that the limitations imposed by intellectual property rights are upper-most in the minds of writers, composers, artists, sculptors and so on is delusional. Cultural

133 See Section 5.2.

134 See also Boyle, n 53 above, esp ch 3.

135 For a pithy account of the argument that commodification imposes a burden on future creativity, see, e.g., Boyle, n 53 above, ch 2.

136 And, it should be said, of much scientific research, see, e.g., M A Heller & R S Eisenberg, "Can Patents Deter Innovation? The Anticommons in Biomedical Research" (1998) 280 *Science* 698–701.

production, innovation and creativity are not just things that take place through the formation of copyright end products. They also have countless other lives, some of which are community-based, and many of which are also commercial.[137] The live music scene – and many other arenas of live performance – is as good an example of this as any.[138] Of course, clear lines delineating property rights are important for creative activities that depend on substantial investment in their production and distribution. Once capital is involved, property rights matter and this certainly might cause a blow-back on how some creative activities are conceived and undertaken. Nevertheless, to fall into the trap of thinking that acts of primary creativity (literary, dramatic, musical and artistic ones, to pick some random examples) are highly sensitive to where property boundaries are drawn is to adopt copyright's vision of the world in which what is considered creative must satisfy the needs of capital. The other misunderstanding that is implicated in the idea that strong and clearly drawn property lines stimulate cultural innovation and creativity is the relatively simple fact that in some way all such activity is located in, derived from, reacting against, inspired and influenced by, what went before it. There is an excellent literature on this, which in some cases produces a genealogy of particular well-known works and the debt that they owe to their undoubted, and often openly acknowledged, forbears.[139] As this literature makes clear, property rights interfere with this process. This does not necessarily finish in an argument against the existence of any property rights in creative output, but rather in one that favours the importance of a non-propertized space of cultural production.

The fact that this non-propertized space goes by a collection of possible names – including the public domain, the commons, the cultural commons – reflects its indeterminate character and uncertain legal status. It is, as Liang says, a residual memory of the commons in physical space, an imagined space.[140] As an imagined space, its contents and dimensions are unclear, but the general idea is that it is the repository of material that constitutes freely available resources and building blocks for acts of creativity and innovation. As Fisher notes, there are various possible ways of understanding its "raw materials". One of these might be that it is composed of "our cultural heritage – the set of artifacts (novels, paintings, musical compositions, movies, etc.) that we 'share' and that gives our culture meaning and coherence". However, as he goes on to note, such an

137 Murray, Piper & Robertson, n 70 above.

138 And see the excellent case studies in Murray, Piper and Robertson, n 70 above, esp (but not only) ch 8.

139 See esp K McLeod, *Owning Culture: Authorship, Ownership and Intellectual Property Law* (New York: Peter Lang, 2001); S Vaidhyanathan, *Copyrights and Copywrongs: The Rise of Intellectual Property and How It Threatens Creativity* (New York: New York University Press, 2001); Boyle, n 53 above, ch 6; J Boyle & J Jenkins, *Theft! A History of Music* (CreateSpace Independent Publishing Platform, 2017).

140 Liang, n 64 above, at 176.

understanding cannot be sustained in the light of "contemporary copyright and trademark law, under which much of our cultural heritage – Mickey Mouse, 'Gone with the Wind', the shape of a coke bottle – is owned, not by the community, but by individual persons or organizations".[141] Of course, this is an observation that applies principally to "our" occidental cultural heritage, where the needs of capital have tended to eradicate the interests of community, but it does not necessarily apply to the heritage of non-Western peoples. The next chapter examines the role of the non-propertized domain of intellectual space, focussing on the way in which it manages and affects the relationship between intellectual property and heritage understood as both an occidental and a post-colonial concept.

141 Fisher, n 33 above, at 186.

Chapter 2

Hyperreality and the non-propertized domain of intellectual space

I Introduction: imagining intellectual space

This chapter engages with the frequent assertion that intellectual property's system of private rights over cultural production is, or could be, adequately balanced by some concept of the public domain (or commons or cultural commons) in intellectual space. This hyperreal space has been reified, and then valorized, as the place where community and culture are protected from "property", meaning privately owned property, and where creativity consequently flourishes. However, the chapter argues that while being a place of potential political significance, in the sense that it might offer a bulwark against the creeping propertization of everything, it has proved illusory (as might be expected from its hyperreal nature). Not only has it been so seriously under-imagined that its political potential has not been realized, there is also a concern that it, or the rhetoric that sustains it, is potentially damaging to other rights, including the right to enjoy and control cultural heritage as a community right.[1]

One possible way of commencing the enquiry in this chapter might be to ask for the definition, or at least a description, of this space, known variously as the "public domain", "commons" and/or "cultural commons", about which so much has been written by, amongst others, intellectual property scholars. The lack of consensus over a name for this space, however, gives some indications of the difficulty in coming up with something that might fit the definitional bill. Instead, this chapter approaches the question of definition elliptically by

1 See K Bowrey & J Anderson, "The Politics of Global Information Sharing: Whose Cultural Agendas Are Being Advanced?" (2009) 18 *Social & Legal Studies* 479–504; L Liang, "Beyond Representation: The Figure of the Pirate" in M Biagioli, P Jaszi & M Woodmandsee (eds), *Making and Unmaking Intellectual Property: Creative Production in Legal and Cultural Perspective* (Chicago, IL & London: University of Chicago Press, 2011), esp at 170; F Macmillan, "The Problematic Relationship between Traditional Knowledge and the Commons" in S Pinton & L Zagato (eds), *Cultural Heritage: Scenarios 2015–2017* (Venice: Università Ca Foscari, 2017); L J Murray, S T Piper & K Robertson, *Putting Intellectual Property in Its Place: Rights Discourses, Creative Labor, and the Everyday* (Oxford & New York: Oxford University Press, 2014), ch 1.

focussing on the putative function of what it will refer to for the moment as the public domain. Understood in its most celebratory light, the public domain is that part of intellectual space in which creativity and innovation, community and culture, flower unimpeded by the restrictions of intellectual property law. This is what one might call the optimist's description. Viewed through these rose-tinted spectacles, the public domain appears to be a wholly positive, desirable and even necessary concept – basically a wonderful place to be. However, even an optimist might find themselves assailed by doubts about this happy version of the public domain in intellectual space. While not necessarily doubting the rhetorical and (even) actual importance of such a place in intellectual space, one might wonder about things like its efficacy as a legal concept – particularly when posed against the power of law's property paradigm, its ability to create the conditions necessary to deliver the benefits claimed on its behalf and even its very existence. Each of these questions, when opened up to examination, triggers a plethora of related enquiries. For example, the question of whether the public domain really exists might quickly resolve itself into an enquiry as to whether the intellectual public domain is really just a figment of the imagination of intellectual property scholars? (A question that is, perhaps, unavoidable in a chapter that purports to address, even tangentially, "hyperreality".[2]) Consequent questions might look something like the following: Is the intellectual public domain an imaginary space *in law*? Or just an imaginary space? If creativity flourishes in intellectual public space, then what does it mean to say this space is imaginary? Isn't creativity something real, rather than imaginary? Do real things exist in imaginary spaces? In the absence of any sure answers to these questions, one tentative response might be that real things might exist in the domain of intellectual space, but its architecture has been imagined by law. And perhaps the imagination of law is always hyperreal in the sense that it projects a world in which it is difficult to say which bits are fantasy and which bits might be reality. It projects a world of rules and regulations, which constrain and affect behaviour, but never as much as they claim to – not only because law is inherently unable to penetrate all social relations, but also because, at least in the imaginary domain of intellectual space, the impact of law is constrained by banalities such as its inability to operate effectively above the nation state-based system of jurisdiction.

Surer ground (at least if one is an intellectual property scholar with a primary disciplinary background in law) might be found in attempting to describe intellectual space as imagined by law.[3] One of the characteristics of this space is its division into private and public domains. In this version of intellectual space, the intellectual public domain is under threat from the privatizing and imperialistic

2 See further, e.g., U Eco, *Travels in Hyperreality: Essays* (London: Picador/Secker & Warburg, 1987).

3 Fortunately, not all intellectual property scholars have a primary disciplinary background in law, but it is true in my case and may explain some of the peculiarities of this chapter.

tendencies of intellectual property, as it extends its boundaries horizontally to include new types of intellectual activity and vertically to confer wider powers of control on the relevant rights' holders. One of the implications of this claim with respect to the possibly imaginary domain of intellectual space is that it is composed of a simple binary opposition, which divides the whole of intellectual space between that which is subject to private intellectual property rights and that which is not.[4] The two are envisaged as butting up against one another so that, if we were to conceive of this in physical terms, each fits snugly against the shape of the other. More than this, if the two also take up the whole of intellectual space, altering the contours of intellectual property will alter those of the public domain. In this sense, there is a tendency to imagine the public domain as a largely passive victim of the aggressive presence of intellectual property – so that the boundary between the two changes only when intellectual property rights expand.[5]

Given this simple binary division, one might conclude that intellectual space has been somewhat under-imagined, at least in the minds of intellectual property scholars. Certainly, it is true that law's idea of intellectual space is heavily dependent on a simplistic analogy with physical space. This is, of course, an analogue of the tendency of intellectual property law and theory to rely on comparisons with physical property, which has already been noted in Chapter 1 of this book. A problem with over-reliance on this analogy is that it fails to give sufficient recognition to two particular and distinctive characteristics of things, whether private property or not, in intellectual space: first, that they are non-rivalrous (in the sense that they can be used by more than one person at any given moment in time) and, secondly, that they are non-wasteable (in the sense that they are not exhausted by use). However, physical space and intellectual space do present some similar conceptual problems. For instance, the concept of the whole of intellectual space is no more knowable than is the concept of the whole of physical space. In order to give some sort of purchase to the concept of physical space, we tend to assume boundaries that are constructed by our collective limitations rather than any actual limitations of physical space. We apply the same sort of reasoning in order to bound our concept of intellectual space, despite our understanding of the inherent malleability (or perhaps inexistence) of its borders. Nevertheless, as this chapter will seek to demonstrate, the concept of intellectual space that emerges from intellectual property discourse, what it might contain, how it relates to physical space and the impact of its politics, is much less sophisticated than that applying to physical space. Intellectual space, in this sense, has been generally somewhat under-imagined.

4 E Hemmungs Wirtén, "Out of Sight & Out of Mind: On the Cultural Hegemony of Intellectual Property (Critique)" (2006) 20 *Cultural Studies* 282–291.

5 Or, one could add, if they contract, but only in the case of leaving hyperreality and entering unreality.

2 Intellectual space, intellectual property and the non-propertized zone

Law's imagined public domain in intellectual space is largely drawn from principles of Roman law governing physical space. Some of the conceptual problems that arose with respect to physical space in Roman law have also emerged in the modern notion of intellectual space. At the same time, the metaphorical existence of modern intellectual space lacks the complexity of its Roman law forbear in physical space. The relevant Roman law principles recognized various dimensions of non-exclusive – but not necessarily public – property.[6] The most well-used of these so far as the intellectual property/public domain debates are concerned are *res communes* and *res publicae*. The former referring to things incapable by their nature of being exclusively owned, while the latter referring to things open to the public by operation of law. These seem to have loosely translated into the modern-day debate about property in intellectual space in the form of the concepts of the commons and the public domain. The fact that these expressions are often used interchangeably is probably not much of a surprise, given that the Romans had a similar problem with *res communes* and *res publicae*, which reflected the modern-day tendency "to mix up normative arguments for 'publicness' with naturalistic arguments about the impossibility of owning certain resources".[7] This confusion between the commons and the public domain, *res communes* and *res publicae*, has done nothing to simplify the epistemological basis of the dichotomy between intellectual property and intellectual public space.[8] More than this, it has tended to conceal the fact that, traced back to their Roman law origins, neither of these concepts seems completely up to the task of providing a vibrant public or non-exclusive intellectual space in today's world.

So far as *res communes* is concerned, one might be forgiven for thinking that because of the non-rivalrous nature of things in intellectual space, they are all incapable by their nature of being exclusively owned or appropriated.[9] However, by de-linking the concepts of exclusive possession/use and ownership intellectual property law has put paid to that idea. It may also be the case that the non-wasteable nature of things in intellectual space means that they are less vulnerable to the "tragedy of the commons" according to which resources held commonly are plundered, degraded and eventually exhausted.[10] Certainly, things in

6 See C M Rose, "Romans, Roads and Romantic Creators: Traditions of Public Property in the Information Age" (2003) 66 *Law & Contemporary Problems* 89–110.

7 Rose, n 6 above, at 96, citing A Borkowski, *Textbook on Roman Law* (London: Blackstone, 1994), at 144.

8 See also Hemmungs Wirtén, n 4 above.

9 Except, and for so long as, they are kept secret: Rose, n 6 above, at 95.

10 See G Hardin, "The Tragedy of the Commons" (1968) 162 *Science* 1243–1248, at 1244; E Ostrom, *Governing the Commons: The Evolution of Institutions or Collective Action*

intellectual space are not used up in the same way as things in physical space and this might impact negatively on the justification for foreclosing them. However, things in intellectual space can certainly be plundered and degraded, so they are perhaps vulnerable to the tragedy of the commons in a different sense, a theme to which this chapter will return. In any case, whether or not some sort of tragedy of the commons makes it necessary to create private property rights over things in intellectual space, intellectual property law has done it. Or, at least, it has tried to do it. It may be that there are certain things that not even the might of intellectual property law can convert into property capable of exclusive ownership in any meaningful sense. For example, the ease of copying works available in digital form allied with the difficulty in identifying and proceeding against unauthorized copiers, and the jurisdictional issues to which reference has already been made, may be an indication that this part of intellectual space is incapable of the type of exclusive ownership enjoyed in relation to other types of intangible works. To permit this type of thinking, however, would be to risk the intrusion of reality into law's hyperreal world of intellectual space. In any case, the combined effect of technology and law may render even this part of intellectual space appropriable.

Intellectual property law has not, of course, sought to foreclose all of the intellectual commons. As a body of law, it has declared that certain things are incapable of being owned. Patent law, for example, rejects the concept of ownership over a range of innovations, including discoveries, scientific theories and methods for doing business.[11] However, its imperializing tendency means that it is constantly pushing at the boundaries of these exclusions so that more and more of that intellectual space concerned with inventions and technical innovations is subject to patent rights. Copyright law, famously, rejects the ownership of ideas, embracing the tenuous distinction between the unprotected idea and the protected expression, although this concept seems to be unevenly applied and subject to much erosion.[12] More generally, creative acts that do not fall within the

(Cambridge & New York: Cambridge University Press, 1990), esp ch 1, in which the tragedy of the commons is contrasted with other models of the commons.

11 See, e.g., the UK Patents Act 1977, s 1(2).

12 On the idea/expression dichotomy, see, e.g., *Donoghue v Allied Newspapers* [1938] Ch 106; *Fraser v Thames Television* [1983] 2 All ER 101; *Green v Broadcasting Corporation of New Zealand* [1989] RPC 469 & 700. The two-dimensional/three-dimensional infringement rule in relation to artistic works in, e.g., the UK Copyright Designs and Patents Act 1988, s 17(3), arguably breaches the idea/expression rule: see further F Macmillan, "Artistic Practice & the Integrity of Copyright Law" in M Rosenmeier & S Teilmann (eds), *Art & Law: The Debate over Copyright* (Copenhagen: DJØF, 2005); F Macmillan, "Is Copyright Blind to the Visual?" (2008) 7 *Visual Communication* 97. As do, e.g., the provisions on the protection of preparatory design material for computer programmes in the UK Copyright, Designs & Patents Act 1988, s 3(1)(c). On the erosion of the dichotomy in case law, see, e.g., *Krisarts v Briarfine* [1977] FSR 577; *Ravenscroft v Herbert* [1980] RPC 193; *Designer Guild Ltd v Russell Williams (Textiles) Limited* [2000] UKHL 58.

realm of copyright's listed subject matter are not appropriated.[13] However, copyright (along with intellectual property rights related to it) has been distinguished by a tendency to extend its reach over more and more creative or innovative acts in intellectual space. This occurs in two ways. One of them is through formal legislative extensions to the lists of protected works.[14] The second much more insidious way in which the scope of copyrightable subject matter is extended is through new interpretations of old copyright subject matter.[15] The private property rights of copyright owners are also effectively extended by reductions in the scope of defences or exceptions to copyright, which occur either by legislation or by judicial decision-making. Technically, this further form of extension of the reign of copyright is a consequence of shrinking limitations on the enforceability of copyright so that fewer new acts of creativity fall outside the propertized zone of intellectual space. Attempting to analogize from Roman law concepts, this looks more like a constriction of *res publicae* than of *res communes*, and it illustrates their tendency to converge in the context of today's intellectual space. To the extent that intellectual property laws continue to exclude certain parts of intellectual space from the propertized domain, it is far from clear whether their exclusion is because they are, by their legal nature, incapable of being owned, and therefore part of the commons, or because they should not be brought into the private domain of intellectual property but should be kept in the public domain.

In an attempt to describe or understand the relationship between the propertized and non-propertized zone of intellectual space these exclusions from the realm of intellectual property rights have spawned a whole set of metaphorical allusions. So that the relationship between the non-propertized and propertized domains of intellectual space is described as being, or being like, the relationship between raw materials (non-propertized domain) and manufactured products (propertized domain); knowledge (non-propertized domain) and innovation (propertized domain); idea (non-propertized domain) and

13 See, e.g., *Merchandising v Harpbond* [1983] FSR 32; *Komesaroff v Mickle* [1988] RPC 204; *Creation Records Ltd v News Group Newspapers Ltd* [1997] EMLR 445; *Norowzian v Arks Ltd (No 2)* [2000] FSR 363 (CA).

14 The history of copyright is marked by exactly this type of piecemeal legislative extension; see L Bently & B Sherman, *The Making of Modern Intellectual Property Law* (Cambridge: Cambridge University Press, 1999). For more recent examples, see the inclusion of computer programmes and preparatory design work for them within the definition of protected "literary works" (see, e.g., Directive 91/250/EEC on the legal protection of computer programmes & the UK, Copyright, Designs & Patents Act 1988, s 3(1)) and the database right established under Directive 96/9/EC on the legal protection of databases.

15 Examples abound, but two cases that have recently caused much comment are the so-called *Blurred Lines* case, *Williams v Gaye*, No 15-56880 (US Court of Appeals, 9th Circuit, 2018) and the *Katy Perry "Dark Horse"* case, *Gray v Hudson*, No (US Federal Court, California, 2019), verdict reversed in March 2020. On *Blurred Lines*, see further, e.g., J P Fishman, "Music as a Matter of Law" (2018) 131 *Harvard Law Review* 1861–1923.

expression (propertized domain); nature (non-propertized domain) and culture (propertized domain). It is not necessarily clear whether the problem here is generated by confusion between competing ideas about what belongs in the non-propertized zone, the failure of the analogies, the imprecision of metaphors or, conversely, the tendency of analogies and metaphors to expose uncomfortable truths. And the uncomfortable truth that seems to be exposed in this case is that the non-propertized zone can just as easily be understood as part of the market economy rather than a place of resistance to that market economy.[16] Even admitting this, the suggestion that culture (whatever that might mean in this context) is in the propertized domain gives pause for thought. Is this hyperreality or it is reality? This is a question to which this chapter will return.

Arguably, because things in intellectual space are all incapable of ownership in the sense that things in physical space may be owned, but are all – or nearly all – quite capable of being appropriated in another way by force of law, the concept of the commons derived from *res communes* is a difficult one to apply to intellectual space. At least, it is difficult once we concede any concept of ownership in intellectual space, unless by referring to the commons we merely mean to be descriptive and refer to those things that, as a matter of fact, have not for whatever reason been subsumed into the intellectual property regime.[17] Despite its vagueness, or maybe because of it, the concept of the commons has enjoyed considerable purchase in intellectual property theory. It is a foundational concept for Lockean theorists of intellectual property.[18] For copyright maximalists who locate their concept of fundamental property rights in a reading of Locke, it may very well be that a rather vague and weak notion of the commons does them good service.[19] However, the concept of the commons or the cultural commons, either in the sense of *res communes* or blended with other concepts of openness such as those deriving from *res publicae*, has also been critically elaborated in much stronger forms by a range of intellectual property theorists and commentators.[20]

16 See further Murray, Piper & Roberston, n 1 above, ch 5 on Exchange Practices among Nineteenth-Century Newspaper Editors, esp at 91, quoting Y Benkler, "Between Spanish Huertas and the Open Road: A Tale of Two Commons?" (Paper presented at the *Convening Cultural Commons* Conference, New York University, September 2011) & at 106: "A case study such as this reminds us that commons are not innocent or isolated from capital".

17 See also W Fisher, "Theories of Intellectual Property" in S R Munzer (ed), *New Essays in the Legal and Political Theory of Property* (Cambridge: Cambridge University Press, 2001), at 186–188, reflecting on the possible modern interpretation of the Lockean "commons".

18 As a result of Locke's famous proviso on the limits to private appropriation: John Locke, *Second Treatise of Government* (London: Awnsham & Churchill, 1690), ch 5. See also Fisher, n 17 above.

19 On this maximalist position, see ch 1, section 4.

20 See, e.g., J Boyle, *The Public Domain: Enclosing the Commons of the Mind* (New Haven, CT & London: Yale University Press, 2008); M Bruncevic, *Law, Art and the Commons: Space, Materiality and the Normative* (Oxford & New York: Routledge, 2018); E Hemmungs Wirtén, *Terms*

The concept of the *res publicae*, where there is a scope for what Rose describes as "normative arguments for 'publicness'", seems to offer greater promise for a more complex architecture in intellectual space.[21] The primary reason for this, at least in relation to physical space, is that being *res publicae* implies appropriability, if not actual appropriation. Unlike the concept of *res communes*, *res publicae* in physical space does not reject the notion of private property. According to Rose, *res publicae* is always open to the possibility of ownership "subject to the requirements of reasonable public access".[22] One consequence of this is that it is necessary for something or someone to defend *res publicae*. In physical space, *res publicae* is regarded as normatively justified by the need to ensure productive synergistic interactions that would otherwise be obstructed by denying public access.[23] The irony in the application of this concept to intellectual space is that precisely because things in intellectual space are non-rivalrous, there are not many reasons why productive synergistic interactions should not take place.[24] That is, there are not many reasons apart from intellectual property law itself. By regarding things in intellectual space as capable of appropriation and not therefore *res communes*, intellectual property law has created a system of obstructions to synergistic interactions. Then, in response to these obstructions, it has created its own mechanisms to defend *res publicae*. The reasoning animating this somewhat circuitous process is that without the grant of property rights productive synergistic interactions might not take place in unfettered intellectual space because, in the absence of an incentive, appropriate investment and effort might not be made.[25] The ways in which arguments of this type misunderstand acts of primary creativity have already been the subject of some comment in Chapter 1. Even accepting this argument with respect to investment in creative production and distribution, and accepting that the most appropriate form of "incentive" is the creation of intellectual property rights,[26] it seems reasonably clear that to

of Use: Negotiating the Jungle of the Intellectual Commons (Toronto: University of Toronto Press, 2008).

21 Rose, n 6 above, at 96.

22 Rose, n 6 above, at 99. On the attributes of *res publicae*, see, Rose, *ibid.*, at 96–100.

23 Rose, n 6 above, at 96–98.

24 See also Rose, n 6 above, at 102–103.

25 On the incentive theory of copyright, see ch 1, section 4. On the relationship between the "static inefficiencies" of intellectual property and "dynamic benefits" (or, more precisely, the lack thereof), see J E Stiglitz, "Economic Foundations of Intellectual Property Rights" (2008) 57 *Duke Law Journal* 1693–1724, at 1702–1704.

26 A point that is not universally accepted: see, e.g., J Smiers, "The Abolition of Copyrights: Better for Artists, Third World Countries & the Public Domain" in R Towse (ed), *Copyright & the Cultural Industries* (Cheltenham: Edward Elgar, 2002); M van Schijndel & J Smiers, "Imagining a World without Copyright: The Market & Temporary Protection a Better Alternative for Artists & the Public Domain" in H Porsdam (ed), *Copyright & Other Fairy Tales* (Cheltenham: Edward Elgar, 2005); J Smiers & M van Schijndel, *La fine del copyright. Come creare un mercato culturale aperto a tutti* (Viterbo: Stampa Alternativa, 2010). And see also ch 1, section 4.

achieve productive synergistic interactions, there needs to be a carefully calibrated balance between property rights in intellectual space and rights that preserve *res publicae*. In intellectual property law, this is generally achieved through three mechanisms: disclosure requirements, limits on duration and exceptions to the exercise of the exclusive rights. With respect to the first two mechanisms, the provisions of the law automatically defend the *res publicae*, whereas in relation to the last, those seeking to use the exceptions must make a case. Despite the existence of these mechanisms, it would be straining credulity to suggest that the balance between property rights and rights that preserve *res publicae* in intellectual space is carefully calibrated.[27] The history of intellectual property law has marked a progressive extension of the duration of intellectual property rights and the contraction of their respective exceptions and defences.[28] This suggests, of course, that to be effective, that part of the non-propertized domain that is represented by *res publicae* may need some improved legal architecture.

3 The power of property in intellectual space

So what if the non-propertized part of hyperreal intellectual space is contracting? The reason that preserving a non-propertized zone has come to matter so much in the debate about intellectual space and its creeping propertization is not just because of some intuitively appealing ideas about the importance of balance between it and the propertized domain; it is rather a consequence of the dangers posed by the power of those few who hold so much of the really bankable property in intellectual space.[29] Intellectual space is no longer divided between a non-propertized zone and a propertized zone in which a rich diversity of author-originators and inventor-originators each wields exclusive rights over a small plot. To be sure, these people still exist as owners of intellectual property rights. But, as Chapter 1 argues, the commodifiable nature of intellectual property rights means that vast tracts of prime intellectual space have been bought up

27 For an excellent account of the history of the public domain and its contraction, see Boyle, n 20 above.

28 See, e.g., L A F Bently & T Aplin, "Whatever Became of Global Mandatory Fair Use? A Case Study in Dysfunctional Pluralism" in S Frankel (ed), *Is Intellectual Property Pluralism Functional?* (Cheltenham: Edward Elgar, 2018). Although (for optimists) the fair dealing/fair use right continues to have some liberatory potential, especially in Canada: see, e.g., R J Coombe, D Wershler & M Zeilinger (eds), *Dynamic Fair Dealing: Creating Canadian Culture Online* (Toronto: University of Toronto Press, 2014); A Drassinower, "From Distribution to Dialogue: Remarks on the Concept of Balance in Copyright Law" (2009) 34 *Journal of Corporation Law* 991–1007; E L Rosenblatt, "Fair Use as Resistance" (2019) 9 *UC Irvine Law Review* 377–400.

29 For a full exposition of this argument in relation to the copyright industries, see F Macmillan, "Public Interest and the Public Domain in an Era of Corporate Dominance" in B Andersen (ed), *Intellectual Property Rights: Innovation, Governance and the Institutional Environment* (Cheltenham: Edward Elgar, 2005). And see ch 1, esp sections 3, 5.1 and 5.2.

by powerful multinational corporate interests.[30] Here, the analogy with physical space similarly held is alarming – and rightly so. This power, which resides to a considerable degree in the hands of concentrated corporate sectors, means that its members are able to exert undue control over the direction of significant areas of cultural and technical development.[31] Even more seriously, the power that has been acquired by the corporate players, partly although not exclusively on the back of intellectual property rights, means that they are able to exert more and more control over the shape of intellectual property law itself.[32]

In the imaginary world of intellectual space, the non-propertized zone of intellectual space is the place in which the power of the corporate giants can be challenged and resisted. One of the reasons why the power of the concentrated corporate sectors over the development and direction of intellectual property law is a matter of such concern is that intellectual property has a symbiotic relationship with its non-propertized counterpart. That is, in intellectual space, the propertized zone shapes the non-propertized zone, which might be conceived of alternatively as its progeny, rather than being in a binary opposition to it.[33] In this lies the tragedy of the modern public domain/commons in intellectual space. If the formation of intellectual property law is subject to the power of those who dominate the propertized part of intellectual space, then it seems likely that this part will expand and the non-propertized part will consequently contract. As the aforementioned discussion has attempted to demonstrate, this is exactly what has happened. Concepts of the commons or the public domain have been unable to put up much resistance to this. *Res communes* may be weakly analogized to that part of the non-propertized zone in intellectual space that intellectual property law deems incapable (for now) of appropriation. However, as already noted, intellectual property law has shown a tendency to deem more and more of what we might have considered *res communes* as capable, after all, of appropriation. The concept of *res publicae* in intellectual space, which is justified

30 See ch 1, esp sections 3, 5.1 and 5.2.

31 See Macmillan, n 29 above; S Vaidhyanathan, *Copyrights & Copywrongs: The Rise of Intellectual Property & How It Threatens Creativity* (New York: New York University Press, 2001); L Lessig, *Free Culture: How Big Media Uses Technology & the Law to Lock Down Culture & Control Creativity* (New York: Penguin Press, 2004); D Bollier, *Brand Name Bullies: The Quest to Own and Control Culture* (Hoboken, NJ: John Wiley & Sons, 2005).

32 The classic example of this is the negotiation and conclusion of the WTO Agreement on Trade-Related Aspects of Intellectual Property Rights (TRIPs Agreement): see S K Sell, *Private Power, Public Law: The Globalization of Intellectual Property Rights* (Cambridge: Cambridge University Press, 2003). And see Report of the Special Rapporteur in the field of cultural rights, F Shaheed, *Copyright Policy and the Right to Science and Culture*, UN Doc. A/HRC/28/57, 24 December 2014, para 19.

33 See also Boyle, n 20 above, at 50:

> It may sound paradoxical, but in a very real sense protection of the commons was one of the fundamental goals of intellectual property law. In the new vision of intellectual property, however, property should be extended everywhere; more is better.

by the importance of productive synergistic interactions, is defended (or not) by intellectual property's own variable and constantly changing rules on duration and a progressively weakening range of defences and exceptions. It may even be that the very idea of intellectual space analogized to physical space creates the social and political conditions under which private property rights and their enthusiastic enforcement flourish in response to the fear of anarchy or of the thief or trespasser.[34] The role of the non-privately propertized zone here is to act as "mere supplement, in the Derridean sense, confirming the power of the IP system even if it may be declared an 'outside'".[35]

Perhaps, however, there is a degree of exaggeration in the foregoing argument: exaggeration being an easy, if not an obligatory, thing to do in hyperreality. Is intellectual property really the only thing that law has imagined to govern the relationship between the propertized and non-propertized domains in intellectual space? The answer to this must surely be that, despite the imagined binary world of intellectual property and its non-propertized progeny, there are other legal tools for the regulation and order of activity in intellectual space. These include, for instance, censorship, obscenity and blasphemy laws, defamation, laws governing national security and laws protecting human rights, including the right to free speech.[36] It seems that at least some of these laws have the effect of altering the boundary between the propertized and non-propertized zones. For example, there is some evidence that courts will refuse to enforce intellectual property rights in material that is regarded as obscene, or has been produced contrary to national security obligations.[37] In these sorts of cases, it is arguable that artefacts in intellectual space are being forced out of the propertized zone and into the non-propertized zone, where they will become subject to other forms of regulation designed to ensure that intellectual space remains orderly and, perhaps, productive. Of course, it might be argued that intellectual property law has attempted to internalize considerations of morality and public policy with the result that it has pushed material

34 See Liang, n 1 above, at 176:

> Emerging from the early history of the enclosure of the commons, the idea of the trespasser has shown remarkable resilience and adaptability to the changing ideas of property and value. The trespasser has resurfaced in the information era along with other familiar figures from the history of property ... As with the historical expansion of material property, the expansion of intellectual property relies on strategies by which various categories of illegality are mobilized both to justify IP and to argue for stronger enforcement regimes.

35 Murray, Piper & Robertson, n 1 above, at 8.

36 See also Liang, n 1 above, at 170: "The linking of public domain theories to freedom of speech is not accidental, and the model of the public domain as the sphere of rational communication borrows from existing accounts of the public/private divide" (footnote omitted).

37 On obscenity, see, e.g., *Glyn v Weston Feature Films* [1916] 1 Ch 261. On national security, see, e.g., *AG v The Guardian Newspapers (No 2)* [1988] 3 All ER 542; see also F Patfield, "The House of Lords Decision in the Spycatcher Litigation" (1989) 1 *European Intellectual Property Review* 27.

that transgresses certain norms into the non-propertized zone where it may be regulated by areas of law more suited to the purpose.[38] The distinction between exactly what is pushed out by intellectual property law and what is pulled out by other areas of law is, however, rather obscure. This is perhaps particularly the case with respect to the relationship between intellectual property rights and free speech.[39] And it is not necessarily clear that what intellectual property law pushes out into the non-propertized domain has a significant degree of identity with that which other areas of the law might seek to pull into it. More than this, the non-propertized zone of intellectual space lacks the legal architecture to defend its border with the propertized zone.

4 Cultural property/heritage in intellectual space

The absence of legal architecture to defend the border of the non-propertized zone is one of the most obvious drawbacks in relying on the concepts of the public domain and/or the commons to regulate the relationship between intellectual property and cultural property/heritage. Not only is much of what might be described as cultural heritage/property already subject to the dominion of intellectual property, and especially copyright, the border is also highly contested and the claims of intellectual property to colonize new space by pulling that space into the propertized domain often fall on what might otherwise be conceived of as cultural heritage/property. Perhaps because of the absence of any strong legal concept of cultural property or heritage, and certainly as a consequence of the apparently overlapping subject matter of intellectual property rights (especially, but not exclusively, those granted by copyright) and some types of cultural artefacts, there has been a remarkable persistence in legal claims to associate, rather than distinguish, intellectual property and cultural property rights.[40] This is despite the fact that the system of intellectual property rights is in conflict with many of the rights that might be described as cultural rights.[41] This persistent confusion, which goes to the heart of the argument in this book, arises from the fact that what is common to intellectual property, especially copyright, and

38 See, e.g., UK Patents Act 1977, s 1(3); UK Copyright, Designs and Patents Act 1988, s 171(3).

39 See F Macmillan, "Commodification and Cultural Ownership" in J Griffiths & U Suthersanen (eds), *Copyright and Free Speech: Comparative and International Analyses* (Oxford: Oxford University Press, 2005); Liang, n 1 above; & for a salutary example of the issues here, see & S Teilmann-Lock, "Corporate Interests & Artistic Voices: The *Plesner* Case" in L Belder & H Porsdam (eds), *Negotiating Cultural Rights: Issues at Stake, Challenges and Recommendations* (Farnham: Ashgate, 2017).

40 Legal concepts of cultural heritage are subject to more examination in ch 3.

41 See further F Macmillan, "The UNESCO Convention as an Incentive to Protect Cultural Diversity" in H Schneider & P van den Bossche (eds), *Protection of Cultural Diversity from a European and International Perspective* (Mortsel: Intersentia, 2008); F Macmillan, "Copyright Policy and the Right to Science and Culture – Report 2015 (A/HRC/28/57/)" in Belder & Porsdam, n 39 above.

cultural property is that both make an appeal to the preservation or reservation of property rights in cultural artefacts in some form. There is also a political aspect to this apparent confusion and claimed association of intellectual property and cultural property/heritage. For many communities, especially Indigenous communities, in the absence of strong rights over cultural heritage, intellectual property has presented itself as the only device that might confer some community control over cultural heritage. In the absence of anything else, intellectual property has been the device upon which the hope of avoiding the plunder and degradation of cultural property/heritage otherwise left in the commons has been placed. However, as is further investigated in subsequent chapters, it is not fit for the purpose. In the context of the present chapter, it is worth noting that cultural property/heritage claims tend to explode the boundaries between the hyperreal world of intellectual space and the rest of the world. Claims to cultural property claims are not confined to intangible things or intangible space. They vault over this division, problematizing its existence, living in both intellectual and tangible spaces at the same time.[42] In this way, they create a crisis in the hyperreal fabric of intellectual space – or, at least, in the way that this space has been imagined by intellectual property law.

A central claim of this book is that the regime of protection for cultural property and cultural heritage is unable to defend itself from the predatory impulses of the intellectual property system. The international legal regime governing cultural property and heritage will be further examined in Chapter 3, and its own entanglement in the distinction between the tangible and the intangible is considered in Chapter 5. One of the key features of the concept of cultural property or cultural heritage embodied in this regime is the recognition of claims by a state or by a community (somehow defined) that the relevant cultural property or heritage belongs to them (in some sense). Where international law recognizes these rights as belonging to community, it often identifies that community as global, or as humanity in general. Nevertheless, as is the nature of international law, whether these are some form of global rights of humanity or are envisaged as rights of particular communities, they must be enforced through the agency of states. National laws often make similar claims to artefacts falling within the general rubric of "heritage". In these cases, a wide range of rights are asserted, from full state ownership, through rights of preservation exercised by the state, to rights vested in the state to control physical movement of artefacts. The last is often particularly important in state regimes relating to tangible cultural property. States may, for example, attempt to prevent certain artefacts leaving their territories on the ground of their significance as "heritage". Obviously, some of these types of rights do not map onto intangible cultural property, which is the

42 Without accepting that it contains the first and/or last word on the meaning of intangible cultural heritage, see, e.g., the definition of UNESCO Convention for the Safeguarding of the Intangible Cultural Heritage 2003 (CICH), Art 2.

territory over which the real tug of war with intellectual property rights occurs. Nevertheless, whether cultural property is tangible or intangible, the essential features of cultural property are as follows: first, that certain rights in relation to it are "owned" in common or, at least, publicly; and secondly, that the rights focus on things like preservation, access and the sharing of benefits associated with it.

Claims to intellectual property are, of course, quite different since they focus on a private property right. Further, unlike cultural property/heritage, they are not claims to tangible objects, but rather claims to intangible rights – albeit claims that often implicate tangible objects (and thus create some small anomalies in the border between the hyperreal and the real).[43] In general, this means that although there maybe tangible objects that simultaneously attract claims for intellectual property rights and cultural property rights, we are not usually in danger, in a theoretical sense, of confusing or eliding the two types of property claims. Things are otherwise, however, in the realm of intellectual or intangible space. Here, the dangers of confusing, eliding and overlapping cultural heritage/ property rights and intellectual property rights are considerable. Since, at least theoretically, cultural property is publicly owned or otherwise owned in common, it would seem to fall outside that part of intellectual space that is subject to intellectual property rights.[44] This, at least, is the argument that is being asserted here – despite the problematic metaphorical suggestion, to which reference has already been made, that the difference between the non-propertized and privately propertized zones can be captured in a parallel distinction between nature and culture. Under these circumstances, one might have thought that a central role of cultural heritage/property rights must surely be to protect the non-propertized domain from the encroachments of the privately propertized domain, not to mimic those encroachments by confusing and eliding intellectual and cultural property.

It is at this point that we start to come up against some of the limitations of the rather simple concept of imagined intellectual space that is reflected in the binary division between the propertized and the non-propertized zones. One of the most obvious problems is that the division between intellectual and physical spaces, between the intangible and the tangible, becomes ever more difficult to sustain. Cultural property/heritage, even the concept of intangible cultural property/heritage as reflected in the international legal regime, does not respect this boundary. And intellectual property rights often implicate tangible

43 The relationship between intellectual property and tangible objects is often problematic. The most obvious example of this relates to the intellectual property protection of works of visual art: see Macmillan (2008), n 12 above.

44 *Cf* Bowrey & Anderson, n 1 above. However, it should be noted that to the extent that this chapter argues in favour of a non-propertized zone in intellectual space, it should not be regarded as supporting the version, or its method of operation, that is criticized by Bowrey & Anderson, *ibid*.

objects and exercise control over them. Where there are tangible objects, there are also those who may hold private property rights in them.[45] However, even if we were to set aside for a moment the admittedly perplexing problem of the constant movement between the intangible and tangible, and the viability of the distinction between them, and confine ourselves to the hyperreal world of intangibles imagined by intellectual property law, we would hardly be out of the metaphorical woods. For one thing, it is not difficult to imagine intangible artefacts that are subject to both intellectual and cultural property/heritage rights, so perhaps binary intellectual space would start to look more like a Venn diagram with a substantial area of overlap between the privately propertized and non-propertized zones. But we would still have the problem of the lack of much sophisticated architecture in the non-propertized zone and, even more, a problem with the idea that the non-intellectual-propertized zone is really a non-propertized zone (as this chapter has been so far suggesting) or, at least, a zone where nothing belongs to anyone. Admittedly, if cultural property/heritage is something that belongs to everyone, then we might be tempted to try getting away with the argument that it also belongs to no one in particular. The stumbling block in this argument is that the widest class of "everyone" that I would be prepared to concede in this context would be humanity in general. For me, this would not include non-human legal persons such as corporations (or, at least, not those types of corporations that engage in the commodification of cultural property/heritage), so there would still be the problem of defending rights in cultural property/heritage in the non-intellectual-propertized zone. However, if we concede that cultural property/heritage might often belong to communities that form less than humanity in general, then the general legal free-for-all of the non-propertized zone starts to look a little more problematic. As Murray, Piper and Robertson note, the concept of the commons "has often amounted to expropriation from local populations and reallocation to those who would 'develop' the 'raw material' in line with the agendas of capital".[46]

As this book will argue in subsequent chapters, this is not only a problem of Indigenous Peoples, but their experience with it in a post-colonial world dominated by Western legal concepts is particular.[47] This experience has resulted in the claim to some sort of hybrid space in the intellectual domain in which cultural property – often described under the rubric of traditional cultural

45 Saki's story about the unfortunate Deplis, with which this book commenced, plays with exactly this idea pitting Deplis' rights over his own body against the range of intellectual property and heritage rights created in (or on) it, thanks to the artistry of the famous tattooist Pincini: Saki (H H Munro), "The Background" in *The Chronicles of Clovis* (London & New York: John Lane, 1912), 60–66. And see ch 1, section 1.

46 Murray, Piper & Roberston, n 1 above, at 8.

47 See also Bowrey & Anderson, n 1 above, for an elegant argument on the way in which the discourse of the commons has amounted to a new post-colonial expropriation for Indigenous Peoples.

expressions and knowledge – owned on a communal basis, is protected through a property device that mimics, or is, private intellectual property. These claims, being claims by a community forming less than the public as a whole, to cultural property in the form of intellectual property, strike right at the heart of the hidden or obscured relationship between intellectual property and cultural heritage/property. They are founded on the assertion that cultural heritage/property can only be preserved through its transformation into private property. This, in other words, is an argument that at least in some circumstances, community cultural property/heritage should be treated as part of the privately propertized zone of intellectual space. Arguments of this type start to make a muddy mess of the concept of intellectual space that underlies the liberatory discourse of the public domain, commons and cultural commons. Nevertheless, they provide a useful entry point into a consideration of the appropriate role of cultural heritage/property rights in preserving and maintaining cultural property in the realm of intellectual space.

Claims to communal intellectual property rights in so-called traditional cultural expressions and knowledge are, at least so far as they are concerned with preserving cultural heritage/property, premised on the argument that the best defence to the cultural threat posed by the possibility of private intellectual property rights owned by outsiders encroaching onto those cultural rights is to turn those cultural rights into private rights. This argument has an intrinsic appeal. Moreover, the post-colonial political context of these claims is not easy to ignore. However, if we recognize so-called traditional cultural property as intellectual property, do we do some damage to the preservation of that property – that is, to the preservation of culture and heritage of a particular group or community? Treating cultural property as intellectual property means corralling it into the shape of Western intellectual property law.[48] This will mean that different levels of protection will apply to different types of "traditional" or non-Western knowledge and culture. If the item of cultural property is a story, music or artwork, then it has to be fitted into copyright law; designs and symbols must fit into the netherworld of the relationship between copyright, designs and trademarks; knowledge about local flora and fauna must be fitted somewhere into patent law, plants breeder's rights and geographical indications. And anything else just falls out of the scheme altogether. In short, the end result is that occidental intellectual property law comes to constitute non-Western culture and heritage.[49] In so doing, it changes the shape of that heritage in ways that are not necessarily the consequence of the reflexive cultural practice that in

48 See M Blakeney, "The Protection of Traditional Knowledge under Intellectual Property Law" (2000) 22 *European Intellectual Property Law Review* 251–261.

49 P Fitzpatrick & R Joyce, "Copying Right: Cultural Property and the Limits of (Occidental) Law" in F Macmillan (ed), *New Directions in Copyright Law: Volume 4* (Cheltenham: Edward Elgar, 2007).

fact constitutes the so-called traditional cultural expressions and knowledge.[50] This seems to be inimical to the very purpose of protecting cultural heritage/ property.

The danger here is not only with respect to Indigenous and other non-Western knowledge and culture. There is also a more general concern, which is the possibility that accepting the protection of non-Western knowledge and culture through the use of private intellectual property rights will create a type of "blowback" onto the shape of Western law governing the relationship between the non-privately propertized domain and the privately propertized domain in intellectual space. Will we, then, come to accept that "culture", "cultural rights", "cultural property" and "cultural heritage" are best protected as some type of private rights? Or perhaps we have already done that (in which case we need to reconsider the situation).[51] At the same time, however, treating non-Western, and especially Indigenous, cultural property as exceptional means that we pass up the opportunity to learn lessons from its holders about the balance between individual and community rights in cultural property/heritage. As Murray, Robertson and Piper observe, "the respectful impulse to treat indigenous cultural property laws and practices as *sui generis* has limited their critical reach and comparative power".[52] There are important geo-political and cultural differences between the West and the rest that must not be discounted, particularly those that arise from the post-colonial condition of so much of the non-Western world. But by ignoring completely the way in which the non-Western world deals with questions of balance between individual and community rights in cultural property and heritage while simultaneously navigating the imposed conditions of Western intellectual property law, we continue with a long tradition of Western blindness and stupidity. In other words, we put ourselves in danger of believing that Western intellectual property law can do everything, even satisfying the colonial mandate "to bring the blessings of Western civilisation to the inhabitants of the tropics and to activate neglected resources in 'backward' countries for the benefit of the world economy".[53] (One of the tragedies of the post-colonial Western world is the widespread failure to have ever even thought about the possibility that a "neglected resource" of the non-Western world might lie in innovative solutions to legal, cultural and political conundrums.)

This book will return at various other points to the question (and the answers) of Indigenous and non-Western cultural property/heritage. The brief

50 As Fitzpatrick and Joyce argue, n 49 above, at 171–173, the so-called "traditional knowledge and culture" would never have survived if it had not been "dynamically generative and relational" and "capable of being utterly responsive, comprehensively self-transgressive".

51 See ch 3, section 4.

52 Murray, Robertson & Piper, n 1 above, at 4.

53 (Lord) F J D Lugard, *The Dual Mandate in British Tropical Africa* (Frank Cass & Co, 1922); see J Osterhammel, *Colonialism: A Theoretical Overview* (Princeton: Markus Wiener, 1997, trans S L Frisch), at 109–110.

examination in this chapter is intended to expose a couple of important points about the so-called public domain, commons or cultural commons, and to pose a couple of consequent questions. What (hopefully) emerges is that whatever the nature of this imagined space, it is woefully short of legal architecture, not only to control the constant encroachments of private property rights into its territory, but also to understand and protect the complex nature of public and community rights in cultural property/heritage. Strangely, the only relevant legal architecture that we seem to have in intellectual space is intellectual property itself, with its own devices for limiting its reach and pushing some things that might otherwise be subject to it out into the non-propertized domain (but often only for limited times and purposes). How should we deal with this state of affairs? Do we leave cultural heritage/property, widely defined, in the non-propertized domain where it can be freely mined as raw material for intellectual property, but where it might not be adequately conserved or preserved as cultural property? Or, do we privatize it through intellectual property rights and progressively destroy its distinctive character as cultural property and heritage? These questions are, of course, part of a much larger and unresolved problem about the preservation and conservation of intangible cultural property in intellectual space. Nevertheless, the suggestion that the best method of preservation and conservation of intangible cultural heritage/property is by its privatization in the form of intellectual property does seem naive. Not only is intellectual property ill-equipped to protect cultural rights, it is clearly implicated in their constriction and possible destruction.[54]

5 While we're talking about the Romans ...

It is clear that in order for concepts like the public domain, the commons or the non-propertized zone of intellectual space to do all the things they are celebrated for and, at the same time, to protect rights over cultural property/heritage, we need a more complex articulation of the intellectual or intangible domain. Specifically, we need to start moving away from the simplified binary divide of the intellectual private domain of intellectual property law and the intellectual public or common domain. Instead, as already suggested, what appears to be required is some legal architecture in the imaginary domain of intellectual space, particularly that part of this imaginary domain that is not subject to private intellectual property rights. I have argued in this chapter that the ideas of the public domain and the commons, as they have been derived from the Roman law concepts of *res publicae* and *res communes*, have not been adequate to protect the non-privately propertized part of intellectual space. Whatever we want to call this non-privately propertized zone, the solution to the problem posed

54 See Macmillan (2017), n 41 above.

by the imperial reach of intellectual property and, especially of copyright, over cultural property/heritage – both Western and non-Western must – be to get rid of intellectual property (or copyright), to reduce its reach substantially and/or to introduce other rights that are as strong as it.

To the extent that the solution lies in the last of these options, it might be worth noting, while we are talking about Roman law, that it has been rather under-used in the modern re-construction of non-privately propertized space. Part of the problem clearly is, as it often seems to be in relation to intellectual property discourse, that the analogy with real or tangible property does not necessarily work well.[55] Nevertheless, given the role of intellectual property law in constructing our understanding of the non-privately propertized zone of intellectual space – and the endless problems of understanding what is (reality, if it exists) and what should be (normativity or, perhaps, desire), especially in what is in any case a hyperreal concept – it seems that the possible utility of other Roman law concepts has been underestimated. What is important about these concepts is perhaps not exactly how they were applied by the Romans, but how they allow us to focus on the some of the pertinent issues. The first of these, as the Romans also knew, is that we need to make a clear distinction between what is publicly or collectively "owned" in intellectual space and what is by its nature unable to be owned. In other words, the difference between the Roman law concepts of *res publicae* and *res communes* must be recognized despite the challenges. An associated recognition is that some things can never be owned, at least privately, because of their cultural or other social significance. The Roman law concept of *res divini juris*, which is grounded in the idea that the potency of some symbols gives too much power to those who might seek to appropriate them, might be redeveloped in a modern form in order to form the basis of this claim.[56] Relying on copyright law's uncertain approach to questions about whether parodies or satires are infringing is really not enough here.

And, as this book will argue, we also need to recognize particular rights of groups or communities that form less than the public as a whole without that recognition becoming oppressive for the members of those groups or communities. One approach to this would be the development of group and communal rights, belonging to less than the public as a whole, bounded by property on the outside, but inside promoting freedom and space for creativity, innovation, invention and cultural conservation. The Roman law concept of *res universitatis* recognized exactly this idea.[57] In physical space, this concept merges the

55 See, e.g., the comments on Lockean-based intellectual property discourse in ch 1, section 4.

56 *Res divini juris* referred to things that cannot be owned because of their sacred or religious nature: Rose, n 6 above, at 108–110. For a more developed version of this argument, see F Macmillan, "Many Analogies, Some Metaphors, Little Imagination: The Public Domain in Intellectual Space" (2010) 2 *Pòlemos* 25–44.

57 For a description of *res universitatis*, see Rose, n 6 above, at 105–108.

advantages of productive synergistic interaction with the need to avoid the tragedy of the commons. In intellectual space, as discussed earlier, there is no need to avoid the tragedy of the commons, so the utility of *res universitatis*, or the bounded commons, must be to preserve productive synergies and protect these when necessary through the exercise of rights against outsiders.[58] The so-called creative commons movement embraces a version of this idea, but it is probably not the best version. It and other communities like it are perhaps capable of indirectly tilting against the power of the corporate giants by developing an alternative space for creativity and innovation. However, not only is their ability to form the basis of a direct attack on the monolith of corporate power is open to question, but they also may lead to the indirect extension of the power of intellectual property by propagating the idea that a licence is always necessary, and consequently that there is in fact no non-privately propertized zone in intellectual space.[59]

Some (other) type of modern instantiation of *res universitatis* might very well form part of a legal architecture to protect rights in some type of hybrid sort-of-propertized part of intellectual space. Would it and modern variations on other concepts drawn from Roman law limitations on private property rights in physical space be enough to protect the cultural property/heritage of communities and to recognize the rights they have in it? Or conversely, might even these ideas of the public domain, the commons and cultural commons threaten such rights? Before starting to answer such a question, it is necessary to know more about what we are talking about when we talk about cultural property/heritage and the rights that exist over it.

58 For a more developed version of this argument, see Macmillan, n 56 above. Such a space would also supply the incentive, if it is really needed, to produce such synergies.

59 There are serious questions around the ideological roots of the creative commons movement: see Murray, Piper & Robertson, n 1 above, at 23–29. On its tendency to reinforce the power of the intellectual property system, see S Dusollier, "The Master's Tools v. The Master's House: Creative Commons v. Copyright" (2006) 29 *Columbia Journal of Law & the Arts* 101–123; Murray, Piper & Robertson, n 1 above, at 27. And for an example of a particular part of intellectual space where there is no version of the commons, see E Hayot & E Wesp, "Solomon's Bluff: Virtual Property and the Aesthetics of Modern Worldmaking" in P K Saint-Amour (ed), *Modernism and Copyright* (Oxford & New York: Oxford University Press, 2011).

Chapter 3

Heritage, law and community

1 Introduction: the UNESCO regime in geo-political context

Disputes involving the sorts of things that are claimed to be the cultural stuff of one community or another mark and tarnish the recorded history of humanity. It is, therefore, unsurprising that the philosophical and legal concept of cultural heritage/property can be traced back to antiquity, and in particular from a legal perspective, to the famous *Verrines* of Cicero.[1] Then, as now, it is clear that these disputes were primarily generated by the unattractive human propensity to plunder, loot, steal, pillage, (mis)appropriate and destroy. Under these circumstances, there is a certain inevitability in the fact that cultural heritage first became a recognized concept in post-Westphalian international law at the time of the Vienna Treaty of 1815, which was imposed by the British victors after the conclusion of the Napoleonic Wars.[2] The precise motivations for the British insistence that France atone for the destruction of heritage and return the movable artefacts looted by Napoleon during his campaigns might reasonably be regarded as being obscured by the passage of time. However, given the context, it seems reasonable to assume that the relevant clause was punitive. More interesting for present purposes is the likelihood that it was influenced by the concurrent rise of a discourse that linked people, territory and cultural objects.[3] That this was an entirely Eurocentric and imperial discourse is hardly a great surprise: at the same time as Britain was championing the return of European cultural artefacts, it continued to plunder the cultural artefacts of its colonies with impunity.[4] By

1 See M M Miles, *Art as Plunder: The Ancient Origins of Debate about Cultural Property* (New York: Cambridge University Press, 2010).

2 A F Vrdoljak, *International Law, Museums & the Return of Cultural Objects* (Cambridge: Cambridge University Press, 2008), at 23–29.

3 Vrdoljak, n 2 above, Pt 1.

4 Special Rapporteur, Mohammed Bedjaoui, who was responsible for the preparation the work that eventually lead to the conclusion of the Vienna Convention on Succession of States in respect of State Property, Archives and Debts (1983) found that the removal of cultural objects

the end of the Second World War, however, this colonial free-for-all was coming to an end. Britain had been replaced by America as the dominant world power, the regimes of international law were being remade, and the period of decolonization was commencing.[5] Even though the current international law regime for the protection of cultural heritage was born out of the rupture that marked the end of the British period of world dominance and inaugurated the American one, it is nevertheless marked by both its historical antecedents and contemporaneous movements in the geo-political order.[6]

Of these contemporaneous geo-political movements, two are particularly important to the argument in this chapter. First of all, there is the very process of decolonization itself and the political aspirations that accompanied it. At the international law level, this process was managed in a rather *ex post facto* fashion by something that eventually became the Vienna Convention on the Succession of States in Respect of State Property, Archives and Debts of 1983. In the current context, there are two key (low) points of this treaty. The first of these is its failure to recognize the distinctive position of Indigenous Peoples within former colonial subject states. This, of course, is a serious problem with which the international law system continues to struggle. In part, it is a consequence of the strongly state-based thinking that characterized the development of international law in the post-war period. This explanation (the inadequacy and injustice of which needs no elaboration), however, cannot serve to explain the second important aspect of the Vienna Convention, which is the absence of any rules on restitution of works of art or artefacts to the former colonial states. Instead, the question of the return of works of art and artefacts was to be governed by bilateral negotiations under the auspices of a UNESCO Committee, the operation of which has continued up until to the present period.[7] One of the things that makes this particularly pernicious is the stark contrast between the arrangements that the colonial powers, comprising a number of European states, made with respect to the return of artefacts to their former colonies and the arrangements that they made for the return of what they considered to be their own artefacts under the Allied Restitution programmes that followed the conclusion of the Second World War.[8] As this chapter

during the colonial period was generally not "in accordance with the canons of justice, morality and law": UN Doc.A/CN.4/292, quoted in Vrdoljak, n 2 above, at 202. Of course, Britain's championing of the return of European cultural stuff tended to be more rhetorical than anything else: see F Macmillan, "The Protection of Cultural Heritage: Common Heritage of Humankind, National Cultural 'Patrimony' or Private Property?" (2013) 64 *Northern Ireland Legal Quarterly* 351–364, at 356–357.

5 G Arrighi, *The Long Twentieth Century: Money, Power and the Origins of Our Times* (London: Verso, 1994), at 47–74 and ch 3.

6 On the historical antecedents, see also, e.g., Miles, n 1 above, at 1–12.

7 For a critical assessment of the work of this committee, see Vrdoljak, n 2 above, at 211–217.

8 Vrdoljak, n 2 above, at 202. And for an account of the Allied Restitution programmes in this context, see Vrdoljak, *ibid.*, at 140–148.

and those following it will argue, a significant part of the current political concern with the question of the protection of cultural artefacts is a consequence of the failure of international law properly to address the wrongs of the colonial period.[9]

The second important political current in the post-colonial period was the re-institutionalization of the concept of free trade along with the remaking of the international law regime after the Second World War. The concept of international free trade had been floating around in international law since at least the Treaty of Westphalia of 1649.[10] While the economic freedoms of Westphalia were not observed during the Napoleonic Wars, they were restored in the Settlement of Vienna of 1815 and the Congress of Aix-la-Chapelle of 1818.[11] These freedoms were then restored again, after the cataclysms of the First and Second World Wars, at the Bretton Woods diplomatic conference, starting the international legal system(s) on a process that leads eventually to the World Trade Organization (WTO).[12] The strength of this discourse, and the political and economic baggage that it has dragged in its wake, has had a particular effect on the way in which the relationship between public, community and private rights has played out in relation to cultural artefacts. This is the case with respect to both tangible and intangible artefacts, although there seems little doubt that the conclusion of the Agreement on Trade-Related Aspects of Intellectual Property (TRIPs Agreement) as one of the WTO-covered agreements has considerably upped the ante in this respect in relation to intangible cultural stuff.

At the same time as all this was going on, the other part of the post-war international law regime, which grew out of the negotiations at the Dumbarton Oaks diplomatic conference, was the site for the emergence of bodies of law governing human rights and the protection of "culture". The regime for the protection of culture is the focus of this chapter, but it is worth noting its entanglement, actual and putative, with its human rights bedfellow. Both of these bodies of law are managed under the general auspices of the United Nations, although instruments for the protection of culture are generally (but not exclusively) the province of UNESCO. There is, therefore, a clear historical and institutional relationship between these two bodies of international law. However, the extent of the legal, political and philosophical relationship between them is open to more conjecture. Certainly, twenty-first-century UNESCO Conventions make rather florid claims to some type of association, but the extent to which the UNESCO Conventions can be regarded as a direct expression of international

9 For an argument on the significance of this failure in relation to identity and sovereignty, see Macmillan, n 4 above.

10 Arrighi, n 5 above, at 43–44.

11 Arrighi, n 5 above, at 52.

12 See further F Macmillan, "The World Trade Organization and the Turbulent Legacy of International Economic Law-Making in the Long Twentieth Century" in J Faundez & C Tan (eds), *International Law, Economic Globalization and Developing Countries* (Cheltenham: Edward Elgar, 2010).

human rights law is unclear.[13] The provisions of international human rights law that are usually cited in support of this claim are probably most convincingly construed as a right to cultural self-determination.[14] Under these circumstances, perhaps the most that can be said for the claim that human rights law is the wellspring of the UNESCO regime is that a right to cultural self-determination suggests the valorization of the sort of concepts, such as cultural heritage, cultural property and cultural diversity, with which the UNESCO regime is concerned. However, it is also apposite to note that the same body of international human rights law is often argued as providing the normative justification for the system of intellectual property rights.[15] If, as this book argues, the intellectual property system as a system of private rights poses a threat to community rights in cultural heritage/property, then it might be concluded that not all that much is gained by attempts to invoke human rights rhetoric – let alone human rights law itself – in support of claims for stronger cultural property rights.

While some sort of link to human rights has recently featured in what Laurajane Smith describes as the authorized heritage discourse, as noted earlier, this discourse also has much older and deeper influences.[16] Thanks to both its historical antecedents and its geo-political context, the authorized heritage discourse provided a pretty clear idea of what cultural heritage was considered to be. Based on Cartesian dualisms of nature and culture, tangible and intangible, there was a reasonable sense of certainty in the world of international policy and law-making about the objects of the various efforts at protection.[17] Of course, imbricated in that certainty were particular ideas of nation, class and ethnicity.[18] But this could hardly be regarded as a surprise for a concept that was cooked up in the West and

13 See Convention on the Safeguarding of Intangible Cultural Heritage (CICH), Recitals 1–2; Convention on the Protection and Promotion of Cultural Diversity (CCD), Recitals 1–5 & Arts 2.1 & 5.1.

14 Universal Declaration of Human Rights, Art 27; United Nations Charter Covenant on Civil & Political Rights, Arts 1, 19 & 27; United Nations Charter Covenant on Economic, Social & Cultural Rights, Art 15: see F Macmillan, "The UNESCO Convention as a New Incentive to Protect Cultural Diversity" in H Schneider & P van den Bossche (eds), *Protection of Cultural Diversity from a European and International Perspective* (Mortsel: Intersentia, 2008). For a more extensive and nuanced consideration of this question, see L Belder, "The Right of Access to and Enjoyment of Cultural Heritage – Report 2011 (A/HRC/17/38)" in L Belder & H Porsdam (eds), *Negotiating Cultural Rights: Issues at Stake Challenges and Recommendations* (Cheltenham: Edward Elgar, 2017).

15 This is the case with respect to the Universal Declaration of Human Rights, Art 27.2 & UN Charter Covenant on Economic, Social & Cultural Rights, Art 15.1.

16 See L Smith, *Uses of Heritage* (London & New York: Routledge, 2006), from which I draw this expression and concept. As (I hope) a legitimate development of this concept, I place emphasis in this chapter on the role of the relevant international legal texts as both authorizing and being authorized by this discourse.

17 On the Cartesian dualisms of the authorized heritage discourse, see R Harrison, *Heritage: Critical Approaches* (London & New York: Routledge, 2013), ch 9.

18 Smith, n 16 above, at 29ff; Macmillan, n 4 above.

embedded in the post-Second World War regime of international policymaking and heritage law, represented by bodies like ICOMOS (International Council on Monuments and Sites) and UNESCO.[19] Under this regime, and reflecting its Western philosophical roots, the authorized heritage discourse took on the characteristics of what must have seemed like the only comparable Western legal concept. Consequently, with a couple of exceptions, the international legal regime for the protection of cultural heritage came to reflect occidental property law distinctions.[20] One of these is the distinction between things that are said, by law, to be "fixed" to a particular place and those that are said to be moveable. Another, of course, is the distinction between tangible and intangible things.

So far as the UNESCO Conventions themselves are concerned, they started off with a concern for the protection of cultural property during armed conflict (UNESCO Convention on the Protection of Cultural Property in the Event of Armed Conflict [Hague Convention, 1954]), moved on to a concern for restitution to states of movable cultural property (UNESCO Convention on the Means of Prohibiting and Preventing the Illicit, Import, Export and Transfer of Ownership of Cultural Property [1970]) and then the preservation of immovable cultural heritage (UNESCO Convention Concerning the Protection of the World Cultural and Natural Heritage [1972]).[21] In this century, while the rate of international law-making with respect to the protection of culture and cultural heritage has increased, the focus of protection has moved to a concern for underwater cultural heritage (UNESCO Convention on the Protection of the Underwater Cultural Heritage [2001]), intangible cultural heritage (UNESCO Convention for the Safeguarding of the Intangible Cultural Heritage [2003]) and the concept of "cultural diversity" (UNESCO Convention for the Protection and Promotion of the Diversity of Cultural Expressions [2005]).

The trajectory and content of the UNESCO Conventions have been affected by the contemporaneous political, economic and legal developments in two principal ways. First, despite using the language of the cultural heritage of mankind/humanity, the regime is intensely statist, which is also (obviously) a consequence of its location in the system of international law. This, of course, reflects the strongly statist ideology that characterized the period of decolonization.

19 For account of the relationship between ICOMOS (International Council on Monuments and Sites) and UNESCO, and its role in relation to the authorized heritage discourse, see Smith, n 16 above, ch 1.

20 See further F Macmillan, "Cultural Property and Community Rights to Cultural Heritage" in T Xu & J Allain (eds), *Property and Human Rights in a Global Context* (Oxford & Portland, OR: Hart Publishing, 2015), at 47, in which I note that the Convention for the Protection of Cultural Property in the Event of Armed Conflict (1954) and the Convention for the Protection of Underwater Cultural Heritage (2001) stand in some respects outside this classification.

21 The Hague Convention locates itself within the context of the 1907 Hague Regulations on Law & Customs of War: see UNESCO Convention on the Protection of Cultural Property in the Event of Armed Conflict 1954, Preamble, para 4.

There are now some small breaches in this discourse as witnessed at the general level of public international law, for example, in the United Nations Declaration on the Rights of Indigenous Peoples (DRIPs) of 2007 and reflected in the UNESCO Convention for the Safeguarding of the Intangible Cultural Heritage (CICH) and the UNESCO Convention for the Protection and Promotion of the Diversity of Cultural Expressions (CCD).[22] Second, at the same time, and arguably running counter to this strongly statist approach, the ambit of the UNESCO regime is circumscribed by the dominance of free trade ideology and the associated importance of private ownership rights. One classic example of this is the UNESCO Convention on the Means of Prohibiting and Preventing the Illicit, Import, Export and Transfer of Ownership of Cultural Property, which makes its provisions on the return of moveable cultural property subject to ensuring compensation for "innocent" purchasers and persons "who have valid titles" to the relevant artefacts.[23] The CCD is also marked by the dominance of free trade ideology. In one way, its very existence can be considered a reaction to the international legal implementation of that ideology in the WTO agreements because one of primary motivations of the Convention's promoters was to compensate for the absence of a general cultural exception in the WTO agreements.[24] However, it might also be regarded as accommodating aspects of the ideology underpinning the WTO through its uncritical acceptance of the role of private property rights, in the form of intellectual property rights, in sustaining the type of cultural creativity that it regards as essential to the flourishing of cultural diversity.[25] A similar uncritical acceptance characterizes the CICH.[26] Given the historical intertwining of the trade regime and the UNESCO regime, it is probably not surprising that UNESCO's increasing concern with the protection of intangibles has been matched by an enormous

22 The CICH recognizes in recital 6 "that communities, in particular indigenous communities, groups and, in some cases, individuals, play an important role in the production, safeguarding, maintenance and recreation of the intangible cultural heritage"; and also recognizes the role of communities and groups in art 2.1. The CCD makes repeated references to "traditional cultural expressions" and notes in its recital 15

> the importance of the vitality of cultures, including for persons belonging to minorities & indigenous peoples, as manifested in their freedom to create, disseminate & distribute their traditional cultural expressions & to have access thereto, so as to benefit them for their own development.

23 UNESCO Convention on the Means of Prohibiting & Preventing the Illicit, Import, Export & Transfer of Ownership of Cultural Property (1970), Art 7(b)(ii).

24 See further C B Graber, "The New UNESCO Convention on Cultural Diversity: A Counterbalance to the WTO?" (2006) 9 *Journal of International Economic Law* 553–574.

25 According to recital 17, the CCD recognizes "the importance of intellectual property rights in sustaining those involved in cultural creativity"; see Art 20. For a further analysis, see Macmillan, n 14 above.

26 See CICH, Art 3(b).

growth in the scope and application of intellectual property rights, which are now part of the WTO package in the form of its Agreement on Trade Related Aspects of Intellectual Property (TRIPs Agreement). What might be considered more surprising is the fact that the power of the intellectual property system to trump community rights to cultural heritage/property is often advanced and, when necessary defended, as an exercise of human rights. At least in this sense, it might be said that UNESCO's embrace, at the same time, of both human rights and intellectual property rights – in the CICH and the CCD – is not internally inconsistent.

The foregoing serves to provide the background against which this chapter considers the interplay of public, community and private interests in cultural stuff as it is governed by the current international law regime. The chapter is concerned with the way international law understands the relationship between heritage, sovereignty, identity and community. It investigates these issues in three parts. First, it focusses on, and critiques, the international law concept of "cultural heritage" and its protection. Second, it deepens this analysis by considering the protection of intangible cultural heritage under the CICH and its relationship with the protection of intellectual property. The chapter then opens up a discussion of the post-colonial dimensions of the current international law regime, focussing on the protection of the cultural property/heritage of post-colonial ("developing") states and of Indigenous Peoples.

2 The concept of cultural heritage

2.1 The UNESCO regime

Since this book has so far tested the patience of readers and author alike by the largely interchangeable use of the expressions "cultural heritage/property" and (even worse, the highly technical "cultural stuff", at the beginning of this chapter), it is worth noting as a preliminary observation – and in the interests of self-defence – that this indecision also characterizes the UNESCO system. Both the Hague Convention (1954) and the Convention on the Means of Prohibiting and Preventing the Illicit, Import, Export and Transfer of Ownership of Cultural Property (1970) describe their object of protection as "cultural property". However, the use of this expression was subsequently abandoned, in favour of the expression "cultural heritage", which was used in the Convention Concerning the Protection of the World Cultural and Natural Heritage (WHC) (1972). The significance of this is open to speculation, but one possible explanation is that the association with traditional concepts of rivalrous property rights was regarded as inaccurate or problematic.[27] The issue here, assuming this speculation

27 See J Blake, "On Defining Cultural Heritage" (2000) 49 *International & Comparative Law Quarterly* 61–85, at 65–67.

holds water, is not only the rivalrous nature of property as understood by law, but also the possibility that the objects of protection of the UNESCO system might be broader than the traditional objects of property protection. The latter point seems to be true with respect to this century's Conventions on underwater cultural heritage, intangible cultural heritage and cultural diversity. The extent to which it might be thought to apply to the WHC, which marked this change of discourse in 1972, is perhaps more debateable, as its objects are mainly tangible immovables in traditional property parlance. The idea that it was the rivalrous nature of traditional property rights that prompted the change in discourse can, if accurate, be read in at least two ways. One is as an acknowledgement of the importance of community, rather than individual, rights to the concept of cultural heritage. The other is that the cultural stuff that the UNESCO Conventions are concerned with cannot generally be the object of ownership as understood in traditional property law. Yet, another possible explanation for the change in discourse from property to heritage is that the expression "cultural property" makes reference to a form of property that is not generally recognized in Western legal systems.[28]

Whatever the reason for the change in discourse, one of the many interesting things about the UNESCO system, as already noted, is that it follows a taxonomic model that nevertheless seems to owe a substantial amount to that governing rivalrous private property rights. This taxonomic tendency is evident in the way in which the Conventions are divided between those concerned with tangible property, which is further split between movables and immovables, and those concerned with intangible property.[29] Certainly, there are Conventions that stand in some respects outside this classification, but overall the organizational influence of Western legal concepts of property is strong.[30] The question of what types of tangible or intangible property constitute cultural heritage is not consistently addressed at a general level. The Conventions do not define their object of protection by reference to an overarching concept, but rather by closed or open lists of specific objects to which the relevant Convention intends to extend protection. An example of a closed list is provided by the WHC, the first UNESCO Convention to employ the expression "cultural heritage", to describe

28 Many European continental systems recognize this concept, but it has not been a traditional part of the common law systems.

29 The Convention on the Means of Prohibiting and Preventing the Illicit, Import, Export and Transfer of Ownership of Cultural Property (1970) deals with tangible moveables. The WHC (1972) deals with tangible immoveables. The CICH (2003) and perhaps the CCD (2005) deal with intangibles.

30 Convention for the Protection of Cultural Property in the event of Armed Conflict (1954), which does however refer to "movable or immovable property" (Art 1(a)), stands outside this classification, as does the Convention for the Protection of the Underwater Cultural Heritage (2001).

its general object of protection. This Convention provides in Article 1 that for its purposes, "cultural heritage" is:

> **monuments:** architectural works, works of monumental sculpture and painting, elements or structures of an archaeological nature, inscriptions, cave dwellings and combinations of features, which are of outstanding universal value from the point of view of history, art or science;
>
> **groups of buildings:** groups of separate or connected buildings which, because of their architecture, their homogeneity or their place in the landscape, are of outstanding universal value from the point of view of history, art or science;
>
> **sites:** works of man or the combined works of nature and man, and areas including archaeological sites which are of outstanding universal value from the historical, aesthetic, ethnological or anthropological point of view.

The concept that appears to link these different classes of immovables together is the symbolic or intangible element of "outstanding universal value", although the type of outstanding universal value in question undergoes a subtle shift in relation to the protection of "sites".

Reflecting perhaps millennial uncertainties about everything, the CICH employs a more open-ended list prefaced by an attempt to arrive at a wider concept. According to Article 2.1, "intangible cultural heritage" means:

> the practices, representations, expressions, knowledge, skills – as well as the instruments, objects, artefacts and cultural spaces associated therewith – that communities, groups and, in some cases, individuals recognize as part of their cultural heritage. This intangible cultural heritage, transmitted from generation to generation, is constantly recreated by communities and groups in response to their environment, their interaction with nature and their history, and provides them with a sense of identity and continuity, thus promoting respect for cultural diversity and human creativity.

This is followed in Article 2.2 by an open-ended list (further considered in Section 3.3) of things that fall within this general definition. Open or closed lists of things are also common when the concept of cultural heritage is invoked in general cultural and political discourses, although such lists often appear at odds with the concepts and lists of cultural heritage in the UNESCO Conventions.[31] Part, and probably a large part, of the reason for this disjunction is the absence

31 See, e.g., Macmillan, n 20 above, and its discussion of the 2014 European Union *Heritage Plus* funding call: *Cultural Heritage: A Challenge for Europe* (JPI Cultural Heritage and Global Change – Heritage Plus Call, 2014).

of any overarching concept of cultural heritage in the UNESCO Conventions themselves.

2.2 An overarching concept?

One of the things that makes cultural heritage a rhetorical moving feast in all sorts of legal, political, cultural and bureaucratic discourses is the difficulty in pinning down an overarching concept of cultural heritage.[32] Looking to the UNESCO Conventions for inspiration – or even information – in the search for such a concept suggests a number of related possibilities. One would be, as the WHC suggests, to focus on stuff that is of "outstanding universal value" historically, artistically, scientifically, ethnologically or anthropologically. There is an obvious problem here of working out who decides what is of relevant "outstanding universal value" according to a range of disciplines that have a strong whiff of European enlightenment thought and thus might be regarded as, in any case, suspect in the context of the "universal". The Convention on the Means of Prohibiting and Preventing the Illicit, Import, Export and Transfer of Ownership of Cultural Property, which deals with the protection of tangible movables and employs similar concepts to those in the WHC, presents a possible solution to this problem. Article 1 provides that the subject matter of protection is "property which, on religious or secular grounds, is specifically designated by each State as being of importance for archaeology, prehistory, history, literature, art or science" and which belongs to a closed list of categories. Despite the certainty that flows from designation by a state, it is suggested that this manifestation of statist thinking is an unsuitable solution in a world where not all peoples and communities enjoy the benefit of statehood.[33]

A second possibility, suggested by the UNESCO Conventions, for a broad concept of cultural heritage would be to generalize the statement in Article 2.1 of the CICH. This would produce something to the effect that cultural heritage is what is transmitted from generation to generation by communities and groups in response to their environment, their interaction with nature and their history, thus providing them with a sense of identity and continuity. The more up-to-date language of this second approach has clearly influenced twenty-first-century commentators (including me) who have proposed an overarching concept of cultural heritage as being expressions of creativity (moveable and immoveable, tangible and intangible) that a community or people consider worth handing on

32 See also T Flessas, "Cultural Property Defined and Redefined as Nietzschean Aphorism" (2003) 24 *Cardozo Law Review* 1067–1098.

33 This seems to have been recognized in the UNIDROIT Convention on Stolen or Illegally Exported Cultural Objects (1995), which seeks to give private international architecture to the UNESCO Convention. The definition in the UNIDROIT Convention, Art 2, of the subject matter of protection is almost identical to that in the UNESCO Convention except that it refers to cultural objects, rather than property, and it leaves out the requirement for state designation.

to the future.[34] There is, of course, an obvious political element in identifying what is considered to be worth handing on to the future and this carries with it a degree of malleability and slipperiness.[35] Thus, what we understand to be cultural heritage/property reflects current political concerns. This gives it an obvious potency in cultural and political discourses.

2.3 *Identity, community, property*

This potency owes a substantial debt to the strong relationship between community and/or national identity and cultural heritage/property.[36] Perhaps because the question of identity has become so important in our globalizing and homogenizing world, claims to cultural heritage/property are imbricated with the politics of identity. Depending on how the world is understood, there are various ways of expressing this relationship. Not all cultures express it as a claim to ownership, but in an international political and legal context that is dominated by occidental ways of seeing the world, this is a frequent claim. Whether it is always a claim to some type of property in the heritage itself is not clear. What is, however, much clearer is that the claim is one made by a community.[37] At least, it is clearer until one reads the UNESCO Conventions closely. There are at least two reasons why the community nature of cultural heritage/property claims is obscured in the UNESCO Conventions. One is their constant references to the cultural heritage of (hu)mankind. While this can be taken as a claim to some sort of universal ownership, it is probably better understood as a justification for protecting cultural heritage.[38] Second, the pervasive influence of state-based thinking in the early UNESCO Conventions tends to obscure the concept of community, although it is possible to understand the Conventions as referring to a community that is co-extensive with the nation state.[39] The more recent Conventions, however, more readily accept the relationship between community

34 F Macmillan, "Arts Festivals as Cultural Heritage in a Copyright Saturated World" in H Porsdam (ed), *Copyrighting Creativity: Creative Values, Cultural Heritage Institutions and Systems of Intellectual Property* (Farnham: Ashgate, 2014),citing Blake, n 27 above, at 68–69. See also the CCD, Art 4.1–3.

35 See also Blake, n 27 above, at 68.

36 See further Macmillan, n 4 above, at 352–356. See also, e.g., E Hobsbawm, *Fractured Times: Culture and Society in the Twentieth Century* (London: Little Brown, 2013), ch 12, esp at 148ff.

37 See, e.g., UN Declaration of the Rights of Indigenous Peoples, Arts 11.1, 12.1, 13.1 and 31.1.

38 Macmillan, n 4 above.

39 See, e.g., UNESCO Convention on the Means of Prohibiting and Preventing the Illicit, Import, Export and Transfer of Ownership of Cultural Property (1970), Recitals 3–5:

> **Considering** that cultural property constitutes one of the basic elements of civilization and national culture ... **Considering** that it is incumbent upon every State to protect the cultural property existing within its territory ... **Considering** that ... it is essential for every state to become increasingly alive to the moral obligations respecting its own cultural heritage and that of all nations.

and cultural heritage. The CICH, for example, recognizes "that communities, in particular indigenous communities, groups and, in some cases, individuals, play an important role in the production, safeguarding, maintenance and recreation of the intangible cultural heritage".[40] It is notable, however, that this Convention does not talk about the claims or rights of such communities to their cultural heritage.

There is a constant movement, and not only in the UNESCO Conventions,[41] in the discourse of cultural heritage between the cultural heritage of humanity, nation states, peoples and communities. This complicates the question of the interplay of traditional concepts of public and private in this context, especially if one associates the concept of the public with that of the state. There is an argument that the protection of cultural stuff calls, instead, for a distinction between private and non-private. At the same time, there are good arguments for the concept of the public and so we abandon the public-private distinction at our peril, in this context, as in others.[42] In the context of cultural stuff where we are in some netherworld, floating between concepts of rights, ownership, custodianship, belonging, we are also never very far away from some idea of property, even if it is not the traditional Western concept of rivalrous private property. This is why we need to keep hold of the public-private distinction, as well as the distinction between what is private and what is not. The traditional concept of (private) property is not only heavily loaded with an elevation of the private over the public good, it is also part of the process by which all values become subject to the logic of the market.[43] In these circumstances, hanging on to the distinction between public and private, or at least non-private and private, may be a way to retain social and political values that rise above those of the market.[44] This is, of course, a theme to which this book will return on many occasions.

Cf UNIDROIT Convention on Stolen or Illegally Exported Cultural Objects (1995), which is based upon the UNESCO Convention on the Means of Prohibiting and Preventing the Illicit, Import, Export and Transfer of Ownership of Cultural Property (1970), of which recital 3 makes reference to "the cultural heritage of national, tribal, indigenous or other communities".

40 CICH, recital 6. See also CCD, recitals 7 & 8, referring to respectively "peoples and societies" & "indigenous peoples".

41 Hobsbawm, n 36 above, ch 12.

42 See E Christodoulidis, "On the Politics of the Public/Private Distinction: What Does It Mean to Sustain the Politics of a Lost Distinction?" *ESRC Seminar Series: The Public Life of Private Law* (Kent Law School, 18 January 2013), http://backdoorbroadcasting.net/2013/01/emilios-christodoulidis-on-the-politics-of-the-publicprivate-law-distinction-what-does-it-mean-to-sustain-the-politics-of-a-lost-distinction/, accessed 03/09/2014; S Veitch, "Law and the Public/Private Distinction" in E Christodoulidis, R Dukes & M Goldoni (eds), *Research Handbook on Critical Legal Theory* (Cheltenham: Edward Elgar, 2019).

43 Christodoulidis, n 42 above.

44 See also Christodoulidis, n 42 above.

3 Intangible cultural heritage

3.1 Defining intangible cultural heritage

Given the great variety of cultural artefacts that now, thanks to the UNESCO regime, are included within the concept of heritage, perhaps it is no surprise to find that the authorized heritage discourse does not seem to contain an overarching idea of heritage that holds together all its disparate strands. The distinctions between movable and immovable, and between tangible and intangible, tend to have obscured the development of a uniting concept. This is not only the inevitable result of the theoretical process of division and compartmentalization, but also a consequence of the way in which the authorized heritage discourse has ignored the artificiality, and even meaninglessness, of these distinctions. For example, the history of the looting, sacking and removal of cultural objects makes it abundantly clear that plenty of things that law regards as immovable are, in fact, quite evidently movable.[45] If the failure of the authorized heritage discourse to appreciate this point seems troubling, then we need to find a much stronger adjective to describe its complete confusion around questions of tangibility and intangibility.

Until the twenty first century, the distinction between tangible and intangible heritage appears to have given very little trouble to the authorized heritage discourse as embodied in the ICOMOS-UNESCO regime. Its overwhelming focus on tangible stuff, fixed or moveable, denominated as heritage by reference to a set of intangible values, provided a neat way of dealing with the tangible/intangible distinction, without losing the similarly overwhelming occidental focus on the tangible heritage object. This is well demonstrated by both the Convention on the Means of Prohibiting and Preventing the Illicit Import, Export and Transfer of Ownership of Cultural Property, dealing with movables, and the WHC, dealing with legally denominated immovables. The WHC, for example, as has been noted earlier, limits its concept of protected tangibles by reference to obviously occidental concepts such as "outstanding universal value from the point of view of history, art or science" and "outstanding universal value from the historical, aesthetic, ethnological or anthropological point of view".[46] According to both Conventions, which dominated the international legal protection of heritage in the twentieth century, heritage was what the state said it was, or in the case of the WHC, what the state said it was as endorsed by a UNESCO listing.[47] And

45 If an example of this is needed, the so-called "Elgin Marbles", previously part of various buildings on the Athenian Acropolis, would fit nicely, as would the Bruno Schulz wall paintings that have been relocated from Drohobych in the Ukraine to the Yad Vashem Museum in Jerusalem: see further, ch 5, section 4.

46 WHC, Art 1.

47 Convention on the Means of Prohibiting and Preventing the Illicit, Import, Export and Transfer of Ownership of Cultural Property 1970, Art 1, which protects "cultural property" falling

what the state said was heritage was governed by prevailing national discourses that tended, and still tend, to privilege the largely Western ideas that dominant elites have about things that are important to history, art, literature, science, anthropology and ethnology.[48] The possibility that the intangible could take flight on its own account and start to fray this straitjacket may have been raised from time to time in international contexts – and especially by subaltern voices – but for a considerable period it was in little danger of toppling the operation of the authorized heritage discourse.[49] The process leading to the 2003 CICH and the 2005 CCD started chipping away at all this certainty. Now that both these Conventions have come into force it seems that the limits on the possible expansion of the heritage concept that were imposed by the former linkage between the tangible and the intangible have been abandoned.

This, of course, has created some problems in defining the concept of intangible cultural heritage. Strangely, however, the question of what is intangible seems comparatively less problematic than the question of what we mean by heritage. Perhaps the long occidental obsession with the tangible/intangible distinction turns out to be some help after all. This is because, as much as it is true that all tangible heritage is inherently connected with the intangible values that make it heritage and not just a pile of old junk, it is also arguably the case that all – or nearly all – intangible heritage is connected to the tangible or material world. The types of intangible practices that likely constitute intangible cultural heritage are, as Harrison argues, "thoroughly embedded in a set of physical relationships with objects, places and other people".[50] (While forms of cultural heritage that are digital may present some challenges to this characterization, an intangible place – like cyberspace – might still count as a place.) Nevertheless, the intangible world – connected or not to the tangible world – seems to offer a vast palette, especially when linked to the undefined concept of heritage and the undefinable idea of culture. Viewed from this perspective, intangible cultural heritage might be just about anything at all intangible to which we might attach descriptions like "culture" or "cultural".[51] Needless to say, if everything intangible that we do is intangible cultural heritage, then at least one consequence of this is that the idea of subjecting it to some sort of regime of legal protection or recognition is problematic. This risk is, of course, recognized by the authorized heritage discourse, which seeks to put some limits on the concept of intangible

within a closed list of categories all subject to the prerequisite that it is "on religious or secular grounds ... specifically designated by each State as being of importance for archaeology prehistory, history, literature, art or science"; WHC, Art 11.

48 See, e.g., Smith, n 16 above; Harrison, n 17 above.

49 Smith, n 16 above, at 106–113.

50 Harrison, n 17 above, at 14.

51 Which provides hardly any limit at all bearing in mind the totalizing nature of the concept of "culture": see, e.g., Blake, n 27 above, at 67–68, quoting G M Sider, *Culture and Class in Anthropology and History* (Cambridge: Cambridge University Press, 1986), at 6.

cultural heritage and thereby resists disintegrating under the weight of its own expansion. However, as this chapter argues, we should be wary of assuming that this authorized discourse, as embodied in things like the CICH, correctly identifies what is intangible cultural heritage or properly protects it.

Intangible cultural heritage is caught in a strange temporal loop. On the one hand, as with all so-called cultural heritage, it reflects the contemporary obsession with the past. On the other, it must negotiate the equally obsessional quest to call everything that seems to be a present-day "cultural" practice intangible cultural heritage. Both of these ideas involve a type of *pas de deux* between past and present, the first more obviously so, which is reflected in modernity's relationship with time. As Harrison writes of modernity:

> [I]t constantly creates the present as "contemporary past" whilst it anticipates the future as embodied within its present. In other words, modernity creates for itself a past that is perceived to be both immanent (contained within) and imminent (impending) in the present ... One important outcome of this rather peculiar relationship with time is that in its obsessive attempts to transcend the present, modernity becomes fixated on the past in several distinctive ways. In the first instance, it is haunted by the idea of decline or decay ... Secondly, in attempting to define itself in opposition to tradition and the past, modernity becomes concerned with defining and categorising it.[52]

While this obviously addresses what I have described as the obsession with the past, it also links this with concerns about the value of contemporary cultural practices. The critical point is that this *pas de deux* between past and present is immanent in the very notion of heritage, which is always contemporary and also always past. It is always contemporary because it is only in the present that it is recognized as heritage, but also always past because even what we might describe as contemporary intangible heritage, in the sense of contemporary cultural practices, has to have already happened, even if it has only just happened, for us to be able to reflect on it and identify it as heritage.[53] This element of reflection is essential to the concept of cultural heritage/property that has been outlined in Section 2 and which, so far as the UNESCO Conventions are concerned, has its clearest instantiation in Article 2.1 of the CICH. That is, that heritage is constituted by those things we select from the past (including presumably the near past) as having the sort of value that makes them worth passing on to the future.

52 Harrison, n 17 above, at 25–26 (references omitted).

53 See also, e.g., Harrison, n 17 above, at 14: "heritage is formed *in the present* and reflects inherited and current concerns about the past" (italics as in the original).

3.2 Intangible cultural heritage and community

It is clear that, given free reign, this concept of heritage poses some challenges to, and introduces some dissonances in, the authorized heritage discourse contained in the UNESCO Conventions. We should not shrink away from acknowledging this. As Smith argues:

> Heritage *is* dissonant – it is a constitutive social process that on the one hand is about regulating and legitimizing, and on the other hand is about working out, contesting and challenging a range of cultural and social identities, sense of place, collective memories, values and meanings that prevail in the present and can be passed on to the future.[54]

The questions of whose identity prevails, whose collective memories survive and who gets to decide what is passed on to the future are all intensely political questions "tied to claims to and expressions of power" by a community.[55] And it is in this mutually constitutive relationship between heritage and community that the particular power and importance of heritage lies. Not only does cultural heritage belong to communities, but it also defines them and confers them with cultural, social and political power.[56] This mutual relationship between heritage and community tends to reinforce the essentially intangible nature of all heritage.[57] It also means that some understanding of the nature and identity of community is an essential part of any attempt to conceptualize cultural heritage/property. At the same time, it is precisely at the interface of cultural heritage/property and community that a particular challenge is flaunted in the face of the authorized heritage discourse as it is contained in the international legal instruments. While this will be addressed in more detail in the next chapter, it is, perhaps, useful to preface the current discussion by noting that, for most purposes, the authorized heritage discourse understands the cultural heritage community as being national. In order to suppress dissonance, it *often* ignores the fact that community identities are formed at multiple levels and in multiple layers.[58] It *necessarily* ignores the fact that one of the more contentious levels of community identity may be that of the nation state.

Before considering in more detail how the authorized heritage discourse deals with the concept of community, it is worth emphasizing the fact that community only makes sense here when it is understood as a contemporary phenomenon. This raises a necessary relationship between any meaningful concept of cultural property/heritage and contemporary cultural practices. If heritage belongs to a

54 Smith, n 16 above, at 82.
55 Smith, n 16 above, at 192.
56 See Smith, n 16 above, at 288.
57 See also Smith, n 16 above, at, e.g., 3 and 307.
58 See also Smith, n 16 above, at 53.

community, then it is also true that a community only exists and identifies itself through a common process of remembering and forgetting those things and practices that are essential to its identity. Cultural heritage/property, therefore, is drawn from a current and ongoing process of selection and identification, which reflects contemporary concerns and values.[59] And because it is reflexive, it changes with community practice.[60] Cultural practices that are no longer the values and practices of a contemporary community are not heritage. As a result, all cultural practices of communities, which those communities consider worth continuing, are the intangible cultural heritage/property of those communities. But it is also the case that the more recent the cultural practice, and the formation of a community around it, the more unstable its identity is likely to be and the less likely it is that it will have a coherent capacity to reflect on the processes of identity-making, memory and reflection that produce and constitute its intangible cultural heritage.

Focusing in more detail on how the UNESCO regime deals with the issue of community, we see (as already noted in Section 2.3) that it at least rates a mention in the CICH. Its sixth recital recognizes "that communities, in particular indigenous communities, groups and, in some cases individuals, play an important role in the production, safeguarding maintenance and recreation of the intangible cultural heritage". Given the role of this Convention in the authorized heritage discourse, one might speculate, quite reasonably, that this mention is a type of inoculation against criticisms of the international legal regime for its statist nature. However, much as the authorized discourse may protest, the introduction of the concept of community into this instrument is compromised by the inescapably statist nature of the system. The results of this are clearly exclusionary. Despite their special mention in the CICH, in the post-colonial context, Indigenous Peoples, not constituting a state in international law, provide a salutary example of the problems of being a stateless community. But the CICH does not limit its rhetorical concern for communities to those formed by Indigenous Peoples. This much is clear from the Convention's definition of "intangible cultural heritage" in Article 2.1, which is reproduced in (coincidentally) Section 2.1.

Even though it uses the community word, the CICH does not seek to define the concept of community. Nor does it attempt to indicate expressly how a community might be recognized by the law, although perhaps the reflexive relationship between community, types of intangible things ("practices, representations, expressions, knowledge, skills") and a tangible or spatial dimension ("instruments, objects, artefacts and cultural spaces") in this definition provide

59 Smith, n 16 above, at 3; see also Harrison, n 17 above, at 14, quoted in n 53 above.

60 P Fitzpatrick & R Joyce, "Copying Right: Cultural Property and the Limits of (Occidental) Law" in F Macmillan (ed), *New Directions in Copyright Law: Volume 4* (Cheltenham: Edward Elgar, 2007).

some orientation points.[61] Further, there is also the hope of what Zagato describes as a "(fruitful) contamination" between the meaning of "community" in the CICH and the more fully articulated concept of "heritage communities" in the Council of Europe's 2005 Framework Convention on the Value of Cultural Heritage for Society (Faro Convention).[62] Without labouring the point unduly, it is clear that what constitutes "practices, representations, expressions, knowledge, skills – as well as the instruments, objects, artefacts and cultural spaces associated therewith" in Article 2.1 of the CICH must be understood to be in a reflexive relationship with the community to which they belong. The risk that we enter into an endless circularity of vague uncertainty is mitigated to some extent by Article 2.2 that provides an inclusive definition of the intangible objects of protection to which further reference will be made in the following section of this chapter. Armed with this guidance on the type of stuff that constitutes intangible cultural heritage, and tactfully avoiding the problem of community identification, to which this book will return in Chapter 4, we might say that the CICH makes quite a reasonable job of identifying the sorts of intangible things that might be the reasonable object of protection as forms of heritage. This even extends to its acknowledgement of the role of the tangible and spatial dimensions of this type of heritage.[63]

Or, at least, things seem this way until one turns from the gilded cage of the CICH's text to its real operative life. At this point, things start to look a bit less rosy for three reasons in particular, all of which are part and parcel of the essentially state-based nature and occidental framing of (not only) this Convention (but also all international law). First, the patterns of state adherence to the CICH may reasonably be interpreted as expressing the continuing unease that the authorized heritage discourse has with the concept of intangible cultural heritage.[64] At the time of writing, the CICH has 178 states parties, which is a good overall level of adherence.[65] There is a significant level of adherence amongst non-Western states. However, there are some interesting omissions amongst the parties to the Convention, especially if it is compared with other UNESCO Conventions pertaining to cultural heritage. Australia, Canada, New Zealand, the United States and the United Kingdom, for example, are not parties to the CICH. Smith notes that for countries such as these, in addition, to

61 See also L Zagato, "The Notion of 'Heritage Community' in the Council of Europe's Faro Convention. Its Impact on the European Legal Framework" in N Adell, R F Bendix, C Bortolotto & M Tauschek (eds), *Between Imagined Communities and Communities of Practice: Participation, Territory and the Making of Heritage*, Göttingen Studies in Cultural Property, Volume 8 (Göttingen: Göttingen University Press, 2015), at 153.

62 Zagato, n 61 above, at 153 and see esp 153–159.

63 But without, of course, challenging the Cartesian dualism that permeates the UNESCO Conventions: see Harrison, n 17 above, at 137.

64 Smith, n 16 above, at 55.

65 https://ich.unesco.org/en/states-parties-00024, accessed 03/05/2020.

unease with the idea of intangible cultural heritage, there is also doubt about its relevance: "one official in a leading government heritage organization in the United Kingdom having asserted the irrelevance of the Convention as the 'UK has no intangible heritage'".[66] But even for those occidental states that are parties, it is evident that very little (comparatively speaking) has been listed. Non-Western states have made an overwhelmingly greater use of the provisions to list intangible cultural heritage on the Representative List of the Intangible Cultural Heritage of Humanity and the List of Intangible Cultural Heritage in Need of Urgent Safeguarding, which are established under Articles 16 and 17, respectively, of the CICH. A comparison with the use made by Western states of the listing facility under the WHC, of which they have made extensive use, points up a notable lack of Western interest in intangible cultural heritage even on the part of signatory states to the CICH. This phenomenon, Smith suggests, "relates to the inability of intangible heritage to 'speak to' or find synergy with the dominant sense of historical and social experiences" on which the (Western) authorized heritage discourse is based.[67]

Of course, the very notion that listing something contributes in some way to its protection is part of the Western authorized heritage discourse that is largely concerned with materiality and monumentality. In the authorized heritage discourse, these concepts represent values that can be captured in a list, frozen in time and rendered immutable. It is far from clear that it is meaningful to attempt to capture the vitality and mutability of intangible heritage in this way. Concerns have similarly been expressed that even the use made by non-Western states of the listing facility tends to favour things having the quality of "folklore" or of "traditional" practices: "the colourful and the exotic, those things that the West tends to romanticize".[68] More than this, these "colourful and exotic" things are being listed by states, not by communities within those states. Consequently, in the non-Western world, as much as in the Western world, alternative voices and communities forming less than the state as a whole are not necessarily well-represented, despite the existence of provisions in the CICH designed to encourage community participation in the identification and safeguarding of cultural heritage.[69] As always, this has tended to penalize Indigenous Peoples,

66 Smith, n 16 above, at 109. If there are changes to this position, they have not yet resulted in adherence to the CICH.

67 Smith, n 16 above, at 109.

68 Smith, n 16 above, at 112, citing R Kurin, "Comments" (2002) 43 *Current Anthropology* 144–145; R Kurin, "Safeguarding Intangible Cultural Heritage in the 2003 UNESCO Convention: A Critical Appraisal" (2004) 56 *Museum International* 66–76; B Kirshenblatt-Gimblett, "Intangible Heritage as Metacultural Production" (2004) 56 *Museum International* 52–64.

69 CICH, Art 11 requires states parties to "identify and define the various elements of the intangible cultural heritage present in its territory, with the participation of communities, groups and relevant non-governmental organizations". Art 15 requires states parties to "endeavour to ensure the widest possible participation of communities, groups and, where appropriate, individuals

in particular. Adding insult to injury, some of the Western states that have been noted earlier as not having adhered to the CICH are states that have significant and politically active Indigenous Peoples. The complications of colonial and post-colonial cultural appropriation, political contention (if not outright hostility), confusion about identity and about community formation at the state and sub-state levels, have perhaps made the idea of an authorized discourse of intangible cultural heritage too hot to handle for these states.

Despite the not unpromising text of the CICH, the reality of its operation does not suggest that it provides a particularly fertile ground for the protection of intangible cultural heritage generally, and especially the sorts of intangible cultural heritage/property that might be described as involving contemporary cultural practices. The more contemporary the practice, the more mutable it is, and the more fluid (or unstable) the community built around it, the less likely it is, in any case, to find its way to a listing under the CICH. Added to this, occidental discourses of heritage, which mostly seem to understand intangible heritage as something that "they" (non-Western states and Indigenous Peoples) have, and the state-centric nature of both the CICH and its listing process, all militate against such recognition.[70] In particular, when communities can be formed online without any particular territorial limits, the artificiality of imagining the intangible cultural heritage community as co-terminus with the state becomes even more obvious. Although it is worth noting that the phenomenon of the trans-statal heritage community is not new, a number of Indigenous Peoples fall within this description. In any case, the important point to note here is that the types of things likely to be listed as cultural heritage are those that are represented by dominant narratives within a state. Communities that are less than, and contained within, the state as a whole, or have transcended the limits of state boundaries are unlikely to get much of a look-in.

3.3 *Intangible cultural heritage and intellectual property*

How much do all these criticisms matter? Do vibrant vital cultural practices need the protection of law? What could law possibly offer that is of use to them? It seems hardly worth lingering over the safeguarding obligations on states with respect to listed intangible cultural heritage that are contained in the CICH. It might be going too far to describe the protection granted under the CICH as

that create, maintain and transmit ... [intangible cultural] heritage, and to involve them actively in its management". See further Kirshenblatt-Gimblett, n 68 above, at 57, quoted in Smith, n above, at 112.

70 See J R Slaughter, "Form & Informality: An Unliterary Look at World Literature" in R Warhol (ed), *The Work of Genre: Selected Essays from the English Institute* (New York: English Institute in Collaboration with the American Council of Learned Societies, 2011).

tantamount to leaving that heritage in the unregulated commons, but it also seems pretty clear that the protection conferred by this Convention cannot do all the things that a real community right to its cultural heritage/property might imply. Safeguarding is, apparently, a different thing to protecting. The safeguarding obligations under the CICH, according to Article 2.3, require states to put in place "measures aimed at ensuring the viability of the intangible cultural heritage, including the identification, documentation, research, preservation, protection, promotion, enhancement, transmission ... as well as the revitalization of the various aspects of such heritage". The very nature of these obligations tends to emphasize the folkloric and static nature of the things that are likely to be listed, and perhaps also their value in attracting tourism. Maybe there is a symbolic importance for the communities to which such heritage belongs in having it listed under the auspices of an international instrument. Assuming, of course, that where the community is not co-extensive with a state, they manage to get the states in which they live to apply for listing in a way that recognizes the cultural importance and political impact of the intangible cultural heritage in question in the constitutive processes of community building.

However, if the object of protecting intangible cultural heritage is more than rhetorical or symbolic, then my suggestion is that the form of legal protection that might conceivably matter for intangible cultural heritage, particularly in relation to some types of contemporary cultural practices, is one that is notably absent, at least in such specific terms, from the CICH: protection from the exercise of private intellectual property rights over cultural production in relation to the protected heritage. While the concept of safeguarding might be wide enough to encompass such measures, it would be more than an optimistic overstatement to read the CICH as mandating them. Article 13(d)(ii) requires states to "adopt appropriate legal, technical, administrative and financial measures aimed at ... ensuring access to the intangible cultural heritage while respecting customary practices governing access to specific aspects of such heritage".[71] Perhaps the ambiguous expression "customary practices" might be wide enough to give some scope for limiting the type of appropriation by those outside the relevant cultural heritage community that occurs through the device, unknown to many customary practices, of appropriation in the form of private intellectual property. But there seems to be no evidence of this so far.

While attempting to avoid falling into the trap of assuming that the definition of intangible cultural heritage in the CICH is the last word on this question (even though, as a definition it has something going for it), at this point it is

71 If any notice is taken of this at all, it seems more likely that it will result in the protection of forms of intangible cultural heritage that are considered to be somehow sacred: see, e.g., P Yu, "Cultural Relics, Intellectual Property and Intangible Heritage" (2008) 81 *Temple Law Review* 433–506.

worth having a closer look at the inclusive list of the domains of intangible cultural heritage in Article 2.2 of the CICH, which provides:

The "intangible cultural heritage", as defined in paragraph 1 earlier, is manifested inter alia in the following domains:

a oral traditions and expressions, including language as the vehicle of the intangible cultural heritage;
b performing arts;
c social practices, rituals and festive events;
d knowledge and practices concerning nature and the universe;
e traditional craftsmanship.

As this list makes clear, the concept of intangible cultural heritage with which the CICH is concerned is, like the concept of cultural heritage/property generally, strongly associated with the creative arts.[72] In Chapter 1, it was argued that one of the markers of the social acceptance of a practice as part of the creative arts in occidental society is, similarly, that the practice then came to be protected as a copyright work.[73] Bearing this in mind, it seems strange that the possible dissonance between the cultural heritage and the intellectual property regimes is not addressed by the CICH. It is even stranger when the non-exclusive list in Article 2.2 mentions things like "the performing arts" and "craftsmanship", and when the reference to "knowledge and practices concerning nature and the universe" looks like exactly the type of the so-called traditional knowledge that has been the subject of debates around its use in patent specifications. There is a type of backhand acknowledgement in the CICH that some conflict could arise, but the possibility of the conflict is resolved by giving precedence to "the rights and obligations of States Parties deriving from any international instrument relating to intellectual property rights … to which they are parties".[74] The CICH Operational Directives, however, suggest a more positive spin on the heritage-intellectual property relationship.[75] Paragraph 104 directs states parties to the Convention

> to ensure, in particular through the application of intellectual property rights, privacy rights and any other appropriate form of legal protection, that the rights of the communities, groups and individuals that create, bear and transmit their intangible cultural heritage are duly protected when raising awareness about their heritage or engaging in commercial activities.

72 See also Hobsbawm, n 36 above, ch 12.
73 L Bently & B Sherman, *Intellectual Property Law* (Oxford: Oxford University Press, 5th edition, 2018), ch 2. And see ch 1, section 2.2.
74 CICH, Art 3(b).
75 CICH Operational Directives 7.GA (2018), which are made by the General Assembly pursuant to CICH, Art 7.

This provision does not elide cultural heritage and intellectual property rights, but it comes quite close, and it certainly suggests some sort of mutually beneficial resonance.

The question of the relationship between cultural heritage/property and intellectual property is a particularly fraught one.[76] The central tension rests on the fact that while cultural heritage/property is something that "belongs" in some way to a community, intellectual property including copyright is a rivalrous form of private property. Consequently, these two systems involve two very different ways of expressing value. As has been argued in Chapter 1, copyright – and sometimes also other intellectual property rights – commodifies creative forms so that their value can be expressed through the market. As the next chapter will argue in more detail, the value of cultural heritage/property is tied to that of the community. So while copyright as a private property right locates all relationships in the context of the market, the context of cultural heritage/property relationships is the community, of which the market forms a part but does not (or should not) control the whole. Of course, not everything that might be considered to be intangible cultural heritage/property falls inside the copyright net and vice versa. Understanding heritage as a constitutive process of community formation puts it at odds with copyright's market-based focus on an end product.[77] However, it is also clear that copyright can intervene in the constitutive process appropriating pieces of it, not only changing the identity of what has been appropriated but also changing the heritage process.[78] And then, there are other aspects of copyright that mean that if we were to compare everything that might be considered intangible cultural heritage/property and everything that is subject to copyright, there would be a great amount of stuff that does not fall into the area of overlap. For instance, there is intangible cultural heritage/ property that falls outside the copyright net because, even if its "authors" are

76 See Macmillan, n 4 above; Macmillan, n 34 above; F Macmillan, "Arts Festivals: Property, Heritage or More?" in K Bowrey & M Handler (eds), *Law & Creativity in the Age of the Entertainment Franchise* (Cambridge: Cambridge University Press, 2014); Macmillan, n 20 above; F Macmillan, "Heritage, Imperialism and Commodification: How the West Can Always Do It Best" (2017) 74 *Europa Ethnica* 114–124.

77 For discussions around this point during the drafting process of the CICH, see L Lixinski & L Buckingham, "Propertization, Safeguarding and the Cultural Commons: The Turf Wars of Intangible Cultural Heritage and Traditional Cultural Expressions" in V Vadi & B De Witte (eds), *Culture and International Economic Law* (London & New York: Routledge, 2015).

78 Fitzpatrick & Joyce, n 60 above; L Liang, "Beyond Representation: The Figure of the Pirate" in M Biagioli, P Jaszi & M Woodmansee (eds), *Making and Unmaking Intellectual Property: Creative Production in Legal and Cultural Perspective* (Chicago, IL & London: University of Chicago Press, 2011), at 176:

> The epics, stories, songs, and sagas that represent in some ways the collective heritage of humanity have survived only because their custodians took care not to lock them into a system of end usage; instead they embellished them, adding to their health and vitality before passing them on to others.

identifiable, any copyright interest will have disappeared into the mist of the copyright duration rules. Similarly, not every banality – and there are plenty bearing in mind that the "originality" requirement in copyright is *de minimis* – to which copyright gives protection can claim the type of importance to constitutive processes of community that might qualify it as cultural heritage/property.

It is at this point that one might start to unravel the apparent strangeness in the fact that the CICH ignores the possibility of an overlap between its objects of protection and those of copyright. Implicit in the underlying idea of the CICH is not only the idea that intangible cultural heritage is something that "they" (non-Western states and Indigenous Peoples) have, but also that what we have instead is intellectual property.[79] As Slaughter argues, what we in the West, heartland of international law construction, think of as intangible cultural heritage or property is stuff that is no longer in copyright protection and has stood the test of time somehow becoming "heritage" in the process.[80] And we don't really think it needs any other sort of protection once it comes out of the end of the copyright machine. According to this approach, intangible cultural heritage – if it exists at all – is, like its tangible counterpart, basically something old. At least so far as the authorized heritage discourse goes, this resolves the problem of the protection of contemporary intangible property/heritage practices. And, in particular, it resolves what would otherwise be the conflict between the identity of at least some things as intangible cultural property/heritage and their character as copyright works. And so, the privatization and commodification of all our contemporary cultural practices can proceed apace.

4 Cultural property and decolonization

So much for the situation of the West/Global North when it comes to the protection of that part of its cultural heritage/property that would be labelled as intangible according to the authorized heritage discourse. What about the position of the post-colonial world, composed of the states and communities that were not present at the remaking of the international law system at the end of the Second World War? Given the relationship between cultural heritage/property and identity, it is not surprising that "ownership" of cultural heritage is also a part of the contested territory of sovereignty, and challenges to sovereignty, in a world that is not perhaps quite as globalized (for better or worse) as one might sometimes be tempted to think. This raises the question of how we mediate the claims of the authorized heritage discourse that cultural stuff is the common heritage of humanity with the particular claims of "developing" countries and Indigenous Peoples. Another challenge that these claims make to the authorized heritage discourse arises as a result of its organization around a taxonomy that resembles the Western ordering of property. When the cultural stuff in question

79 Slaughter, n 70 above.
80 Slaughter, n 70 above.

is not Western, it becomes even more difficult (not to mention somewhat ridiculous) to fit it into Western systems of thought. This is particularly noticeable in relation to the distinction between tangible and intangible cultural heritage/property, and tends to expose in an even starker fashion the problems in this distinction. And, of course, in the post-colonial context, the perennial question of the appropriation of cultural heritage/property through the device intellectual property has the additional dimension that non-Western cultural stuff is frequently appropriated by interests from the global North.

4.1 Claims of developing countries and Indigenous Peoples

There are some common issues that arise when considering the question of the mediation of general claims to the common heritage of humanity with particular claims of developing countries and Indigenous Peoples. Nevertheless, such claims by developing countries and Indigenous Peoples are distinct and should not, therefore, be elided. For developing countries, whose very existence as states is often a post-colonial construct, attempting to build a national identity, sometimes from scratch, and to forge it around often invented/artificially constructed national symbolism, the failure to return significant forms of what the authorized discourse considers movable tangible cultural heritage/property has been in some cases viewed as a denial of the right to exist.[81] Despite the statist focus of the UNESCO Conventions, they have been of little assistance to developing countries with respect to tangible cultural heritage because of their resolutely non-retroactive effect. The irony of this is particularly marked in relation to the Convention on the Means of Prohibiting and Preventing the Illicit Import, Export and Transfer of Ownership of Cultural Property, Article 2 of which provides:

> The States Parties to this Convention recognize that the illicit import, export and transfer of cultural property is one of the main causes of the impoverishment of the cultural heritage of the countries of origin of such property and that international co-operation constitutes one of the most efficient means of protecting each country's cultural property against all the dangers resulting there from.

The fact that the Convention and its more recent partner the UNIDROIT Convention on Stolen or Illegally Exported Cultural Objects of 1995 apply to

81 For a discussion of the importance of the restitution of cultural artefacts to former colonial states, see Vrdoljak, n 2 above, at 200–206. Post-colonial states also increasingly regard intangible heritage as essential to nation building, see C Antons & W Logan (eds), *Intellectual Property, Cultural Property and Intangible Cultural Heritage* (London & New York: Routledge, 2018), Part III Intangible cultural heritage, law and nation building.

movable tangible property and that both Conventions clearly envisage that such property is national in nature would seem to make them well-adapted to the task of recognizing at least some of the cultural interests at play here.[82] However, the Conventions only apply to acts undertaken from the time they came into force, which means that they are more or less irrelevant, in a strictly legal sense, to the claims of countries from the global South for restitution of objects removed during the colonial period.[83] However, symbolically, they might be regarded as stating an ethical position that should be recognized by the international community.[84] In this respect, it is interesting to note that the UNIDROIT Convention provides that, despite its lack of retrospectivity, it

> does not in any way legitimise any illegal transaction … which has taken place before the entry into force of this Convention … nor limit any right of a State or other person to make a claim under remedies available outside the framework of this Convention for the restitution or return of a cultural object stolen or illegally exported before the entry into force of this Convention.

For Indigenous groups, the question of the right to control cultural heritage is linked to questions of identity, survival and the political project of self-determination, in a world that is dominated by the Westphalian state-based system of sovereignty and law-making. Representing some changes in political awareness, the 1995 UNIDROIT Convention recognizes the existence of "national, tribal, indigenous or other communities" and introduces some procedural rules about claims to movable tangible heritage in the light of this recognition. Its applicability is, of course, limited by the problem of retrospectivity. Another problem for Indigenous Peoples is that the Convention envisages the need for a co-operative relationship between these groups and the state or states in which they live in relation to the international claims for return with which it is concerned. It is also the case that, as the Convention only deals with international claims, it says

82 The UNIDROIT Convention on Stolen or Illegally Exported Cultural Objects introduces a more complex legal architecture in order to support the UNESCO Convention on the Means of Prohibiting & Preventing the Illicit Import, Export & Transfer of Ownership of Cultural Property.

83 UNESCO Convention on the Means of Prohibiting & Preventing the Illicit Import, Export & Transfer of Ownership of Cultural Property, Art 7; UNIDROIT Convention on Stolen or Illegally Exported Cultural Objects of 1995, Art 10.

84 Although the Convention on the Means of Prohibiting & Preventing the Illicit Import Export & Transfer of Ownership of Cultural Property, Art 4, makes cultural property that has been removed with the consent of the competent authorities (paras (c) & (e)) or "been the subject of a freely agreed exchange" (para (d)) part of the patrimony of the state in which it is located. The application of this provision to artefacts taken during the colonial period would be the source of endless conflicts about what was "looted" and what was not. In the post-colonial context, this is not only difficult to substantiate, but more importantly beside the point.

nothing about claims by Indigenous Peoples against the states in which they live. It is interesting, perhaps, to note that, in any case, at the time of writing, a number of states with substantial populations of Indigenous Peoples, including Australia, Canada and the United States, are not parties to the Convention.[85]

All this is, of course, quite consistent with the proposition that the endlessly inconclusive work of the World Intellectual Property Organization's Intergovernmental Committee on Intellectual Property and Genetic Resources, Traditional Knowledge and Folklore (WIPO IGC) is intended by the international legal community as the primary site for debates about the protection of the heritage of Indigenous Peoples.[86] Apart from its aforesaid inconclusiveness, a problem with the relocation of this debate to the halls of WIPO is that the WIPO IGC's work is very much focussed on the protection of end products of this heritage, rather than having the more open and holistic focus of the CICH.[87] This dovetails with the symbolism of locating this work in the domain of WIPO, where the (at least) implicit assertion of some relationship between intellectual property and the heritage of Indigenous Peoples seems to be a foregone conclusion. The same asserted relationship also appears quite explicitly in the 2007 United Nations Declaration on the Rights of Indigenous Peoples (the DRIPs), which is one of the results of the long campaign of Indigenous Peoples for the recognition and remediation of the treatment meted out to them in the colonial and post-colonial periods.

While being careful to make no claims with respect to political self-determination, the DRIPs should be understood as being linked to this agenda.[88] It recognizes the connection between heritage and identity, and contains numerous manifestations of the importance attached to this relationship, which traverse rights in both tangible and intangible heritage.[89] These concepts are found in Articles 11.1, 12.1 and 13.1, which provide, respectively:

> [Article 11.1:] Indigenous peoples have the right to practise and revitalize their cultural traditions and customs. This includes the right to maintain, protect and develop the past, present and future manifestations of their

85 https://www.unidroit.org/status-cp, accessed 03/05/2020.

86 See Lixinski & Buckingham, n 77 above.

87 See also Lixinski & Buckingham, n 77 above.

88 DRIPs, Art 46.1 provides:

> Nothing in this Declaration may be interpreted as implying for any State, people, group or person any right to engage in any activity or to perform any act contrary to the Charter of the United Nations or construed as authorizing or encouraging any action which would dismember or impair, totally or in part, the territorial integrity or political unity of sovereign & independent States.

89 While at the same time making reference to the ubiquitous concept of the common heritage of humankind in a preambular statement that affirms that "all peoples contribute to the diversity and richness of civilizations & cultures, which constitute the common heritage of humankind".

> cultures, such as archaeological and historical sites, artefacts, designs, ceremonies, technologies and visual and performing arts and literature.
>
> [Article 12.1:] Indigenous peoples have the right to manifest, practise, develop and teach their spiritual and religious traditions, customs and ceremonies; the right to maintain, protect, and have access in privacy to their religious and cultural sites; the right to the use and control of their ceremonial objects; and the right to the repatriation of their human remains.
>
> [Article 13.1:] Indigenous peoples have the right to revitalize, use, develop and transmit to future generations their histories, languages, oral traditions, philosophies, writing systems and literatures, and to designate and retain their own names for communities, places and persons.

Articles 11.2, 12.2 and 13.2, meanwhile, impose obligations on states with respect to the protection of these rights, as well as redress and restitution in cases where the rights have been infringed. The Declaration's main assertion with respect to cultural heritage, however, is in Article 31.1, which also has the effect of linking cultural heritage and intellectual property rights:

> Indigenous peoples have the right to maintain, control, protect and develop their cultural heritage, traditional knowledge and traditional cultural expressions, as well as the manifestations of their sciences, technologies and cultures, including human and genetic resources, seeds, medicines, knowledge of the properties of fauna and flora, oral traditions, literatures, designs, sports and traditional games and visual and performing arts. They also have the right to maintain, control, protect and develop their intellectual property over such cultural heritage, traditional knowledge, and traditional cultural expressions.

4.2 *Tangibility, intangibility and the privatization of cultural heritage*

In general cultural terms, the significance of the distinction between tangible and intangible heritage can be easily exaggerated. This is because what makes a tangible item heritage is precisely its symbolic value. In other words, even tangible items are only heritage because of an intangible connection.[90] Despite itself, UNESCO's authorized heritage regime has been unable to completely ignore the problems posed by attempts to divide cultural heritage/property between tangible and intangible stuff. Both the CICH and the CCD disrupt to some extent the previous practice of attempting to separate the tangible and the intangible. As already noted earlier, the CICH includes within its definition of

90 See Blake, n 27 above, at 67–69.

intangible cultural heritage "instruments, objects, artefacts and cultural spaces" associated with "practices, representations, expressions, knowledge, skills ... that communities, groups and, in some cases, individuals recognize as part of their cultural heritage".[91] The CCD recognizes that both the tangible and intangible are part of the diversity of cultures.[92] Neither Convention, however, has much to offer to either Indigenous Peoples or developing countries when it comes to the protection of their intangible cultural heritage/property from Western appropriation, which has occurred in relation to a wide range of things such as traditional medical or environmental knowledge, know-how, stories, artistic styles, music, dance, festivals, carnivals and other ceremonies. This (mis)appropriation, apart from being problematic in itself, has raised problems with respect to inappropriate use.[93] There are also circumstances in which this (mis)appropriation can interfere with the ability of Indigenous Peoples or communities in the developing world to access, use and reflect upon their own cultural heritage/property. One of these circumstances is where it is privatized without the consent or participation of the relevant community. Considerations such as these are apparently responsible for the provision in Article 31.1 of the DRIPs that proposes treating the shield as a sword by granting intellectual property rights in cultural heritage. Given the fact that turning cultural heritage/property into intellectual property is exactly how cultural heritage is misappropriated, this provision might be thought of as a little dangerous. Apart from the clear and justified sensitivity to the particular historical and political circumstances of Indigenous Peoples, one of the reasons that that claim in Article 31 of the DRIPs has gone under the critical radar is that the proposed holders of the intellectual property in cultural heritage envisaged in Article 31 are the members of the same heritage community. But, at the same time, the provision begs the question of how a cultural heritage community can also be the holder of intellectual property rights.[94]

4.3 Public v private claims to cultural heritage

The problem of mediating co-existing claims to private and some form of public or communal ownership of cultural property/heritage is one that exists with respect to both those things designated as tangibles by the authorized heritage discourse and those things designated as intangibles. As already noted in the introductory section of this chapter, the importance of respecting private property rights in relation to movable heritage was regarded as so paramount by the metropolitan powers that the UNESCO Convention on the Means of Prohibiting

91 CICH, Art 2.1.

92 E.g., through its recognition of the role of "cultural goods": CCD, Art 4.4.

93 For a full discussion of this problem, see Yu, n 71 above.

94 A similar question, but in a more generic context, is posed by the CICH Operational Directives 7.GA (2018), paragraph 104: see Section 3.3.

and Preventing the Illicit Import, Export and Transfer of Ownership of Cultural Property makes special provision to ensure that it is respected and that proper compensation is paid to a property holder. If anything, the situation with respect to the protection of private property rights over intangible forms of cultural heritage is even more biased in favour of the private right holder, with this century's UNESCO Conventions simply ceding the ground.[95] Certainly, this accommodating approach does nothing to contradict claims that appropriation through intellectual property is the new form of imperialism.[96] For developing countries and Indigenous Peoples, not only is there the problem of the appropriation of cultural heritage/property through a discourse that claims their heritage as the patrimony of humankind – some sort of global patrimony – but also the problem of the appropriation by private corporate interests, usually in the global North, of their intangible heritage. Some of the types of intangible cultural heritage that might be appropriated through intellectual property rights have already been mentioned in Section 4.2. So far as, for example, traditional medical knowledge is concerned, there is a plethora of examples of the way in which this type of intangible heritage can be appropriated by pharmaceutical corporations through the use of patents. Similarly, for example, with respect to stories, songs and music, there are serious issues about the appropriation of intangible heritage by, for example, the entertainment industry represented by the Hollywood machine.[97]

Not only does all this add another possible layer onto the question of "who owns cultural heritage?", but it also means that somehow the relationship between the private rights and the public or communal rights inherent in identifying something as cultural heritage/property must be negotiated. A negotiation of this type must depend upon some choice as to which rights should prevail. In the post-colonial context, there is strong argument in favour of giving precedence to cultural heritage/property rights over intellectual property rights and other private property rights. Three arguments might be cited in support of this proposition. The first is simply that the importance of cultural heritage to processes like nation building and self-determination, as well as its importance for the identity of Indigenous Peoples, should be regarded as giving it precedence over private rights on the grounds of ethics, justice and the right to development. Second, it could be argued that, in relation to tangible heritage, the international community has already made a political choice to favour cultural heritage/property rights over private property rights. This choice is expressed in the both UNESCO Convention on the Means of Prohibiting and Preventing

95 See n 25 above and Section 3.3.

96 See, e.g., M Rendix, "Copyright as Moral Strategy of Reclaiming the Past: The Return of the Icelandic Sagas" in H Porsdam & T Elholm (eds), *Dialogues on Justice: European Perspectives on Law & Humanities* (Berlin & Boston, MA: De Gruyter, 2012), at 191–192; Slaughter, n 70 above, esp at 198–199.

97 See, e.g., B Ivey, *Arts, Inc: How Greed and Neglect Have Destroyed Our Cultural Rights* (Berkeley: University of California Press, 2008).

the Illicit Import, Export and Transfer of Ownership of Cultural Property and the UNIDROIT Convention on Stolen or Illegally Exported Cultural Objects of 1995, in which private property rights are recognized by a right to compensation in certain circumstances, but cannot be relied upon to prevent the return of stolen or illegally exported cultural artefacts. This approach dovetails with the third argument in favour of preferring cultural heritage/property claims over private property claims, which is that this approach gives scope to both types of claims, whereas giving precedence to private property claims effectively extinguishes cultural heritage/property claims. This is an argument, of course, that also holds water outside the post-colonial context.

There is plenty of evidence that the intellectual property machine has permitted the appropriation and commodification by Western corporate interests of the cultural practices and knowledge of Indigenous Peoples and communities in the global South.[98] But it would be misleading to think that the problem here is only a problem of these communities and so another manifestation of the conflict between the West and the rest. All communities generate what the authorized heritage discourse identifies as intangible heritage. (This is the case whether the UK heritage organization officials think so or not.[99]) The idea that any community does not have intangible heritage probably owes much to the fact that we in the West think of intangibles as being the province of private intellectual property rights. In this way, while we may have greatly enriched certain Western-based corporate interests in a material sense, we have at the same time degraded our own sense of community in the Western world by allowing private intellectual property rights to sever our communities from their own cultural practices. While the idea that all non-Western cultural property is open to private appropriation is unjust and outrageous, it might also be noted that the notion that the West lacks intangible cultural property is socially (and culturally) impoverishing.

5 Asking too much of heritage?

What does it mean, in the end, to say as UNESCO instruments do with such predictable regularity, that cultural heritage is the common heritage of humanity? Is it a claim to ownership or is it a justification for special status and protection? Is it a ground upon which to argue, for example, that heritage is what makes us human? Or a ground upon which to argue that wanton acts of destruction harm the humanity of us all? As Blake notes, there is an "inherent contradiction" in characterizing something as the common heritage of humanity "while at the same time noting its power in asserting the cultural identity of the community

98 See Macmillan, n 4 above.
99 See text acc n 66 above.

which produced it".[100] Yet, the assertion of a general claim on the basis of common humanity is not without value.

History shows us that it is not possible to de-couple cultural heritage/property from particular identities, national, communal or otherwise. But it is not clear that this always implies the right to make a claim for "ownership", which might in any case be better understood as a form of stewardship.[101] Political context is clearly significant here. The post-colonial context, with its urgent demands for justice, makes claims for return of artefacts by Indigenous Peoples in Australia different to claims to some form of national cultural sovereignty by right-wing governments or political parties in Europe.[102] However, the pressing need to recognize that cultural heritage/property is critical to identity, nation building and sovereignty, and that any notion of a right to development is meaningless without these things, does not just mean that the claims by developing countries to the return of their artefacts taken during the colonial period must be taken seriously by the international community. It also requires a recognition that they have rights over their intangible heritage which impact on, for example, its wholesale appropriation as part of the Hollywood machine.

"Too much", Lowenthal writes, "is asked of heritage. In the same breath we commend national patrimony, regional and ethnic legacies and a global heritage shared and sheltered in common. We forget that these aims are usually incompatible".[103] If the cultural heritage/property claims arising from the oppressive legacy of the colonial period were accepted on the basis that in the name of a right to sovereignty and a globally just process of development they are politically distinguishable from other types of claims, we might find this problem easier to resolve. Attention could then be turned to asking even more of cultural heritage/property – or at least of rights in relation to it. Before, however, I take this line of thought further, there are two issues that have been raised constantly in the discussions of international law in this chapter. One is the question of the role of community in developing a stronger concept of cultural heritage/property, and its possible occlusion by the modern nation state. The other is the problems posed for the concept of cultural heritage/property by the unresolved and indeterminate distinctions that the authorized heritage discourse makes between nature and culture, moveable and immoveable, tangible and intangible, and the way in which these Cartesian dualisms link with the geo-political divisions between the West and the rest. These two issues, respectively, are addressed in the next two chapters.

100 Blake, n 27 above, at 64.

101 See K A Carpenter, S Katyal & A Riley, "In Defense of Property" (2009) *Yale Journal of Law* 100–204.

102 H Porsdam, "Cultural Heritage and Law: The Case of Cultural Looting" in Porsdam & Elholm, n 96 above; Macmillan, n 4 above. And see generally ch 5.

103 D Lowenthal, *The Heritage Crusade & the Spoils of History* (New York: Viking, 1997), at 227, cited in Blake, n 27 above, at 64.

Chapter 4

Community and cultural property

1 Introduction: critical heritage studies v the authorized heritage discourse

The authorized heritage discourse, embodied in the international legal regime for the protection of cultural heritage, is heavily invested in Western tropes based on a collection of Cartesian dualisms – including those of nature and culture, tangible and intangible, moveable and immoveable – which also locate heritage as being always in the past.[1] As Chapter 3 argues, this has a number of consequences for the way in which the authorized heritage discourse understands the object of its protection. These consequences include the idea that heritage can be reduced to lists of stuff; in other words, that it is (strangely, not unlike intellectual property) focussed on some sort of end product. This concept of heritage has been subject to a sustained challenge by critical heritage scholars who instead propose a concept of heritage as

> a constitutive social process that on the one hand is about regulating and legitimizing, and on the other hand is about working out, contesting and challenging a range of cultural and social identities, sense of place, collective memories, values and meanings that prevail in the present and can be passed on to the future.[2]

Heritage, understood in this way as a process, invokes the concept of community as the site of this constitutive social process.[3] This foregrounding of community in critical heritage discourse sits at serious odds with the current regime of international law.

1 The expression and concept of the authorized heritage discourse are drawn from L Smith, *Uses of Heritage* (London & New York: Routledge, 2006). On the Cartesian dualisms of the authorized heritage discourse, see R Harrison, *Heritage: Critical Approaches* (London & New York: Routledge, 2013), ch 9.

2 Smith, n 1 above, at 82.

3 See ch 3, section 3.2.

While the exact nature of the relationship between the nation state and the constitution of international law is a matter of debate, there is little real hope of escaping from the conclusion that the juridical actors of international law are the states themselves and the supranational, international and intergovernmental organizations created through the mutually interdependent process of international law-making.[4] Communities, despite being recognized in political theory as constituting the common political identity that forms the basis of the nation, and perhaps also the common cultural identity that precedes a common political identity, have traditionally received little formal attention in international law precisely because their identity has been submerged into that of the nation state.[5] This concept of international law and of international law-making is clearly exclusionary. One of its consequences is that in the post-colonial context, Indigenous Peoples, not constituting a state in international law, have found themselves without a voice at the international law-making table. In the specific context of the protection of cultural heritage in international legal instruments, this also means that the concept of a community, which is a critical counterpart to that of cultural heritage, can mostly only be understood in the relevant international law instruments as being a nation state. This means that the concept of community – if it exists at all – must be considered to be co-extensive with the nation state. It is true that more recent Conventions, notably the 1995 UNIDROIT Convention on Stolen or Illegally Exported Cultural Objects and the 2003 UNESCO Convention for the Protection of the Intangible Cultural Heritage (CICH), appear to recognize the critical connection between cultural heritage and community, where community is understood as including something different from the nation state. However, neither of these Conventions gives us much to go by in trying to identify such a community.[6] Even more importantly, the ability of communities that are not nation states to vindicate rights to their cultural heritage using these Conventions is extremely limited.

This chapter is dedicated to an investigation of the concept of community in the cultural heritage/property context. It commences with an attempt to unravel some of the relevant strands that make up the concept of community, focussing in particular on the question of the recognition of the cultural heritage/property

4 *Cf* A Carty, "Myths of International Legal Order: Past and Present" (1997) 10 *Cambridge Review of International Affairs* 3–22; P Fitzpatrick, "'The New Constitutionalism': The Global, the Postcolonial and the Constitution of Nations" (2006) 10(2) *Law, Democracy and Development* 1–20.

5 On the relationship between community and nation, see B Anderson, *Imagined Communities: Reflections on the Origin and Spread of Nationalism* (London & New York: Verso, 2006, revised edition; first published 1983).

6 See further F Macmillan, "Contemporary Intangible Cultural Heritage: Between Community and Market" in C Waelde, M Pavis & H Enright (eds), *Intangible Cultural Heritage and Contemporary Culture* (Cheltenham: Edward Elgar, 2017).

community. It then passes to a consideration of the challenges and possibilities that the concept of community in this context poses and offers, respectively, to law. Finally, the chapter shifts its focus from cultural heritage/property to copyright, investigating the relationship of copyright to community and contrasting this relationship with that of heritage and community.

2 Recognizing community

If there is a concept that is more difficult and unwieldy, especially in a work of what is primarily legal scholarship, than "culture", then probably that concept is "community". Readers will perhaps understand, therefore, the practical reasons for burying a chapter that attempts to take on both concepts right in the middle of the book where, one might hope, its defects will be skated over by hasty readers (whether they have started reading from the back cover or, as is more conventional, from the front). However, the middle is also close enough to being the core (or heart) of the book, to indicate the symbolic significance of the placement of this chapter. The book's overall argument depends on an elaboration of the idea of community, at least in the cultural heritage/property context. But even with the attempt to anchor discussions of community in this particular context, it is clear that we are in conceptual and philosophical trouble. In fact, one could go further and say that the very attempt to anchor a consideration of community within a political and legal context is symptomatic of the problem. This impossible problem is embodied in the opening lines of Esposito's examination of community:

> Nothing seems more appropriate today than thinking community; nothing more necessary, demanded, and heralded by a situation that joins in a unique epochal knot the failure of all communisms with the misery of new individualisms.[7] Nevertheless, nothing is further from view; nothing so remote, repressed, and put off until later, to a distant and indecipherable horizon.[8]

The problem Esposito argues is not the absence of philosophies of community, but rather the problem of translating them into

> a political-philosophical discourse that forces community into a conceptual language that radically alters it, while at the same time attempts to name it: that of the individual *and* totality; of identity *and* the particular; of the

7 Citing J-L Nancy, *The Inoperative Community* (Minneapolis, MN: University of Minneapolis Press, 1991, trans P Connor, L Garbus, M Holland & S Sawhney).

8 R Esposito, *Communitas: The Origin and Destiny of Community* (Stanford, CA: Stanford University Press, 2010, trans T Campbell), at 1.

> origin *and* the end; or more simply of the *subject* with its most unassailable metaphysical connotations of unity, absoluteness, and interiority.[9]

At the same time, as Esposito's comment suggests, like culture, it is a concept that is constantly invoked in all sorts of political and social discourses. This is as true for the cultural heritage/property context as for any other. As already noted, the international Conventions governing cultural heritage/property have increasingly made reference to the role and rights of community.[10] Is it possible to give any life to this concept outside the by now well-known and abused (or, at least, misused) equation of community and nation state? And, if we can, is it possible to save the concept from the oppression and tragedies with which, even in very recent history, it has been so often a fundamental part? And if these questions are too big to be taken on here, perhaps we can reduce them to a slightly smaller one: what would it mean to recognize what Esposito calls "the constitutively concave character" of the cultural heritage/property community while avoiding, as Esposito cautions us to do, "its affirmative entification"?[11]

I want to start this impossible and, at the same time, necessary task, by considering Anderson's famous critique of the assimilation of the idea of community into that of nation.[12] Anderson proposes that the central foundational concepts around which community rotates are identification and memory, which are reflexively linked to one another. For Anderson, communities are always imagined.[13] By this, he means not that they are fake or false, but rather that they are created by being imagined. Accordingly, he observes that "[c]ommunities are to be distinguished not by their falsity/genuineness, but by the style in which they are imagined".[14] I read this as a reflection on the subjective nature of all community constitution.[15] Anderson's observations are important because they do much to enrich the foundational relation of identification and memory There are three, in particular, that go to the heart of how community is imagined. First, Anderson notes the "deep horizontal comradeship" that characterizes (imagined) community – something that might also be referred to as solidarity

9 Esposito, n 8 above, at 1 (footnote omitted, italics as in the original). Esposito's examination of the concept takes us on a journey from Plato, via Augustine and Machiavelli, through to a critical exposition of Hobbes, Rousseau, Kant, Heidegger and Bataille.

10 See ch 3, section 2.3.

11 Esposito, n 8 above, at 15.

12 Anderson, n 5 above.

13 With the possible exception of "primordial villages of face-to-face contact": Anderson, n 5 above, at 6.

14 Anderson, n 5 above, at 6.

15 And on this basis I question the claim of De Angelis that Anderson's imagined community can be distinguished from "a community of cognitive and symbolic structures underpinned by lived spaces and social processes": M De Angelis, *Omnia Sunt Comunia: On the Commons and the Transformation to Postcapitalism* (London: Zed Books, 2017), at 123.

and so invoking the idea of reciprocity.[16] Secondly, he places emphasis on the temporal aspect of community, "this sense of parallelism or simultaneity".[17] The temporal dimensions here are both horizontal and vertical: horizontal because comradeship and solidarity carry with them some notion of a shared temporal space; vertical because if memory is critical to the imagined community, then this implies a shared concept of the community's history and its temporal progression. Following on from this, the third aspect of Anderson's study that has particular resonance is exactly this question of how a community imagines its relationship with its own past. Thus, we arrive at the critical question of the reflexive relationship between community and memory. This process of remembering and forgetting lies at the heart of the discourse of community.[18] And remembering here also means remembering to forget about the things that have been excluded – or, at least, forgetting to remember them.

Anderson's concept of the imagined community resonates with the idea of community that tends to emerge from more recent attempts to give some sort of definition to the concept of cultural heritage and, in particular, with perspectives from critical heritage studies.[19] As Chapter 3 argued, in the light of these perspectives, the process of remembering and forgetting things is the way in which the heritage community forms its identity, selecting as its cultural heritage/property those things from the past – including the very recent past – that it wants to celebrate and pass on to the future. This is reflected in Smith's argument that heritage is best understood as "a constitutive cultural process that identifies those things and places that can be given meaning and value as 'heritage' reflecting contemporary cultural and social values, debates and aspirations".[20] How a community imagines, or remembers, its past is an important question in the cultural heritage context because it goes directly to the troubling question of the difference between history and heritage. In other words, from a cultural heritage perspective, how the past is remembered is part and parcel of the question of how it is forgotten, or what part of it is forgotten. As Anderson says: "All profound changes in consciousness, by their very nature, bring with them characteristic amnesias. Out of such oblivions, in specific historical circumstances, spring narratives".[21]

16 Anderson, n 5 above, at 7. See also Smith, n 1 above, at 303; E Christodoulidis, "Social Rights Constitutionalism: An Antagonistic Endorsement" (2017) 44 *Journal of Law and Society* 123–149, at 127–129, citing A Supiot, "Grandeur and Misery of the Social State" (2013) 82 *New Left Review* 99–113; H Brunkhorst, *Solidarity: From Civic Friendship to a Global Legal Community* (Cambridge, MA: MIT Press, 2005, trans J Flynn), at 60.

17 Anderson, n 5 above, at 188.

18 Anderson, n 5 above, ch 11; E Hobsbawm, *Fractured Times: Culture and Society in the Twentieth Century* (London: Little, Brown, 2013), at 150–151.

19 See ch 3, sections 3.1 and 3.2.

20 Smith, n 1 above, at 3.

21 Anderson, n 5 above, at 204.

Already, at this point, we should understand enough about the process of community construction to have some scepticism about claims that are made in its name. Even taking into account the selective and subjective nature of historical accounts, the privileging of a selective narrative of community over such accounts rings alarm bells. The idea of the cultural heritage/property community that is described earlier also seems to run contrary to the etymological reading of community (as *cum munus*) that is presented by Esposito, who takes particular exception to the use of the concept of community in political philosophy.[22] For Esposito, community is not the polar opposite of nihilism, but rather it is the site "of the superimposition between thing and no-thing".[23] It is the place of the loss of identity where its members "are no longer identical with themselves but are constitutively exposed to a propensity that forces them to open their own individual boundaries in order to appear as what is 'outside' themselves".[24] This, for Esposito, means that the presence of community is "constitutively inhabited by an absence of subjectivity, of identity, of property".[25] Community is the relation that makes its members "no longer individual subjects"; it is lack, debt and obligation.[26] And here, the (apparent) death-blow to many modern theorists of community:

> *[C]ommunitas* is utterly incapable of producing effects of commonality, of association … and of communion. It doesn't keep us warm and it doesn't protect us; on the contrary, it exposes us to the most extreme of risks: that of losing, along with our individuality, the borders that guarantee its inviolability with respect to the other …[27]

At least one of the points that Esposito is making here is that community has formed, in relatively recent history – and continues to form – the basis for devastating and oppressive ideologies made political reality. As Enns notes, this negative face of community "is favored by a generation of European thinkers grappling with the legacies of fascism and totalitarianism … [who] are critical of belonging, identification, and the exclusions that appear to be their necessary

22 Esposito, n 8 above, e.g., at 1–2.
23 Esposito, n 8 above, at 137.
24 Esposito, n 8 above, at 138.
25 Esposito, n 8 above, at 138.
26 Esposito, n 8 above, at 139. There is a link here between Esposito's exposition of community and the Roman law meaning of solidarity as "the term for what was effectively a technique of holding co-responsible all those who played a role in the generation of a certain risk": Christodoulidis, n 16 above, at 127, citing Supiot, n 16 above & Brunkhorst, n 16 above, at 2.
27 Esposito, n 8 above, at 140. As Enns, who also quotes this passage, comments: "a rather barren depiction of community": D Enns, "Thinking Community" (Annual Meeting of the Society for Existential and Phenomenological Theory and Culture, Ryerson University, May 2017), https://www.academia.edu/33279929/Thinking_Community, accessed 01/10/2019, at 4.

outcome".[28] Given our recent past, and our disturbing present, this is not a warning to be taken lightly. Where to go from here? Is there anything today that can be drawn for what Esposito describes as this nothingness – or no-thingness – of community? Esposito himself seems to leave open the possibility of a more positive face to community. In his subsequent work on the relationship of community and immunity, arguing that community immunizes itself against what is outside, erecting barriers on both sides of the community wall, he develops the concept of immune tolerance, under the conditions of which community immunizes itself against excess immunization.[29]

Using the concept of immune tolerance and building on Esposito's analogy with the body of a pregnant woman, Enns makes the argument that what is missing in Esposito's analysis is affect:

> [D]espite Esposito's claim to the contrary, experience tells us that what we hold in common forms the basis of our desire for and pleasure in belonging to groups; we crave identifications with a wide spectrum of collectives formed around families, friends, neighbors, and shared interests – cultural, national, religious, intellectual and so forth. Notwithstanding its etymology, I question how much community has to do with obligation and duty, with a gift that "hollows" out the subject through never-ending obligation.[30]

This argument for the positive face of community allows us to make some movement from Esposito's claims that the "common" of community "is only lack, and not possession, property, or appropriation".[31] Where Esposito sees the lack of property held individually, Enns sees the possibility of shared property adding the observation that "[i]n a sense the common owns us – we *belong* to it".[32]

Nevertheless, in embracing the possibility of a positive face of community, we would be unwise (to say the least) not to heed the warning of Esposito, of Nancy, of Agamben and of Lingis.[33] This being the case, it seems worth thinking about what alternatives we have to thinking about forms of community, at least in the particular context of the difference that this book argues should be drawn

28 Enns, n 27 above, at 2, also citing Nancy, n 7 above; G Agamben, *The Coming Community* (Minneapolis: University of Minnesota Press, 1993, trans M Hardt); A Lingis, *The Community of Those Who Have Nothing in Common* (Bloomington: Indiana University Press, 1994).

29 R Esposito, *Immunitas: The Protection and Negation of Life* (Cambridge: Polity, 2011, trans Z Hanafi); R Esposito, *Terms of the Political: Community, Immunity, Biopolitics* (New York: Fordham University Press, 2013, trans R N Welch).

30 Enns, n 27 above, 8–9, citing Esposito, n 8 above, at 17. ("Thus, Kant registers for the first time the antibiological character of *communitas*: its being a gift that does not belong to the subject, indeed that weakens [*reduce*] the subject and that hollows him out through a never-ending obligation, one that prescribes what is prohibited and prohibits what is prescribed".)

31 Esposito, n 8 above, at 139.

32 Enns, n 27 above, at 9.

33 See n 28 above.

between the market and community in the context of cultural production. Three spring immediately to mind. One is simply to forget about attempting to defend rights in cultural heritage/property and to accept that everything that we might otherwise think of as having this quality is open to private propertization by whoever is best able to appropriate it. The second possibility is to go with the status quo and recognize states as the relevant cultural heritage community and thus being in the best position to vindicate rights over such heritage/property. The third is to embrace the cosmopolitan position, which often also seems to be reflected in the UNESCO Conventions, and regard all heritage/cultural property as somehow common to humanity, and so as belonging to us all in our character as humans. For reasons that I hope will be evident to anyone who has read the preceding chapters, I reject the first of these possibilities, which seems to reflect a certain Hobbesian anti-community claim.[34] To embrace it would be to cede the ground to the empire of capital. This book has an entirely contrary political position.

Once this first alternative possibility has been rejected, it seems to me to follow more or less as a matter of course, that the second must meet the same fate. This is not only because states have shown themselves unable or unwilling to resist the creeping private propertization of vast swathes of our cultural life. It is also because, as Chapter 3 has argued, to accept the state as the answer to the problems posed in this book would be to accept a system that is fundamentally flawed by vast imbalances in geopolitical power and in the capacity of states internally to represent the interests of particular groups. The third possibility gives more pause for thought. The promises of cosmopolitanism, with its rejection of narrow sectional interests, should not be disposed of lightly, particularly in a period of human history when the catastrophe of climate change is pressing upon us and when we know that only some version of cosmopolitan solutions can halt its disastrous effects. But perhaps we need to also understand that cosmopolitanism is not a position that can answer every ill or resolve every question.[35] In particular, it may not be able to account for histories of oppression or resist their repetition. In other words, because as human beings we have a common human interest in breathing and otherwise sustaining ourselves physically, what works for the protection of the environment might not work so well when it comes to the protection of cultural heritage/property. So, in the end, I am not sure what alternative we have but to think along the lines of collective resistance to out-of-control private propertization of culture. This could, of course, be a collective resistance that unites us all against the power of capital, but this seems disingenuous. Capital is not some force removed from human agency. Those who resist it also resist those who promote and profit from it. Nor can it be right to think in this simple binary fashion. We live in a world stained by the

34 See Esposito, n 8 above, ch 1 (on Hobbs) & at 112–128 (on Bataille & Hobbs).

35 See M C Nussbaum, *The Cosmopolitan Tradition: A Nobel but Flawed Ideal* (Cambridge, MA: Belknap Press, 2019).

tragedy of colonialism and the ravages of post-colonial capitalism, a world marked and marred by geopolitical injustice.[36] Collective resistances to the appropriation of cultural heritage/property are many, and we need to think a way through to them and for them. If not community, then what else? I do not here reject the possible usefulness of concept of society, or the use of the social, but rather see it as being intrinsically bound up with the current system that accepts states as being the solution to the problem I pose in this book.[37]

We are not yet done with anxiety over community, nor with the question of the cosmopolitan promise. This book will return to the former on many occasions to come, and to the latter in its final chapter. In the meantime, however, it argues for the use of community in the present context and against the type of pseudo-cosmopolitanism that might be thought to characterize at least some of the UNESCO Conventions. This is to say that, in the cultural heritage/property context, this book rejects the proposition that common humanity is community. For one thing, this tends to strip community of any real meaning. Being alive may be common to humans (and a vast number of other non-humans), but much else that flows from the state of human existence is not. For one thing, thinking of common humanity as community ignores the importance of affect.[38] Camus puts the point beautifully (as always):

> Around me were a million human beings who had been alive all this time whose existence had never concerned me. They were alive. I was thousands of kilometres from home. I could not understand their language. They walked quickly, all of them. And as they overtook and passed me, they cut themselves off from me. I felt lost.[39]

Further, to say that the identification and enjoyment of cultural heritage/property is one of the things that makes us human (which is perhaps the best way of understanding the apparently cosmopolitan claims of the UNESCO Conventions) is not to make the claim that as humans we are all in community with each other. In the end, I seem to have little alternative but to make an argument for the cultural heritage/property community forming less than humanity as a whole, more in some circumstances than the general public in one nation state and, in other circumstances, less. All this still leaves us, of course, with the

36 F Macmillan, "Critical Law and Development" in E Christodoulidis, R Dukes & M Goldoni (eds), *Research Handbook on Critical Legal Theory* (Cheltenham: Edward Elgar, 2019).

37 As Esposito's brief engagement with Ferdinand Tönnies' famous dichotomy between community and society (*Gemeinschaft* and *Gesellschaft*) shows, the relationship between society and community is theoretically uncertain: see Esposito, n 8 above, at 135–136. And on philosophical approaches to the social, see also Enns, n 27 above.

38 Enns, n 27 above.

39 A Camus, "Death in the Soul" in E Thody (ed), *Albert Camus: Lyrical and Critical Essays* (New York: Vintage, 1968, trans E Conroy Kennedy), at 40–41.

question of whether there is any real meaning to community, at least in the cultural heritage/property context.

So what can we salvage from the idea of community that is useful in the present context? I return now to the discussion of Anderson (interrupted by the brief and anxious excursus immediately above), which, in its deployment of community as a tool of critique, tends to inoculate us against a reading of community as, to paraphrase Esposito, a warm and cuddly place.[40] The concept of community that is in play in Anderson's analysis is a subjective one. I am not sure that this necessarily runs counter to Esposito's claim that community marks "an absence of subjectivity, of identity".[41] Anderson's analysis is directed towards the formation and identification of community, not its existential condition (and consequences) with respect to individual subjectivity and identity, to which Esposito seems to be referring. Nevertheless, the formation, identification and existence of community are not clearly demarcated and tend to blur into one another When we talk about the reflexive relationship between identification and memory in the context of community formation, whose identification are we talking about? Whose memory? In particular, if the narrative of community built on collective memory is also about forgetting, who is remembering and who is forgetting? It is in relation to questions of this sort that Anderson's insight that communities are imagined is particularly useful. This is because it is clear from his focus on comradeship-solidarity, and his focus on common perceptions of time and history, that the communities he is talking about are imagined *from the inside out* rather than the other way around. This suggests, of course, that not only is community a subjective concept, but also that the identification of oneself as a member of a community is subjective both for the individual and the community. It necessarily rejects the idea that community is marked by the loss of individual subjectivity and identity (which truly is an oppressive and terrifying idea). One of the reasons that this must be the case is that self-identification as part of a community is not exclusive, in the sense that it does not exclude the possibility that an individual will identify as part of other communities. This is to say that community formation is multilevel. Of course, this subjective nature of community formation and existence is complicated by the fact that a community may, and often does, impose apparently objective requirements for community membership. But such requirements cannot work to change the essential nature of community formation. As Christodoulidis argues, community comes about "around a political/ethical understanding both capable of upholding a commitment, and dynamic, always potentially disruptable internally; and with no measure of authority, force, persuasion and violence capable of upholding it externally".[42]

40 See text acc n 27 above.

41 Esposito, n 8 above, at 138; see text acc n 25 above.

42 E Christodoulidis, *Law and Reflexive Politics* (Dordrecht: Springer, 1998), 237, citing R Cover, "Nomos and Narrative" (1983) 97 *Harvard Law Review* 4–68, on the "hermeneutic of principle".

If we are to concede any idea of cultural heritage/property outside the private proprietary relations of copyright, as this book argues we should, then the importance of the concept of community in relation to its identification cannot be overstated. Community and heritage, as already argued in Chapter Three, are mutually constitutive. A community only exists and identifies itself through a common process of remembering and forgetting those things and practices that are essential to its identity. Cultural heritage/property, therefore, is drawn from a current and ongoing process of selection and identification, which reflects contemporary community concerns and values.[43] And because cultural heritage/property is reflexive, it changes with community practice.[44]

3 Community and law

Can this mutually constitutive relationship between heritage and community be captured by law? Does it have the tools to recognize what Graham and Howard describe as "the interconnections of heritages and identities [that] are all around us, entwining the local with the regional, national and global, everyday life with political ideology"?[45] It seems reasonable to speculate that the appearance of the word "community" in the authorized heritage discourse is a type of inoculation against criticisms of the international legal regime for its statist nature. However, much as the authorized discourse may protest, the introduction of the concept (or at least the word) of community into this international discourse is compromised by the inescapably statist nature of the system and the consequent problem that "community" is not a term of art in international law. At the level of national law, however, the reflexive relationship between identity, processes of community building and tangible or spatial dimensions has, in some cases, been recognized and has generated legal provisions geared to the question of community recognition. For example, particularly in states having an Indigenous population that predates the establishment of the state, the Indigenous population is recognized as a community enjoying, at least, a distinct identity and, often, also particular rights. The same is also true in relation to states in which ethnic or linguistic minorities live. To some extent, these types of rights reflect obligations (actual or hortatory) in international law even though their origins might not be directly attributable

43 Smith, n 1 above, at 3; see also Harrison, n 1 above, at 14.

44 P Fitzpatrick & R Joyce, "Copying Right: Cultural Property and the Limits of (Occidental) Law" in F Macmillan (ed), *New Directions in Copyright Law: Volume 4* (Cheltenham: Edward Elgar, 2007).

45 B Graham & P Howard, "Heritage and Identity" in B Graham & P Howard (eds), *The Ashgate Companion to Heritage and Identity* (London: Ashgate, 2008), at 13.

to such obligations. However, there are also other well-known examples in national law of the recognition of community and associated community rights, where community is less than the public at large. It is common, for example, for legal systems to recognize community rights in property based on customary use.[46] An interesting variation on this is the recognition, nationally and internationally, of certain rights associated with the marking of products made in a certain geographical location.[47]

The pivotal question here is not whether we can find a basis in law for delineating a community, which might then lay claim to certain community rights. It follows from the foregoing argument about the nature of community that community comes before the law and so cannot be constituted by it.[48] However, at the same time, we may be able to find some indicia in existing legal accounts around which to build a concept of community that might then be the carrier of certain cultural heritage/property rights and obligations in law. The types of (overlapping) indicia that seem to be important in national systems as they relate to communities that form less than the population of the state as a whole are common political identity; common ethnic identity; common language; common religious identity; common geographical location; common sustenance practices; common history. Although we tend to get stuck in a rather circular line of reasoning here because, as will be evident, with the possible exceptions of common language and common religion, these are all also indicia of the type of communities that constitute nation states in international law.[49] These indicia are also all, in some sense, objective or externally observable criteria, which interact with the subjective indicia of solidarity, identification and memory that have been discussed earlier. And it is precisely here that law's problem with recognizing community formation is exposed. If community is, as argued earlier, a subjective concept, employing objective criteria as part of that subjectivity, then law's problem with it will always be that it will see the objective criteria, but not necessarily their relationship to the subjective identification of community. This is one of the reasons why law has such difficulty in recognizing community outside easily identifiable constellations such as the nation state.

The problem that law has in recognizing community might be understood as part and parcel of the important questions around the legitimacy and politics of

46 A Clarke, "Property, Human Rights and Communities" in T Xu & J Allain (eds), *Property and Human Rights in a Global Context* (Oxford & Portland: Hart, 2015).

47 N Aylwin & R Coombe, "Marks Indicating Conditions of Origin in Rights-Based Sustainable Development" in R Buchanan & P Zumbansen (eds), *Human Rights, Development and Restorative Justice: An Osgoode Reader* (Oxford: Hart, 2013).

48 See Christodoulidis, n 42 above.

49 See Anderson, n 5 above, at 196; Hobsbawm, n 18 above, at 147.

community. As Nancy has observed, reflecting his (well-placed) anxiety about the possible consequences of community:

> These days it is not always possible to say with any assurance whether these identities are intranational, infranational, or transnational; whether they are "cultural," "religious," "ethnic," or "historical"; whether they are legitimate or not – not to mention the question about which law would provide such legitimation; whether they are real, mythical or imaginary; whether they are independent or "instrumentalized" by other groups who wield political, economic, and ideological power…[50]

While this observation brings me no closer to an answer to the question about law's capacity to recognize the cultural heritage/property community, it does catch a number of problems with which any account of community, including accounts in the present context, must wrestle: its relationship to the nation state system; the problem of what "cultural" might mean, and its interaction with seemingly cognate concepts like religion, ethnicity and above all history; whether community requires legitimation through law; whether there are significant differences in this context between real, mythical and imaginary; and finally, of course, the risks in thinking community in political and legal terms. Thus, we are suspended between the impossibility, the threat and the necessity of community. Perhaps, at this point, it might help to identify something that is not community.

4 Community and copyright law

Community is not formed around copyright. This conclusion flows from the foregoing discussion. Community is before the law and for this reason it cannot be formed or held up around a legal right. The private property relations of copyright, which are produced by the law, do not and cannot be regarded as constituting community or controlling all aspects of the relationships within it. The fact that copyright law contains provisions on joint authorship (which it transforms into joint ownership) and, with some changes, might be capable of recognizing collective authorship, or even become a more community-based form of regulation, cannot change this conclusion.[51] Its focus on identifying the

50 J-L Nancy, *Being Singular Plural* (Stanford, CA: Stanford University Press, 2000, trans R D Richardson & A E O'Byrne), at xii–xiii.

51 On copyright's failure and potential in relation to collective authorship, see M Chon, "New Wine Bursting from Old Bottles: Collaborative Internet Art, Joint Works, & Entrepreneurship"(1996) 75 *Oregon Law Review* 257–276; C M Rose, "The Several Futures of Property: Of Cyberspace and Folk Tales, Emission Trades and Ecosystems"(1998) 83 *Minnesota Law Review* 129–182; D Simone, *Copyright and Collective Authorship: Locating the Authors of Collaborative Work* (Cambridge: Cambridge University Press, 2019). On the possibilities for reforming copyright to

owner of the rights over a cultural product means that it is likely to disregard many contributions from the relevant community and to muddle up concepts of origination, ownership and use. As has been argued earlier, community is produced by a reflexive relationship between identity and memory. It imports, however, a concept of solidarity, of mutual obligation. Community is not about the end product and its life in the marketplace, which are the matters upon which copyright is focussed; community is about process. Specifically, as Smith argues, it is a "constitutive social process".[52] It is not that property relations cannot have a place in community, but rather that they should be subject to the mutual obligations of community.

Allowing the possibility that copyright has some role, the context of community cultural production begs the question (of course) of exactly what that role might be. The first thing to say about this is that its role is certainly not fundamental or indispensable in the constitution or regulation of community cultural production. This seems an obvious point since we can point to plenty of examples, both in the pre-copyright period and – despite the close relationship in the Occident between copyright and the "arts" – in the current period, of cultural production without the benefit (at least initially) of copyright. Aside from the well-worn example of computer programming, other cases of Western cultural production outside the copyright kingdom include (for example) street art, graffiti and the large community of body artists and tattooists.[53] As might be expected, these creative communities outside copyright have developed their own norms of behaviour that are also outside the regulatory framework of copyright, including a language that sometimes employs the same expressions as those used by copyright law (for example, "author", "originality", "copy") but not necessarily with the same meanings.[54] In this respect, it is likely that these communities resemble many non-Western creative communities.[55]

make it more "community-based", see J Bellido, "Book Review: *Concepts of Property in Intellectual Property Law*" (2014) 2 *Birkbeck Law Review* 147–156, at 155–156 (reviewing H R Howe & J Griffiths (eds), *Concepts of Property in Intellectual Property Law* (Cambridge: Cambridge University Law Press, 2013).

52 Smith, n 1 above, at 82.

53 On computer programming, see A Barron, "Free Software Production as Critical Social Practice" (2013) 42 *Economy and Society* 597–625. On the norms of the graffiti community, e.g., see M Iljadica, *Copyright beyond Law: Regulating Creativity in the Graffiti Subculture* (Oxford & Portland: Hart, 2016). Although, the recourse of street artists and graffiti writers to copyright may start to change the community-based nature of these cultural forms: see E Bonadio (ed), *The Cambridge Handbook of Copyright in Street Art & Graffiti* (Cambridge: Cambridge University Press, 2019).

54 Iljadica, n 53 above.

55 See, e.g., Robertson's study of the Dafen artists community in China: L J Murray, S T Piper & K Robertson, *Putting Intellectual Property in Its Place: Rights Discourses, Creative Labor, and the Everyday* (Oxford & New York: Oxford University Press, 2014), ch 8.

The ground-breaking empirical research of Murray, Piper and Robertson has made a fundamental contribution to understanding the role of copyright in creative communities.[56] Their six case studies ranging from the world of online knitting communities to the high end international art market confirm what they describe as the "moth-like" rather "than determinative" character of copyright in these communities.[57] The final products of some of these communities enter the market within the regulatory structure of copyright, but copyright is not even instrumental – let alone fundamental – to the community relations that produce them. In relation to her study of the community of visual artists in Kingston, Ontario, Murray comments on:

> the clumsiness or even violence of law, even should it be accessible and redrafted to suit such situations, when people are embedded in ongoing community relationships ... Here, the affective dimension of the act and experience may mean that accommodation is the only possible or positive response, rather than contestation (personal or legal). The idea of rights may be inadequate or beside the point.[58]

And in relation to her study of the contemporary high end art market, Robertson remarks that "[c]opyright may regulate art's passage through some marketplaces, but the economic circumstances of artists involve many other places as well".[59]

As might be expected, the study of the contemporary art market, and some of the other studies show the role of copyright in giving a creative community access to a market, and even the associated significance of market access to the community's idea of itself. Robertson's study of online knitting communities, for example, shows how "a mixed bag of legal and extra-legal frameworks", including intellectual property rights, enables access to a market.[60] And that, in the case of this community where work "has traditionally been seen as a feminized hobby or pastime", access to a market "is exceptionally important to participants ... not only to generate income but also to create a broader sense of value for a formerly belittled practice".[61] In her study of the community of researchers

56 Murray, Piper & Robertson, n 55 above.

57 Murray, Piper & Robertson, n 55 above, at 154. They take the expression "moth-like" from an interview conducted by Murray as part of her study of the community of visual artists working in Kingston, Ontario, in which the interviewee said that "copyright to her is 'like this light little mothy thing that sort of lands every once in a while and then flutters away'": *ibid.*, at 137 (Milly Ristvedt, interview by Sharday Mosurinjohn, 29 April 2012).

58 Murray, Piper & Roberston, n 55 above, at 140.

59 Murray, Piper & Robertson, n 55 above, at 154. And for the study of the contemporary high end art market, see *ibid.*, ch 8.

60 Murray, Piper & Roberston, n 55 above, at 43. And for the study of online knitting communities, see *ibid.*, ch 3.

61 Murray, Piper & Robertson, n 55 above, at 42.

on plant hormones at Canada's National Research Council during the inter-war period and going up to the end of the Second World War, Piper identifies some similar concerns (although not the undervaluing of what is regarded as feminized work) with the role of patents in commercial exploitation.[62] However, locating these concerns within the overall pattern of research community formation and operation, she observes that "[t]he presence of multiple, overlapping rights suggests in both cases that an ethic of working in community is at stake, beyond the strict legal right".[63]

From all this, it is abundantly clear that copyright, like other legal rights, may have a role in community, but does not define or constitute it.[64] This does not mean that copyright is not valuable to individuals working in areas of creative production to which it applies. As observed in Chapter One, not only does it them the possibility of gaining an economic benefit over their creative labour, but it also confers on them the capacity to exercise control over their works (although that control is considerably diminished if copyright does not remain in the hands of the original creator). However, as the studies conducted by Murray, Piper and Robertson show, in order to function effectively, creative communities often suspend or selectively apply intellectual property norms within the confines of the community.[65] Amongst a constellation of valuable insights and observations, it is particularly interesting that Murray, Piper and Robertson note that, consistently with sociological literature, increasing reliance on copyright is often a sign of cracks in the relevant community: "appealing to formal legal mechanisms is generally a sign of either the breakdown of group norms or of outsider presence within those groups".[66] That the formal relations of intellectual property law intervene as the relations of community falter should not be a surprise, although it is interesting to know that this is just as true within the community of legal practitioners (in relation to which the quotation in the previous sentence was made) as elsewhere.[67]

Private property rights like copyright are not a route to building a community of cultural and creative values. Such a community needs to be built by a

62 Murray, Piper & Robertson, n 55 above, ch 4.

63 Murray, Piper & Robertson, n 55 above, at 82.

64 And this is the case, even where an unusual relation between a particular community and copyright law has become part of the narrative of that community: see F Macmillan, "Cultural Heritage and the Unseen Community" in S Whatley, C Waelde, A Brown & S Harmon (eds), *Dance, Disability and the Law: Invisible Difference* (Bristol: Intellect Books, 2018).

65 And see also, with respect to the contemporary dance community, F K L Yeoh, *Copyright Law Does Not Adequately Accommodate the Art form of Dance* (PhD Thesis, Birkbeck, University of London, 2012).

66 Murray, Piper & Robertson, n 55 above, at 121, citing J Loshin, "Secrets Revealed: How Magicians Protect Intellectual Property without Law" (2007) *Social Sciences Research Network*, http://papers.ssrn.com/sol3/papers.cfm?abstract_id=1005564, republished in C A Corcos (ed), *Law and Magic: A Collection of Essays* (Durham, NC: Carolina Academic Press, 2010).

67 See Murray, Piper & Robertson, n 55 above, ch 6.

bottom-up commitment to the value of the artistic or cultural practice. Within such a community, copyright will have a value for individual authors, but it is a value that should be limited by the rights that other members of the community have in their shared cultural heritage/property. In this way, market thinking would cease to be total and the market would become only one artefact of the ties that bind community together. Reflecting the concepts of solidarity and mutual obligation, the proper role of the law here is to give community the means to express its identity and the collective claims that flow from that identity, having reference always to the multiple and overlapping communities that form and give substance to human existence. However, the communities that form around and generate many contemporary cultural forms do not exist in a legal environment that looks much like this. As has been argued in Chapter 1, the international intellectual property law system, which defines ownership and controls the use of many forms of contemporary cultural production, identifies value through a system of total market thinking.[68] Its creation of an extensive system of private property rights over cultural products is designed to make those products into liquid investments. The result is that copyright law, the primary function of which is to protect investment and the accumulation of capital, sustains a system of control of cultural output in the hands of a concentrated group of multinational corporate agglomerations.[69] In the so-called creative industries in which value is generated by the replication of material (books, CDs, DVDs) or dematerialized (digital and/or online) versions of an "original" that is not distinct in market terms from its copies, the property relations of copyright have eviscerated the idea of community cultural production.

5 The complex reality

As Chapter 3 has already argued, the state-based nature of the international law system creates difficulties for it in recognizing communities forming less than the public as a whole in any given state. This chapter has attempted – not without considerable difficulty – to consider the nature of community at a theoretical level and the prospects for its recognition by law outside the nation state system. The purpose of this consideration is to evaluate the extent to which, by recognizing community, law is capable of intervening in the balance between community and market in relation to cultural heritage/property. It is clear that intellectual property law has, particularly in relation to some cultural forms, either destroyed this balance or substantially tipped the scales towards a regime of regulation that concerns itself only with market rights. Is it feasible to look towards some

68 See ch 1, section 5.2.

69 A phenomenon that is becoming increasingly evident, see, e.g., Report of the Special Rapporteur in the field of cultural rights, F Shaheed, *Copyright Policy and the Right to Science and Culture*, UN Doc. A/HRC/28/57, 24 December 2014. See ch 1, section 5, esp 5.2.

sort of non-intellectual property cultural heritage/property regime to tip the scales back in favour of community rights over creative production? Or do we need to find some other way to respond to questions that the concept of community, properly understood, asks in the current system for regulating cultural production?

For its part, international cultural heritage law, at least that portion of it promulgated this century, shows some signs of recognizing that the central function of cultural heritage law should be to provide community with the means to express its identity and the collective claims that flow from that identity. In some senses, this is already a departure from the state-based authorized heritage discourse of international law. Perhaps this breach in the discourse, which has arisen around the question of the protection of intangible cultural heritage, is inevitable because in some ways the very recognition of the concept of intangible cultural heritage creates the sort of noise that this discourse finds hard to absorb or normalize. Not only are the various dualisms on which the discourse is based held up for reconsideration, but the very idea of the legal protection of intangible heritage through a process of listing raises questions around two of what Smith describes as "the underpinning assumptions" of the authorized heritage discourse: "firstly, that management and protection is indeed about, and should be about fossilization; and, secondly, that the inherent values of ... heritage are immutable".[70] This suggests, as Smith continues, that "what the debate about intangible heritage as living culture also throws into relief is the idea that the listing process, either of tangible or intangible heritage, is itself a performance of meaning making".[71] But what then, in relation to intangible heritage, is the meaning that is being made? And how, in relation to what we might describe as contemporary intangible cultural heritage, does that meaning interact with other performances of meaning making, especially the performance that attributes value to it in the form of private property rights?

The law itself makes no attempt to understand the relationship between the way meaning is made in relation to the same cultural practices in the two different systems of intangible cultural heritage protection and intellectual property protection. Consequently, unconstrained by any legally imposed attempt at balance or restraint, the transcendence of total market thinking in the neo-liberal period has prioritized private property rights and their market exploitation over the demands of the contemporary cultural heritage/property community.[72] Current practices of cultural production – instead of expressing the identity, solidarity and mutual obligations of community – are weighed down by private property rights, often exercised by the media and entertainment corporations in

70 Smith, n 1 above, at 111–112.

71 Smith, n 1 above, 112.

72 See further F Macmillan, "Cultural Property and Community Rights to Cultural Heritage" in T Xu & J Allain (eds), *Property and Human Rights in a Global Context* (Oxford: Hart, 2015).

their role as the commodifiers of contemporary cultural output. This form of commodification can, perhaps, be usefully contrasted with other forms of commodification or commercialization of cultural heritage/property. Heritage is, for example, commodified through tourism and I would not be the first to voice the thought that the main function, in reality, of the UNESCO lists of tangible and intangible cultural heritage is as tourist guides. But the difference here is that, whatever the effects of this form of commodification, at least the fundamental character of the heritage as heritage is retained.[73] While it may not always work out this way, the fact that the cultural heritage community may, itself, control this process of tourism commodification is important. In such a case, perhaps we can understand the market as being embedded in community (or, at least, not completely abandon the hope of this). But no such assertion can be made when cultural heritage becomes private property and its fundamental character as a community artefact is overwhelmed and subsumed into the logic of rivalrous individual ownership.

For certain, one of the things that seems to come clearly though this morass of dualisms and distinctions – some of them collapsing into each other and others becoming more starkly delineated – is the essentially Western and post-colonial nature of not only the intellectual property system and its life in the market, but also of the attempts coming from the international law system to recognize the rights of communities over their cultural production. The picture here is messy and requires a highly nuanced response that can no longer depend on the easy separation of the Western and non-Western/post-colonial worlds as though they exist in total isolation from one another. For example, when it comes to the protection of community rights in cultural heritage/property, it is easy to exaggerate the significance of statehood as being a marker that tends to protect the West and ignore the rest, especially the post-colonial rest. This is because, in general, even non-Indigenous cultural property/heritage tends to belong to communities forming less than the state as a whole – that is, communities within a state rather than communities comprising a state. The problems for such communities – or at least some of them – in having their particular rights recognized and pursued at the international level by the state may have something in common with the situation in this respect of Indigenous Peoples. The difference may be, and in some cases certainly is, that the request for protection of cultural heritage/property by non-Indigenous communities does usually not have the same political significance – in the sense that it is not necessarily connected with claims to sovereignty. However, in the end, one common problem that all communities – Indigenous and non-Indigenous – share when it comes to protecting their cultural production is the difficulty of sustaining a community right either by using an individualistic private property right and/or in the face of market system built around such rights. It is facile (and wrong) to confuse the

73 On the effects of this commodification, see, e.g., Smith, n 1 above, at 33–34.

fact that copyright is based on an organization of knowledge production derived from the Western Enlightenment with the claim that all Western creative communities, as opposed to Indigenous Peoples, can be defined by its rules:

> After all computer programmers were not the first Western creators to discover sharing: many other Euroamerican communities have maintained and developed persistent practices and beliefs around creativity and community that sit apart from, and often challenge, presumptions in law ... we reject the binary view that would presume "Western" people to be entirely comfortable or hegemonized by IP law, and indigenous or non-Western people to be alienated from it. The reality is much more complex.[74]

One part of that complex reality is that, when it comes to the protection of cultural heritage/property, in varying degrees we are all victims of what the next chapter describes as a monumental Western tragedy.

74 Murray, Piper & Robertson, n 55 above, at 4.

Chapter 5

The monumental occidental tragedy

1 Introduction: the West v the rest

It can hardly be a surprise that the dominant tropes of thinking about cultural property/heritage, including the approach of international law, are Western. And, this being the case, it is even less of a surprise that these tropes reflect the Western cultural tendency to think about the world in binary distinctions.[1] The authorized discourse of cultural heritage protection is awash with these distinctions, which often have the appearance of empirical validity and yet are conceptually problematic in ways that bring their meaning and validity into question. As should already be evident by this stage of the book, the tangible/intangible distinction has been influential in shaping the authorized discourse. The emphasis on this distinction, and the problem of competing notions of intangibility, is also implicated in the crossover and general confusion between cultural heritage/property and intellectual property. But there is also a range of other critical distinctions that have infected thinking about the protection of cultural heritage/property.

One of these is the distinction between moveable and immoveable cultural heritage/property. This distinction, which – like the distinction between tangible and intangible stuff – reflects the Western juridical order governing interests in property, reverberates through the post-colonial (authorized) discourse of cultural heritage protection.[2] And it is this very reflection of Western property law that makes it conceptually problematic. The sorts of things considered to be immoveable by law are not actually or necessarily immoveable (mountains can be moved in real life, as can pyramids), although certainly they are more difficult

1 At least etymologically, the blame for this has largely been placed on Descartes (see R Harrison, *Heritage: Critical Approaches* [London & New York: Routledge, 2013], ch 9), but the chicken and egg nature of the problem is fairly obvious.

2 Ch 3, section 2.1. See also K Bowrey & N Graham, "The Placelessness of Property, Intellectual Property and Cultural Heritage Law in the Australian Legal Landscape: Engaging Cultural Landscapes" in C Antons & W Logan (eds), *Intellectual Property, Cultural Property and Intangible Cultural Heritage* (London & New York: Routledge, 2018).

to move. The more monumental they are, the more difficult their relocation, and certainly less "immoveable" stuff was relocated to the metropolitan centres of empire during the colonial period. Easily moveable items were much simpler game. Mountains of easily moveable stuff, appropriated during the colonial era, now sit in Western museums – so much, in fact, that very little of it can be displayed.[3] That some of these moveables might be classed by law as fixtures, and therefore part of an immoveable estate in legal terms matters little in the final wash. All of them have been removed from the community and place that generated them and gave them life as cultural heritage/property. All of them have been subjected to the weirdly contradictory Western mania for decontextualization and the so-called preservation of things that it understands as culturally authentic. This is a mania that is only explicable by insisting on a particular invocation of the tangible/intangible distinction that favours the preservation of the tangible object at the expense of its intangible relationship with the cultural community that generated it. At the same time, practices of preservation, often in tandem with policies around access to these objects, invoke another version of the tangible/intangible distinction. In this version, tangible stuff has a second life as intangible digitized objects or "artefacts". While this practice has a particular impact in relation to actually (rather than legally) moveable objects that have been stored in Western museums, it has also been used in situ to solve other heritage/cultural property conundrums and disputes. This blurs the boundary lines of the distinction between what is authentic and what is inauthentic in ways that are unpredictable. Not only does it often reek of a post-colonial desire to continue controlling cultural heritage/property in the face of demands for its return to communities of origin, but it also brings cultural heritage/property back into a new version of its problematic relationship with intellectual property.

Sitting in what seems an almost imperial position over the distinctions between tangible and intangible and between moveable and immoveable is one of the Western world's specialities, the distinction between nature and culture. Embedded in the authorized heritage discourse as a result of the 1972 UNESCO Convention Concerning the Protection of the World Cultural and Natural Heritage (usually called the World Heritage Convention (WHC), but the full name is illustrative of the point), this distinction invites us to think of cultural heritage/property as being independent of the physical and political spaces, geographical locations and relations with the natural world that are, in reality, inextricable from its communities of origin. In the authorized heritage discourse, the possibility that breaking the links between place, community and cultural heritage/property deprives the cultural heritage object of its character

3 See, e.g., P Daley, "There's a New Push for the Return of Looted Aboriginal Artefacts – In the Name of 'Truth Telling'", *The Guardian*, 1 December 2019, https://www.theguardian.com/australia-news/postcolonial-blog/2019/dec/02/theres-a-new-push-for-the-return-of-looted-aboriginal-artefacts-in-the-name-of-truth-telling, accessed 01/12/2019.

as cultural heritage/property has been largely ignored. This discourse also consistently underrates the fact that community cultural practices are not only social processes linked together by stuff that is both tangible and intangible, but they are also critically dependent on relationships to the natural world. It is true that the Convention for the Safeguarding of the Intangible Cultural Heritage (CICH) marks a significant improvement in these respects, but only in the context of the protection of what it defines as intangible heritage.[4] In the world of what the authorized discourse understands as tangible heritage, apart from the WHC's intermediate category of mixed natural and cultural heritage, relationship with place is not understood as going to the intrinsic cultural value of the object of protection. This sits strangely with the fact that for both the things that the authorized discourse denominates as immoveable and those that it denominates as moveable, geographic location or origin is legally significant. This is because, according to this discourse, things belong to one state and not to another. But the idea that cultural heritage/property belongs to a certain state is not the same thing as understanding the intrinsic nature of the links between place, community and cultural heritage/property.

As this chapter will seek to demonstrate, it is not only that these binary distinctions–tangible/intangible,moveable/immoveable,authentic/fake,nature/culture – are unable to be sustained, but also that all of the different concepts they invoke bleed into one another. By seeking to understand cultural heritage/property everywhere according to systems of categorization produced by the Western Enlightenment, we have produced a mish-mash of meaning that defies attempts at regulation or protection. However, the problem we have is not as simple as a mere distinction between the West and the rest, which is, of course, the truly imperial binary in this chapter (and in this book). This is partly because, even in the West, we have done a very poor job at recognizing and protecting cultural heritage/property. But also because the distinction between the West and the rest does not, itself, hold. For reasons that reflect no merit on Western expansionism, historical and contemporary, there are few places and cultures that do not bear its marks. This means that much of the world that we might tend to categorize as non-Western lives, and forms its culture, in some sort of engagement with Western dominance. The negative side of all this, as far as cultural heritage/property is concerned, is that we are all in variations of the same unseaworthy boat. The positive side is that there are things to learn from practices of cultural cohabitation and resistance.

2 Tangibility, intangibility and digitization

The way in which the distinction between tangibility and intangibility has affected the actual and perceived relationship between cultural heritage/property

4 See ch 3, section 3.

and intellectual property has already been noted in this book, as has the ways in which this distinction maps onto the distinction between the West and the rest.[5] As Slaughter observes, the two issues are fundamentally connected:

> [T]he distinction between cultural and intellectual property has generally (once again) been mapped onto the divide between the developing and developed world, trailing behind it a long series of old familiar orientalist oppositions: individual versus collective, personal property vs. group commons, formal versus informal knowledge, and so forth. Accordingly, we in the West produce spontaneous original intellectual property; they in the rest of the world have a rich (though probably burdensome) collective legacy of cultural heritage and traditional knowledge that is, so the logic goes, part of what keeps their societies underdeveloped.[6]

It is, however, critically important that we do not fall into the trap of believing that we can, in reality, divide up the world in this way. Not only do non-Western and Indigenous Peoples have a long engagement with the Western intellectual property system, but it is also the case that the idea that we in the West only have privately owned intellectual property is, besides being culturally impoverishing, questionable. One of the (entirely laudable) principles embodied in the 1995 United Nations Guidelines for the Protection of the Heritage of Indigenous Peoples provides that

> indigenous peoples' ownership and custody of their heritage must continue to be collective, permanent and inalienable; that the free and informed consent of the traditional owners be a precondition of any agreements for the recording, study, use or display of indigenous peoples' heritage: and that concerned peoples be the primary beneficiaries of commercial application of their heritage.[7]

But should it not also be a concern for all of us that our heritage is not "collective, permanent and inalienable", and that we are not afforded the opportunity to consent to the "recording, study, use or display" of our heritage? Are we really supposed to be happy with the idea that when elements of our own heritage are privatized by large media and entertainment corporations, we have to pay to enjoy, use or re-use it, with the result that a large corporation is the "primar[y]

5 See ch 3, section 3, esp section 3.3.

6 J R Slaughter, "Form & Informality: An Unliterary Look at World Literature" in R Warhol (ed), *The Work of Genre: Selected Essays from the English Institute* (New York: English Institute in Collaboration with the American Council of Learned Societies, 2011), at 198–199 (footnote omitted).

7 E/CN.4/Sub.2/1995/26, para 58. And see the discussion of these Guidelines in Report of the Special Rapporteur in the field of cultural rights, Farida Shaheed, *Copyright Policy and the Right to Science and Culture*, UN Doc. A/HRC/28/57, 24 December 2014, para 58.

beneficiar[y] of the commercial application" of our heritage? Does it not matter to us at all that our culture is re-framed and re-interpreted for us according to the values of a gang of corporate giants? Do we think this is alright because we in the global North are all one big (although not happy) community? Perhaps the truly sad (or maybe I mean pathetic) part about all this is that, not having much idea ourselves of how to deal with the balance between community cultural heritage/property and private intellectual property, we in the West continue to talk about, and to, non-Western peoples as though they are somehow more simple than us. We talk about their culture as "traditional", without intending it as a compliment. We seem not to have noticed that, as a result of a long period of living in engagement with the Western world, non-Western peoples know better than us how to strike as a balance between community cultural heritage/property and private intellectual property.

On top of all this, we in the West are patronizing, if not worse, about the significance of cultural heritage/property to identity. Or, if we are not patronizing, then we are threatened by its significance to political identity. We roll out the "common heritage of humanity" mantra of the authorized heritage discourse when it provides a convenient basis for refusing to return something that we would rather keep.[8] If the assertion of intellectual property rights over other people's intangible cultural heritage/property is a new form of imperialism, then we are now upping the ante by inventing yet another form, which has the capacity to re-engage on a new footing with the power of the Western intellectual property system.[9] This new form, the digitization of tangible stuff, extends the empire of the intangible by a further blurring of the distinction between tangible and intangible cultural heritage/property. Now, tangible cultural heritage/property turns out to have a new intangible life, but it is one that raises new possibilities for cultural appropriation and domination.

The idea of digitizing tangible items held in galleries, libraries, archives and museums (the so-called GLAM sector) seems to have commenced with a concern for the preservation of fragile items.[10] But it has now taken on a life of its own, driven by a diverse range of motives, including conservation, documentation of GLAM sector holdings, broadening access and the wish on the part of this generally cash-strapped sector to raise revenue by controlling the intellectual property rights to reproduce digital versions of their holdings.[11]

8 On the use of this concept, or more precisely "the common heritage of mankind" (which is probably intended to be equivalent) in the UNESCO Conventions, see ch 3, section 2.3.

9 On intellectual property as neo-colonialism, see ch 3, section 4.

10 This idea is also reflected in copyright law and policy in some jurisdictions: see, e.g., UK Copyright Designs and Patents Act 1988, s 42, which provides an exemption from copyright infringement for the digitization for preservation purposes of copyright works by libraries, archives and museums.

11 See A Wallace & R Deazley, *Display at Your Own Risk*, https://displayatyourownrisk.org/wallace-and-deazley/, accessed 02/02/2020; A Wallace, "Surrogate IP Rights in the Digital

Another increasingly important driver for digitization of holdings, especially by museums, has been the rising number of claims from parts of the post-colonial world for the return of cultural items relocated to the museums of the imperial powers during the colonial period. These types of claims were the subject of the so-called Sarr-Savoy Report of 2018, commissioned by the French state, which considered claims by African states for the return of items of African origin held in French museums.[12] The Report recommended that these items should be returned, but it also recommended that they should be digitized and that the resulting images and documents should be made freely and openly available online. The Report's recommendations on digitization and online access are the subject of an excellent response, written by Pavis and Wallace, in which a number of arguments against these recommendations are raised.[13] First, the Response draws attention to the fact that the Report's recommendations entail the return of tangible heritage "while retaining control over the generation, presentation, and stewardship of Africa's *Digital* Cultural Heritage for decades to come".[14] Secondly, it draws attention to the contested validity of intellectual property claims over digitized heritage materials.[15] It warns against a discriminatory approach to such materials, observing that hardly any digital cultural heritage of French origin is on open access. It consequently argues that "the French Government should refrain from taking any position that creates a double standard by requiring African Cultural Heritage to be digitized and made available when the same demands are not made of its own national institutions".[16] Thirdly, the Response argues that decisions around digitization of cultural items and access to the digitized versions, which "impact how heritage may be represented, preserved and remembered", are decisions for the communities of origin.[17] In this respect, the Response notes the way in which digitization invokes copyright's concept of authorship in a new guise, implicating "the ability to symbolically appropriate and control the knowledge, personhood and objecthood embodied in

Sector" (PhD Thesis, School of Law, College of Social Sciences, University of Glasgow, September 2018). As both these studies demonstrate, however, not all this digitized material is behind paywalls. This point is further addressed below: see Section 2.3.

12 F Sarr & B Savoy, *Rapport sur la restitution du patrimoine culturel africain: Vers une nouvelle éthique relationnelle* (*The Restitution of African Cultural Heritage. Toward a New Relational Ethics*) (Paris 2018); http://restitutionreport2018.com/, accessed 02/02/2020.

13 M Pavis & A Wallace, *Response to the Sarr-Savoy Report: Statement on Intellectual Property Rights and Open Access Relevant to the Digitization and African Cultural Heritage and Associated Materials* (25 March 2019), https://papers.ssrn.com/sol3/papers.cfm?abstract_id=3378200, accessed 02/02/2020. As the Response records, it was signed by "108 scholars and practitioners working in the fields of intellectual property law and material and digital cultural heritage at universities, heritage institutions and organizations around the world", including me.

14 Pavis & Wallace, n 13 above, Executive Summary.

15 See further, Pavis & Wallace, n 13 above, section 1.

16 Pavis & Wallace, n 13 above, Executive Summary.

17 Pavis & Wallace, n 13 above, Executive Summary.

the material object".[18] Finally, the Response draws attention to the importance of a consistent and coherent policy towards the treatment of all forms of cultural heritage/property – tangible, intangible, archival, digital.[19] As it observes, this is essential to any genuine attempt to decolonize cultural institutions. Giving back the tangible items, while keeping control over their second intangible life, especially in a world that continually feeds itself off digitally transmitted images, seems to be less – or even worse – than a half-measure.

There are three points that are particularly worth emphasizing in relation to proposals for the digitization of tangible heritage items. The first is that digitization creates a new object that nevertheless exists in relation to, and impacts upon, the object from which it was digitized. Secondly, digitization is intimately related to questions of access and use, both of which are culturally determined concepts. And thirdly, the ambiguous intellectual property status of digital artefacts is problematic, not only because of its potential enabling of Western re-appropriation of non-Western cultural heritage/property, but also because of its privatizing potential. These points are clearly interwoven with each other but in an attempt to separate out the strands, each is now dealt with separately.

2.1 Re-representation and co-constitution

Dematerialization by digitization creates new matter, not in the sense of the distinction between material and immaterial, or tangible and intangible, but in the sense of its relevance and pertinence as a cultural and legal object. It is also the case that to represent an object, including by digital means, is both to re-present it and to co-constitute it.[20] So digitization creates a new object, but it does not only create a new object, it also creates a new life for the represented object. In the context of digitized cultural heritage/property, the link between the tangible and the digitized objects means that the respect due to tangible objects must also be accorded to their digitized versions.[21] Damage to this link, and therefore to both objects, occurs if the conditions of use, access and control of the two objects are different in ways that are not the consequence of deliberation by the community of origin. At the same time, the fact that the digitized version is a

18 Pavis & Wallace, n 13 above, section 2; see also M Pavis, "ICH and Safeguarding: Uncovering the Cultural Heritage Discourse of Copyright" in C Waelde, C Cummings, M Pavis & H Enright (eds), *Research Handbook on Contemporary Intangible Cultural Heritage: Law and Heritage* (Cheltenham: Edward Elgar, 2018).

19 On the post-colonial significance of archival material, see A L Stoler, "Colonial Archives and The Arts of Governance" (2002) 2 *Archival Science* 87–109; A L Stoler, *Along the Archival Grain: Epistemic Anxieties and Colonial Common Sense* (Princeton, NJ & Oxford: Princeton University Press, 2009).

20 See J Derrida, *The Paper Machine* (Stanford, CA: Stanford University Press, 2005, trans R Bowlby).

21 Pavis & Wallace, n 13 above.

new legal object renders it vulnerable to being severed from the tangible object it represents. One way, in particular, that this severance may occur is through the authorship/ownership function of copyright law.[22] But an assertion of copyright is not necessary to achieve severance between the two objects. It is enough if decisions about them are made according to criteria that do not respect the intrinsic significance of the link.

Apart from the desire to maintain some sort of control over tangible objects that are the subject of claims for their return to communities of origin, digital images have also been used to represent things that no longer exist in a tangible sense, either because they have been subject to physical destruction or because they have been moved from their place of (physical) origin. Sometimes, these images are reconstructed from fragments of existing artefacts. This includes, for example, projections of lost surface details onto surviving buildings. Sometimes, these projections are more than just surface details, however. For example, 14 years after the giant sixth-century Buddhas of Bamijan in Afghanistan were destroyed by the Taliban regime in 2001, and after long international discussion about their restoration, laser projections of the statues were set up in their place. Given the intensity of the international controversy around the destruction of the Buddhas, it seems likely that this initiative was welcomed in many quarters. However, these projections raise questions about how the network of legal relations created around them mediates their relationship to the formerly existing statutes and their status as cultural heritage/property. The laser projections were created by a private undertaking with the permission of UNESCO and the Afghani government.[23] UNESCO, of course, considers the Buddhas as world heritage.[24] The government of Afghanistan considers them to be Afghani heritage. While the statues have religious significance and historical value, the Buddhist community in the Bamjan Valley disappeared centuries ago so it is not clear what other community interests are at stake here. (And it is important not to discount the possibility, further considered below, that the significance of objects as cultural heritage/property changes over time and invokes different community interests.) The nature of the legal relationship between the undertaking creating the projections, UNESCO and the Afghani government is opaque. It has been reported that the projector was donated by the private undertaking in question, but the question of the relationship between the rights over the projections and the cultural heritage/property interests at play is an open one.[25]

22 See text acc n 18 above.

23 M-A Russon, "Afganistan: Buddhas of Bamijan Resurrected as Laser Projections", *International Business Times*, 12 June 2015.

24 See UNESCO Convention Concerning the Protection of the World Cultural and Natural Heritage (1972) (WHC), List of Heritage in Danger under Art 11(4), whc.unesco.org/en/list/208, accessed 02/02/2020.

25 Russon, n 23 above.

2.2 Access and use

As the second life of the Buddhas of Bamijan demonstrates, the use of digital technologies to reproduce tangible of objects of cultural heritage/property makes them more widely available to whoever wants to see them. In this sense, digitization and open access fit into a discourse about the democratization of cultural heritage/property. This discourse is associated both with the idea of the "encyclopaedic museum", and with UNESCO's concepts of cultural heritage of humanity and cultural diversity.[26] It was also foundational for an earlier iteration of the OpenGLAM Principles, as noted by Pavis and Wallace, which made reference to "the advance of humanity's knowledge" and allowed users to "enjoy the riches of the world's memory institutions, but also to contribute, participate and share".[27] As the OpenGLAM movement seems to have subsequently understood, the discourse of the democratization of cultural heritage/property and its embodiment in the concept of open access are imbricated with Western values and priorities.[28] The unthinking imposition of these values on non-Western cultural heritage/property is simply to perpetuate the colonial mind-set that resulted in the relocation of vast amounts of other people's cultural heritage/property into the "encyclopaedic" museums of the imperial masters. Further, the post-colonial nature of this commitment to making other people's cultural heritage/property available on open access terms is complicated and potentially exacerbated by the variable meanings of "open access". In particular, there is some ambiguity around the relationship between access and use. It is unclear whether the former always implies the latter or, if not, under what circumstances.[29]

26 On the concept of the "encyclopaedic museum", see, e.g., N MacGregor, "Preface" in K Sloan (ed), *Enlightenment: Discovering the World in the Eighteenth Century* (London: British Museum Press, 2004), at 6. See also, N MacGregor, "To Shape the Citizens of 'That Great City, the World'" in J Cuno (ed), *Whose Culture? The Promise of Museums & the Debate over Antiquities* (Princeton, NJ: Princeton University Press, 2009). On the UNESCO's concept of the common heritage of humanity, or "the common heritage of mankind", see ch 3, section 2.3. On UNESCO's concept of cultural diversity and its focus on cultural exchange, see the UNESCO Convention for the Protection and Promotion of the Diversity of Cultural Expressions (2005) (CCD), recital 11 ("*Being aware* that cultural diversity is strengthened by the free flow of ideas, and that it is nurtured by constant exchanges and interaction between cultures"), 16 & Art 7.1(b), although it should be noted that this Convention is alive to the downside of cultural exchange: see recital 19 ("*Being aware* that while the processes of globalization, which have been facilitated by the rapid development of information and communication technologies, afford unprecedented conditions for enhanced interaction between cultures, they also represent a challenge for cultural diversity, namely in view of risks of imbalances between rich and poor countries"); see also UNESCO Convention on the Safeguarding of Intangible Cultural Heritage (2003) (CICH), Art 2.1, which also makes reference to the concept of cultural diversity.

27 Pavis & Wallace, n above, quoting the then version of the OpenGLAM Principles. These principles are currently under revision: see https://openglam.org/, accessed 08/09/2020.

28 Pavis & Wallace, n 13 above, Introduction.

29 Pavis & Wallace, n 13 above, section 2.

The point here is not to demonize democratization discourses around cultural heritage/property, or even UNESCO's commitment to a concept of the cultural heritage of humanity. However, both of these need to be considered in light of the role of cultural heritage/property as a social and political process in a world marked by extreme power imbalances and great inequality. Common humanity as an explanatory concept is weakly understood in our world. The hypocrisy of using this concept to perpetuate power imbalances that continue to create vast differences in the political, cultural and material circumstances of those falling within its definitional scope should not be overlooked. Discourses of democracy have little room to manoeuvre in such circumstances. Even if one accepts a type of democratization discourse that focusses on cultural exchange and understanding, instead of cultural misappropriation, it seems unlikely that this can be achieved by digitizing and making available the cultural heritage/property of other people without their consent and active participation.[30] As Prescott and Hughes observe (in more restrained terms):

> Paradoxically, there is a risk that an emphasis on digitizing cultural treasures will undermine the claim that digitization opens up and democratizes access to cultural heritage. If digital libraries [and other digital collections] merely reiterate and reinforce long-standing cultural narratives and stereotypes, rather than enabling the exploration of forgotten and neglected collections, then they can become agents of cultural exclusion.[31]

2.3 Intellectual property (again)

One of the claims often made in favour of open access for digital artefacts is that this is a way of resisting the power of the (Western) intellectual property rights regime. This is only the case, however, where open access comprises the renunciation of all restrictions over the digitized, or born digital, artefacts. It is not the case that making something open access automatically waives all copyright restrictions over it. Access and use are different concepts in copyright (and in life). To make a digital artefact freely accessible is not to make it freely usable. Since copyright – if it exists – arises automatically, when digital stuff is made freely accessible, the default position is that all other copyright restrictions that are not explicitly waived still apply. This means that digital material on open access always implies the potential to exercise some types of copyright restrictions. Where digitization and open access is managed by institutions in the GLAM sector, then the constant economic pressure on these institutions may result, and

30 This point seems to be accepted in the CCD: see n 26 above.

31 A Prescott & L Hughes, "Why Do We Digitize? The Case for Slow Digitization" [2018] *Archive Journal*, http://www.archivejournal.net/essays/why-do-we-digitize-the-case-for-slow-digitization/, accessed 27/07/2020; see also Pavis & Wallace, n 13 above, section 2[4].

in many cases has resulted, in pressure to exploit these rights for revenue-raising purposes.

Exploitation of copyright restrictions in this context raises a range of problems. Some of them are specific to the post-colonial context, where the complications raised by intellectual property rights leave us between the devil and the deep blue sea. Chapter 3 considers the limitations and problems implicit in claims by Indigenous Peoples to intellectual property over their cultural heritage and property.[32] One of the observations made in that discussion is that the claim by indigenous Peoples to intellectual property in their cultural heritage has slipped under the critical radar. One of the reasons for this is that the ownership of any such intellectual property would be in the relevant Indigenous Peoples themselves. But here the ball game is completely different because digitization raises the possibility – and probably the default position – of intellectual property rights in digitized artefacts belonging to the digitizer. Even where the digitizer renounces all such rights, we are left with the uncomfortable fact that, in the context of cultural heritage/property, the person doing the renouncing is very likely not a member of the community of origin. Rather, such a person has gained the ability to renounce these rights as a result of the intervention of Western law. Of course, collaborations with the community of origin in order to calibrate the desired level of openness, accessibility and reusability are possible and sometimes take place, but such collaborations are purely voluntary and cannot disguise the identity of the person/institution in the driver's seat.

The existence and/or exercise of intellectual property rights over digitized cultural artefacts is a post-colonial problem because it raises the spectre of a second neo-imperialist misappropriation of the cultural heritage/property of others. However, as serious as it is, digitization of cultural artefacts is not just a post-colonial problem, it also raises the same general problems about privatization of cultural heritage/property that have been investigated in Chapter 3.[33] Digitization carried out by GLAM sector institutions of works that are part of the Western canon has the capacity to foreclose and control access to, and use of, what is generally thought to be cultural heritage/property. Effectively, digitization in this context either generates intellectual property rights over works that were never subject to intellectual property protection (because they were made before the concept existed) or gives them a second life as copyright protected items. Either way, the effects of this are to foreclose community rights to access and use cultural heritage/property.[34] Lest this sound unnecessarily paranoid and alarmist, it should be noted that empirical studies of the digitization of works of Western art by GLAM sector institutions have indicated the prevalence of this

32 Ch 3, section 4.

33 Ch 3, sections 3.3 and 4.3.

34 See also G Pesach, "[Networked] Memory Institutions: Social Remembering, Privatization and Its Discontents" (2008) 26 *Cardozo Arts & Entertainment Law Journal* 71–149.

practice and the fact that often the quality of this type of digital data on open access is substantially inferior to that which is under copyright lock and key.[35] (Even paranoids have enemies.) The legal devices used by GLAM institutions to lock up cultural heritage/property of all types, and to prevent the creation of competing digital data, are not limited to intellectual property. They also typically rely on contractual claims to control activities on the physical property of the institution. Nevertheless, intellectual property restrictions have the capacity to play an important part in locking up access to, and use of, cultural heritage/property. And all this, of course, applies not just to GLAM institutions, but to anyone who digitizes cultural heritage/property.

3 Immoveability and monumentality

Not being able to truly let go of the moveable cultural stuff of others that has found its way into a variety of Western places, including GLAM sector institutions, speaks volumes about the post-colonial West and its longing to hold on to the traces of empire. That the authorized heritage discourse embodied in the international Conventions has, in most cases, nothing of use to say about the return of these items is entirely consistent with the well-established instrumentalization of international law as a tool of Western dominance.[36] The fate of what this discourse understands as moveable cultural stuff is too often an object lesson in the authorization of misappropriation, sacking and pillage. Cultural stuff that is, however, understood as immoveable poses a different problem because what is immoveable occupies actual physical space and what occupies actual physical space must be placed in a hierarchical ordering "at the behest of economic, technological, administrative and political power".[37] As Butler argues:

> The position of a particular space within the hierarchy is determined by its position in the conflictive relationship between centres and peripheries which manifests itself in the distribution of power, wealth, resources and information … This hierarchy between centre and periphery is not the random result of an evolutionary process. Rather, it is the product of a strategic logic in which the centre organizes that which is "around it, arranging and hierarchising the peripheries".[38]

35 See n 11 above.

36 See ch 3, section 4.1.

37 C Butler, "Critical Legal Studies and the Politics of Space" (2009) 18 *Social & Legal Studies* 313–332, at 323.

38 Butler, n 37 above, at 323–324, citing M R Martins, "The Theory of Social Space in the Work of Henri Lefebvre" in R Forrest, J Henderson & P Williams (eds), *Urban Political Economy & Social Theory* (Aldershot: Gower, 1982); quoting H Lefebvre, *The Survival of Capitalism: Reproduction of the Relations of Production* (London: Allison & Busby, 1976), at 17.

In the cultural heritage/property context, this ordering of space has been achieved by an obsessional focus on things that are somehow monumental within the Western tradition. UNESCO's emblematic WHC, which is surely the best known of all of its Conventions, addresses itself to three types of structures: monuments, groups of buildings and sites. Only the first of these uses the expression "monumental", in order to include "works of monumental sculpture and painting". However, all of the structures falling within the Convention are defined by reference to a largely Western way of seeing the world that privileges monumentality. Things described by the Convention as "monuments" and "groups of buildings" fall within the scope of the Convention only if they "are of outstanding universal value from the point of view history, art or science"; and "sites" must be "of outstanding universal value from the historical, aesthetic, ethnological or anthropological point of view".[39] These qualifiers are heavily influenced by Western values and Enlightenment thought structures. But what is really striking about them is the way in which they roll the concept of universality into a largely Western perspective. To say that something is of outstanding universal value according to a set of Western concepts is to merge universal and Westerns values in a way that blots out other ways of understanding the world.

In his revolutionary book on the systematic suppression of evidence of extensive and settled land cultivation by Australian Indigenous Peoples, Pascoe observes:

> If the test of sophistication were whether or not all were fed regardless of rank, or whether all contributed to the spiritual and cultural health of the civilisation, Aboriginal Australia might have a much higher rank than some of the nations considered the hallmark of human evolution.[40]

This comment eloquently makes the point that there are other values that might be celebrated as being of fundamental importance in understanding what constitutes cultural heritage/property. But Pascoe's over-arching thesis about the suppression of evidence of settled cultivation is also one among many examples that expose the way in which what is recognized as immoveable cultural heritage is part of the organization and "hierarchisation" of geographical space in order to reflect the distribution of power on a world scale.[41] We all know now – and everyone must have known then, as well – that the colonial claim to Australia as *terra nullius* was a convenient myth. However, it is only after almost 250 oppressive

39 WHC, Art 1. And see ch 3, section 2.1.

40 B Pascoe, *Dark Emu* (Broome: Magabala Books, 2018), at 146.

41 See Butler, n 37 above; Lefebvre, n 38 above. For other examples see L Meskell, *A Future in Ruins: UNESCO, World Heritage, and the Dream of Peace* (New York: Oxford University Press, 2018); L Smith, "Archaeology and the Governance of Material Culture: A Case Study from South-Eastern Australia" (2001) 34 *Norwegian Archaeological Review* 97–105.

years that we now understand the accompanying myth that Indigenous Australians were, prior to colonization, primitive hunter-gatherers with limited ties to territory. According to this fallacious vision of the world, nothing much has been taken from them. Destroying much of the immoveable heritage of Indigenous People in Australia and ignoring what remained has been a critical tool of colonial and post-colonial dominance. For sure, the landmark decision of the High Court of Australia in the *Mabo* case shook the myth because it recognized that Indigenous Peoples may be able to show, according to the rules and principles of the transplanted law of the colonizers, a continuing link with defined geographical spaces.[42] Despite the liberatory potential of this case, Pascoe notes that it provoked further destruction of the immoveable heritage of Indigenous Peoples by landowners anxious to remove any evidence of settled occupation that might result in a *Mabo* claim.[43]

The connection between the failure to recognize these immoveable structures as heritage and the management of colonial and post-colonial claims to land is a clear example of the way in which the production of heritage space has affected territory, sovereignty and the global distribution of power.[44] There are two important aspects of the UNESCO system, and of the WHC in particular, that should not be overlooked in this context. First, as is discussed at length in Chapter 3, the system is a state-based one.[45] It is the state of Australia that must ask for UNESCO listing of its immoveable heritage, not the Indigenous Peoples of Australia. The idea that the Australian state would compromise the legitimacy of continuing occupation and the security of land titles by seeking such listings only needs to be said in order to be understood as being improbable. The second important aspect of the UNESCO system is the way in which the discourse of the common heritage of humanity operates, in any case, to loosen the ties that bind immoveables that are listed as heritage under the WHC to their communities of origin. Sites of non-Western origin that are listed under this Convention are, on the one hand, somehow endowed with Western blessing if they conform to the standards required by the Convention. On the other hand, and at exactly the same time, they are also appropriated into the discourse of universality and the heritage of humankind. Depending on one's perspective, this is either a lose-lose or a win-win situation; and post-colonial history gives us a pretty clear idea of who are the winners and losers.

If we compare the treatment of what the UNESCO system considers to be tangible immoveable cultural heritage with that meted out to tangible moveables

42 *Mabo v Queensland (No 2)* [1992] HCA 23, (1992) 175 CLR 1.

43 Pascoe, n 40 above. On the extensive and complex immoveables constructed by Indigenous Peoples in Australia, see Pascoe, n 40 above, ch 3; & P Memmott, *Gunyah, Goondie and Wurley: The Aboriginal Architecture of Australia* (Brisbane: University of Queensland Press, 2007).

44 See also Meskell, n 41 above.

45 See ch 3, section 2.3.

and intangibles, then it is evident that UNESCO-listed immoveables have, to some extent, been protected from commodification and privatization. This is not a direct legal effect of the WHC obligations.[46] Rather, it seems to be a consequence of the way in which states have implemented their Convention obligations to identify, protect, conserve and transmit listed heritage.[47] Of course, heritage sites have been commodified through tourism; however, they are often fully or partly in state hands or subject to special limits on the usual rights of alienation that apply to privately held property. Moveable tangible and intangible cultural heritage/property has been more fully absorbed into the mechanisms of capital. However, the treatment of immoveable tangibles has a clear connection with the post-colonial world political order. This relationship between heritage, space and power might very well explain the Western obsession with, and privileging of, monumental or immoveable heritage. There is a vicious circle operating here. The privileging of immoveable stuff as a reflection of Western power over the organization of space has meant that cultures that do not produce the sort of stuff that appears to fall within the objects of protection of the WHC, or that do not give it the same importance as heritage, are under-valued. Being under-valued acts as a continuing justification for being subject to a Western idea of how space should be organized. Where, however, non-Western cultures have inconveniently produced the sorts of things that might fall within Western notions of monumentality, their provenance is put into question. This is a widespread colonial phenomenon. As Pascoe notes "the history of colonialism is dense with examples":[48]

> The underestimation of Indigenous achievement was a deliberate tactic of British colonialism. Large structures of North American First Nations people were … ignored, or credited to earlier Europeans; and in South Africa, Cecil Rhodes made it illegal for anyone to mention the huge Shona structures found in what was once Rhodesia and is now Zimbabwe. It was obvious that they were built by the Shona, but in order to legitimise his usurpation it was important that their achievements were denied.[49]

One Australian example of this is treatment of the megaliths at Mount Elephant (clearly not the original name of this place) in the state of Victoria (ditto), in relation to which he observes:

> Colonists recorded inflated accounts of the structures, and then informed the press that only Europeans could have built them … such deceits 'helped

46 See WHC, Art 6(1), which effectively provides that the Convention obligations are "without prejudice to property right (sic.) provided by national legislation".

47 See WHC, Arts 4 & 5.

48 Pascoe, n 40 above, at 219.

49 Pascoe, n 40 above, at 132.

European colonists legitimize their right to inherit the Australian continent. European colonization literally became a process of (re)possession of a lost domain of their heritage'.[50]

4 Moving targets

The Western obsession with immoveable cultural stuff – and its connection with the politics of space, sovereignty and power – should not be allowed to obscure the importance of moveables and intangibles to questions of identity and sovereignty. The relative impunity with which tangible moveable and intangible cultural stuff has been relocated physically or appropriated through intellectual property claims reflects another face of Western colonial and post-colonial dominance. Consequently, it can hardly be a surprise that the "ownership" of moveable tangibles and intangibles is at the heart of the contested territory of sovereignty and challenges to sovereignty. There are myriad competing claims to this type of stuff. Some of the best known controversies relate to the return of tangible items that, whether considered "moveable" in technical legal terms or not, have been in any case removed from their original sites. So far as tangible items are concerned, the preponderance of claims for return relates to things held in Western museums that were relocated from their communities of origin during the colonial period. But not all disputes over tangibles and intangibles fall within this description. For example, the dispute between Poland, Ukraine and Israel over the proper location of the murals of Bruno Schulz is not, at least in the usual sense, a post-colonial question. However, this dispute bears many of the hallmarks of other contested claims to moveable, and even to intangible, cultural stuff – including its link with the infliction of unspeakable horrors by one community of humans on another.

The terrible story of Bruno Schulz is one among the millions of Holocaust tragedies. Schulz, a Polish citizen, was an important cultural figure, both as a writer and as a visual artist. He was born in the city of Drohobycz, then part of Poland and now located in Ukraine. He was also Jewish. During the Second World War German occupation of Poland, he was murdered on his way back the Drohobycz Ghetto by a Gestapo officer. He had been under the "protection" of another Gestapo officer, Felix Landau. The price of this protection was the execution of a series of murals in the nursery of Landau's house, completed shortly before his murder.[51] The murals were subsequently covered and only rediscovered in 2001. Their rediscovery resulted in a conflict between Poland,

50 Pascoe, n 40 above, at 220–221, quoting I J McNiven & L Russell, *Appropriated Pasts: Indigenous Peoples and the Colonial Culture of Archaeology* (Oxford: Altamira Press, 2005), at 113.

51 For an interesting account of Bruno Schulz as a cultural figure, see A Z Newton, *The Elsewhere. On Belonging at a Near Distance: Reading Literary Memoir from Europe and the Levant* (Madison: University of Wisconsin Press, 2005), ch 2.

Ukraine and Israel for the right to possess and control the surviving fragments of the murals. The claims of Poland and Ukraine were based on, respectively, nationality and national cultural significance, and current geographical location. Israel claimed the fragments on behalf of the *Yad Vashem* Museum on the basis that Schulz was a martyr of the Holocaust.[52] What links this dispute to these types of disputes generally are a set of issues around origin and community, decontextualization, conservation and destruction. As always, these issues are linked together. For the sake of clarity, however, in the discussion below, I try to draw out the various individual strands.

4.1 Origin and community (again)

Like disputes over immoveables considered earlier, disputes over moveables typically involve either competing community rights, where community is sometimes understood as nation, or a conflict between community and the interests of humanity in general. Where the latter antagonism is in play, humanity in general is usually a vector for the Western claims, given "universal" status by the authorized heritage discourse.[53] The way in which this issue plays out is, of course, different depending on whether the cultural stuff in question has been moved and how it has been moved. As the Bruno Schulz case demonstrates, at least so far as the conflict between Poland and Ukraine is concerned, there is also the possibility that the stuff itself has not been moved, but its geopolitical circumstances have changed in a way that creates conflicts over its proper location. In fact, one of the rather obvious complications of national claims to cultural heritage/property is that the passage of time, along with the impact of changing political orders and the mutations of nationality and national borders, tends to introduce a certain fragility into some current assertions of national ownership.[54] Disputes over moveables are also more likely to involve a conflict between a community and a private owner. The same is true with respect to disputes over intangible cultural heritage/property, which involve not only the same types of inter-community conflicts as their tangible cultural counterparts, but more often also disputes between community and private intellectual

52 On the dispute over the fragments of the Bruno Schulz murals, see J Gordon, "The Strange Afterlife of Bruno Schulz" (2004) 43(1) *Michigan Quarterly Review*, https://quod.lib.umich.edu/cgi/t/text/text-idx?cc=mqr;c=mqr;c=mqrarchive;idno=act2080.0043.101;rgn=main;view=text;xc=1;g=mqrg, accessed 23/03/2020; M Bruncevic, "The Lost Mural of Bruno Schulz: A Critical Legal Perspective on Control, Access to and Ownership of Art" (2011) 22 *Law & Critique* 79–96; M Bruncevic, *Space, Materiality and the Normative: Law, Art and the Commons* (Oxford & New York: Routledge, 2018), 74–88.

53 See also Section 2.3.

54 See F Macmillan, "The Protection of Cultural Heritage: Common Heritage of Humankind, National Cultural 'Patrimony' or Private Property?" (2013) 64 *Northern Ireland Legal Quarterly* 351–364.

property rights. In this respect, it is interesting to note that had any testamentary legatee or living descendant of Bruno Schulz presented themselves, the case might have also implicated a conflict over the right to control the copyright in his murals.[55]

Thinking about who has the right to "ownership" and possession of cultural heritage/property takes us back into the problematic terrain of community considered in Chapter 4. One of the things that is exposed by a consideration of origin and community in this context is that not all communities are equal – or, at least, not all claims by communities are equal. The post-colonial discourse that forms the basis of claims to the control of cultural stuff by Indigenous Peoples, and by states created in the post-colonial post-war carve up, has attained legitimacy because it recognizes historical and continuing injustice.[56] This historical context, and its current ethical and political implications, provides a clear basis for distinguishing such claims from situations where the assertion of rights over cultural heritage has become the centrepiece of unattractive and dangerous claims to national identity and sovereignty.

There are examples of such claims in the European context where the assertion of national rights over cultural heritage has become part of the policy platform of right-wing and, in some cases, extreme right-wing parties and political movements. The effective claim of these parties and movements is that national identity is so closely tied up with this "heritage" that its relocation is a matter of cultural "right". This discourse, produced by a merger of community with nation state, is exactly what Nancy, Esposito and others warned against and it vindicates their fears about the co-option in politics and political philosophy of the concept of community.[57] A specific instance, which acts as an illustration of this point, is the platform of the Danish People's Party. When accessed in 2013, the Program of this party contained numerous references to the importance of Danish national cultural heritage.[58] The third of four paragraphs that served to introduce the Program stated: "In the Danish People's Party we are proud of Denmark; we love our country and we feel a historic obligation to protect our country, its people and the Danish cultural heritage". And there is a further section concerned specifically with the importance of cultural heritage:

> **The country is founded on the Danish cultural heritage and therefore, Danish culture must be preserved and strengthened.**
>
> This culture consists of the sum of the Danish people's history, experience, beliefs, language and customs. Preservation and further development

55 As far as I can determine, this is not the case.

56 See ch 3, sections 1 & 4.

57 See ch 4, section 2.

58 http://www.danskfolkeparti.dk/The_Party_Program_of_the_Danish_Peoples_Party.asp, accessed 29/01/2013. My thanks to Helle Porsdam for drawing my attention to this material.

> of this culture is crucial to the country's survival as a free and enlightened society.
>
> Therefore we wish to see action on a broad front to strengthen the Danish national heritage everywhere. Outside Denmark's borders we would like to give financial, political and moral support to Danish minorities.[59]

In furthering claims based on this platform, this political party has not hesitated to misappropriate the post-colonial discourse that has sustained the claims of Indigenous Peoples.[60] As Porsdam has shown, this misappropriation is well-illustrated in relation to the controversy over the return to Denmark of the surviving versions of the *Jyske Lov* (Jutlandic Law) of 1241, which was in the possession of the Swedish Royal Library, having either been purchased by it or bequeathed to it in the early eighteenth century.[61] The Danish People's Party claimed that the case was comparable to the dispute in the 1970s over the return to Iceland by Denmark of the Icelandic Sagas.[62] During the nineteenth and twentieth centuries, the Icelandic Sagas had been at the centre of a long campaign by Iceland based on the assertion that these manuscripts were central to their national identity. Greenfield observes:

> The significance of these saga manuscripts to the people of Iceland would be impossible to exaggerate. They have been the root and stock of Icelandic culture, the lifeblood of the nation, the oldest living literature in Europe, enshrining the origins of Icelandic society … Indeed, when the Icelanders took up the struggle for freedom and independence from Denmark in the nineteenth century, the saga literature was both their inspiration and their justification.[63]

There are two things that could be said to distinguish the Danish claims to the Jutlandic Law and the claims of Iceland to the manuscripts of the sagas. One of them is the former imperial relationship between Denmark and Iceland, and the significance of these sagas to Iceland's struggle for independence. The other is

59 Note 58 above (bold as in the original).

60 H Porsdam, "Cultural Heritage and Law: The Case of Cultural Looting" in H Porsdam & T Elholm (eds), *Dialogues on Justice: European Perspectives on Law & Humanities* (Berlin & Boston, MA: de Gruyter, 2012), at 221 & 228–232.

61 Porsdam, n 60 above, at 228–232.

62 As to which, see V Tr Hafstein & M Skrydstrup, "Heritage Vs Property: Contrasting Regimes and Rationalities in the Patrimonial Field" in J Anderson & H Geismar (eds), *The Routledge Companion to Cultural Property* (Oxford & New York: Routledge, 2017), at 48–51; M Rendix, "Copyright as Moral Strategy of Reclaiming the Past: The Return of the Icelandic Sagas" in Porsdam & Elholm, n 60 above.

63 J Greenfield, *The Return of Cultural Treasures* (Cambridge: Cambridge University Press, 1996), at 4, quoted in Rendix, n 62 above, at 180.

the centrality of the sagas to Icelandic identity in the current period. The second point, which follows from the first, should not be overlooked. As has been argued throughout this book, heritage is not about dusty old stuff. Heritage is a contemporary social process that impacts on the present and future.[64]

How, then, should we identify more generally what is an ethically justifiable claim for the return of cultural stuff by a community? One might fall back on an analysis focussed on the relationship between ownership as a legal matter and claims for the return of cultural heritage on the basis of some form of community right. In this case, the focus would be on the lawfulness or otherwise of the acquisition of the item in question. As has already been noted (several times) in this book, history – and, in particular, the history of colonialism – furnishes us with endless examples of looting and other forms of misappropriation of cultural stuff. This behaviour in the so-called outposts of empire during the colonial period has been retrospectively recognized as unlawful.[65] However, many of the appropriations that are subject to controversy in the inter-European context, for example, appear to have at least a claim to legal validity in technical terms. Allowing for the fact that the passage of time tends to obscure some relevant details, it is arguably the case that both the Icelandic Sagas and the Jutlandic Law were legitimately acquired by Denmark and Sweden, respectively.[66] Other salient examples of this are, of course, the long running dispute over the so-called "Elgin" Marbles and the claim by Turkey for the return of sculptures from the Mausoleum of Halicarnassus, which are currently part of the British Museum collection.[67] The problem is that focussing on legality does not allow us to distinguish between claims for the return to Denmark of the Jutlandic Law and those for the return to Iceland of the Icelandic Sagas. It does not allow us any scope for criticizing the extraordinary recalcitrance of certain museums when faced with claims for the return of cultural stuff. None of this should be a surprise. The law is not a reliable guide to ethics, nor is it able to ground a just political position (although in its best moments it can execute such positions).

If the technical "legality" of an appropriation is not a guide, going back to the question posed in the previous paragraph, how can we tell when a claim

64 See ch 3, sections 2 and 3.

65 As noted in ch 3, section 1, this was the conclusion of Special Rapporteur, Mohammed Bedjaoui, who was responsible for the preparation the work that eventually leads to the conclusion of the Vienna Convention on Succession of States in respect of State Property, Archives and Debts (1983): see further, A F Vrdoljak, *International Law, Museums & the Return of Cultural Objects* (Cambridge: Cambridge University Press, 2008), at 202.

66 Rendix, n 62 above, at 181 (Denmark); Porsdam, n 60 above, at 229 (Sweden).

67 For an account of the trajectory of the dispute over the Parthenon Marbles, see Hafstein & Skrydstrup, n 62 above, at 41–42; see also, e.g., www.elginism.com, accessed 21/02/2020. On Turkey's claim, see, e.g., "Turkish campaigners may go to European Court of Human Rights over Mausoleum of Halicarnassus in British Museum", http://www.elginism.com/similar-cases/turkish-compaigners-may-go-to-european-court-of-human-rights-over-mausoleum-of-halicarnassus-in-british-museum/20121217/6770/, accessed 21/02/2020.

by the community of origin for the possession or control of cultural stuff is one to which we ought to pay heed? There are three related things that are worth thinking about in this context: first, the relevance of time, and specifically of its passage, and the extent to which this affects the ties of the cultural stuff in question to the identity of the current version of community of origin; secondly, the relationship between the cultural stuff in question, identity, sovereignty and continuing historical and geopolitical injustice; thirdly, the question of by whom and to whom the claim is addressed. Thinking about these three points might provide a couple of pointers towards the refining of the role of the concept of community in relation to claims getting back cultural heritage/property. One conclusion we might reasonably draw is that claims by communities that are nation states might sometimes be relatively weak in ethical terms precisely because the relationship between their identity and sovereignty has already been recognized in international law, and/or because they are not in a position of relative geopolitical weakness that makes the possession or control of cultural heritage/property critical to identity or survival. Another conclusion, and one that reminds us that we should think about these questions in terms of both tangible and intangible cultural heritage/property, is that claims by communities of origin against those who exploit the cultural stuff of others for private profit might raise ethical and political issues that are qualitatively different to claims against nation states (including national GLAM institutions).

4.2 Decontextualization

Most controversies involving some sort of national, local or community assertion of rights over cultural heritage/property do not, as a matter of logical necessity, involve the rejection of the concept of the common heritage of humankind. Instead, they tend to involve some contingent claim that, for one reason or another, is said to trump or displace other claims. As has already been observed in the foregoing, an outcome of the colonial free-for-all that saw the movement of large amounts of cultural objects and artefacts from the colonial "periphery" to the imperial "centres" is that these types of disputes often involve disputes between a community of origin and large metropolitan museums. There is an ambiguous quality to the position of these museums, which constitute enormous storehouses of cultural stuff, in such disputes. They commonly identify themselves with a sort of discourse of democratization linked to their ability to present an "encyclopaedic" view of the heritage of humankind.[68] Given the way in which the authorized heritage discourse universalizes Western values, the idea of the encyclopaedic museum (or collection) might be understood as creating an

68 See, e.g., MacGregor, "Preface", n 26 above; MacGregor, "To Shape the Citizens of 'That Great City, the World'", n 26 above.

association with this notion of the common heritage of humankind. However, there is a *faux* naivety in this idea of the encyclopaedic collection, as though it was somehow free of the circumstances in which it was formed, and as though all the components of the collection will look exactly the same from wherever they are viewed. Observations made by Slaughter when addressing the concept of "the centre" in the intangible cultural heritage of world literature seem apposite here:

> [T]he core defines the norms and forms that make it the core: it defines itself as center ... We should remember, here at the center, that the core is the core not because it is the *source* of things, but because it is a collection of things ... [T]he center absorbs everything; it ... treats everywhere else and everything else as raw materials to be extracted, exploited, accumulated, and privatized ...[T]he center is never simply a given or merely an object; it is the effect of a certain way of seeing and speaking, of gathering an analyzing data.[69]

Despite attempts by many museums and collections, encyclopaedic or not, to present objects in a way that is in sympathy with their cultural origins and history, the symbolic significance of an article that has been decontextualized and severed from its community of origin is always changed. However, we should be wary in any case when large Western museums and collections align themselves to some idea of the common heritage of humanity. The danger that such a claim is simply another universalization of Western values is ever present. It also ignores the fact that at least some of these museums are a physical and metaphysical embodiment of the history of imperialism.[70] Granting such institutions the status of representing the common heritage of humanity obscures and degrades other histories of the colonial experience. At the same time, recognizing an institution like the British Museum as the incarnation of the British colonial experience could also be taken as the basis for an argument that it has some particular interest, beyond the presentation of an encyclopaedic collection, in keeping all this looted stuff because it is part of British (and, more specifically, English) cultural heritage – although maybe this confuses history with heritage. However, if the British Museum could make such a claim, then how would it relate to claims for the return of artefacts to former colonies, and to communities within former colonies, on the basis of their significance to history and identity? Whose claim trumps whose?

69 Slaughter, n 6 above, at 196.

70 See also M G Simpson, *Making Representations: Museums in the Post-Colonial Era* (London & New York: Routledge, 2001, revised edition, first published 1996); Vrdoljak, n 65 above, esp chs 1 & 2; S Waxman, *Loot: The Battle Over the Stolen Treasures of the Ancient World* (New York: Times Books, Henry Holt & Co, 2008).

My answer to this question is probably obvious to anyone who has read the whole of this chapter (let alone the rest of the book). A question that is a bit harder to answer is what all this means for the concept of the "encyclopaedic" museum. Can we find a version of the museum that embraces the cosmopolitan vision embodied in the idea of the common heritage of humanity and that is somehow able to disentangle itself from the traces of empire and continuing geopolitical injustice?[71] What will not fit this bill is any collection, wherever it is, of other people's stuff removed without their consent and displayed without their permission. An example of an initiative in development that aims to avoid such an approach is the proposed *Museum for the United Nations: UN Live*, which was launched as a digital platform in 2019 and is due to open in physical form at some point in the future.[72] At least so far as its public presentation is concerned, this initiative is in its early stages. However, its concept of an encyclopaedic collection not only rejects the decontextualization of tangible cultural stuff, but also embraces the idea that an encyclopaedic collection cannot be confined to just tangible stuff. The extent to which the *UN Live* initiative manages to avoid the pitfalls of the post-colonial museum, in particular, and the authorized heritage discourse, in general, is a question to be kept under review. However, for the moment, the initiative is interesting for its commitment to avoid decontextualization and its idea of an encyclopaedic museum that also includes intangible cultural heritage/property.

The question of the decontextualization of intangible cultural heritage/property through its presentation in GLAM institutions is a relatively unexplored one. At one level, this question is always implicated in questions around the decontextualization of tangible stuff precisely because, as already argued in this book, what makes tangible stuff into cultural heritage/property is its intangible connection to a community. As has also been explored in Section 2 of this chapter, the digitization of tangible objects creates a new version of the relationship between tangible and intangible, as well as creating new forms of intangible cultural heritage/property. And if the tangible always has an intangible dimension, then the inverse is also true: the intangible is never entirely divorced from the tangible.[73] It is not surprising, therefore, that in the context of an enquiry into decontextualization, there are common complicating features across the tangible/intangible spectrum. Without any doubt, one of these is the

71 See, e.g., D Carden, "My Solution to the Parthenon Marbles Row: A Museum for the 21st Century", *The Guardian*, 21 February 2020, https://www.theguardian.com/culture/2020/feb/21/my-solution-to-the-parthenon-marbles-row-a-museum-for-the-21st-century, accessed 21/02/2020.

72 See https://museumfortheun.org/about/, accessed 24/02/2020. With respect to online museums, see also L De Biase & P A Valentino (eds), *#SOCIALMUSEUMS: Social media e cultura, tra post e tweet* (Milano: Silvano Editoriale, 2016).

73 See ch 3, section 3.1, where it is also noted that this aspect of intangible cultural heritage is integral to its definition in the CICH.

way in which the movement over time of intangible heritage, like its tangible counterpart, creates layers of different community connections. The knowledge and customs around food and drink are a classic example of this. The ease with which knowledge and customs move creates a form of what Goonetilake calls "cultural re-transmission", spawning myriad versions of their antecedents.[74] While cultural re-transmission also applies to tangible objects, it is usually the case that re-transmission of tangibles is composed of successive temporal layers. Knowledge and customs, however, are capable of spreading out everywhere, creating new contexts not only in successive temporal layers, but also in chronologically contemporaneous versions. This is, of course, due to the non-rival nature of intangibles that can be everywhere and enjoyed by everyone at the same time.

There is no doubt that the capacity for re-transmission and re-appropriation of intangible cultural heritage/property has resulted in its decontextualization. And it seems only honest to admit that, despite the fact that it has been produced by "cultural colonization", often its re-contextualization tends to be a reason for celebration.[75] (Books like this would take even longer to write without the cultural re-transmission of tea and coffee drinking.) On the less celebratory side of things, however, the moveability of intangible cultural heritage/property has also led to international disputes over the "ownership" of intangible cultural stuff, including disputes in the context of listings under CICH.[76] Even though we may not be talking here about the way in which cultural heritage/property occupies and structures physical space, its significance in geopolitical power relations should not be underestimated.[77] The CICH, especially when considered together with its twenty-first-century UNESCO sibling, the Convention of the Protection and Promotion of the Diversity of Cultural Expressions (CCD), walks a difficult line between celebrating the cosmopolitan aspects of cultural re-transmission and protecting intangible heritage and cultural diversity from the inevitable mish-mashing effects of globalization. But it also represents a particular configuration of post-colonial state power relations.[78] As has already been discussed in Chapter 3, it has nothing much to say about the specific location of

74 S Goonetilake, "Colonial Culture" (1976) 4 *Social Scientist* 25–40.

75 For an account of "cultural colonization", see Goonetilake, n 74 above.

76 C Antons, "Legal and Cultural Landscapes: Cultural and Intellectual Property Concepts and the 'Safeguarding' of Intangible Cultural Heritage in Southeast Asia" in C Antons (ed), *The Routledge Handbook of Asian Law* (Oxford & New York: Routledge: 2017); C Antons & L Rogers, "Cultural and Intellectual Property in Cross-border Disputes over Intangible Cultural Heritage" in Antons & Logan, n 2 above. With respect to the listing procedure under the CICH, see ch 3, sections 3.2 and 3.3.

77 See H Schreiber, "Intangible Cultural Heritage and Soft Power – Exploring the Relationship" (2017) 12 *International Journal of Intangible Heritage* 44–57; see also N Akagawa, *Heritage Conservation and Japan's Cultural Diplomacy: Heritage, National Identity and National Interest* (London & New York: Routledge, 2014). On the way in which tangible heritage structures physical space, see Section 3.

78 Antons & Rogers, n 76 above; Schreiber, n 77 above.

Indigenous Peoples in this configuration as they attempt to protect their intangible cultural heritage/property from unauthorized and inappropriate use in the face of a saturating cosmopolitan discourse.[79] And, at least so far as Indigenous Peoples and other communities subject to sustained exploitation in the colonial and post-colonial periods are concerned, it has nothing much to say about the relationship between decontextualization, conservation and destruction.

4.3 Conservation and destruction

Much of the justificatory discourse around the retention of other people's cultural stuff by (usually) Western GLAM institutions focusses on the importance of conservation. As is well-known, the British Museum's refusal to return the "Elgin" Marbles was for a long time based on the claim that their physical integrity would be better protected if they stayed under house arrest in London. Whether or not this claim is true, it is as good an example as any of the Western obsession with the "privileging of preservation" at the expense of a dynamic relationship with identity that has often been used to justify retaining (mis)appropriated objects and artefacts.[80] The discourse of conservation is partly based on the patronizing claim that "we know better than you how to look after your cultural stuff", but it also relies on the claim that "in any case it's also our stuff". This might explain why claims for return are still often resisted even when it is clear that conservation is not in issue. For example, even though the Greek state has constructed a climate-controlled museum to house the Parthenon Marbles, the British Museum still refuses to return them.

Conservation, or what is called "safeguarding" in the CICH, is also at the heart of the twenty-first-century authorized discourse in relation to intangible cultural heritage.[81] As Smith and Akagawa observe, this has produced new variations on the tangible/intangible distinction:

> [T]he AHD [authorised heritage discourse] has reworked itself by adding to its lexicon two new key phrases, one tautological and the other absurdly

79 See ch 3, section 4.1. See also K Bowrey & J Anderson, "The Politics of Global Information Sharing: Whose Cultural Agendas are Being Advanced?" (2009) 18 *Social & Legal Studies* 479–504; B de Sousa Santos (ed), *Another knowledge Is Possible: Beyond Northern Epistemologies* (New York: Verso, 2008); C Oguamanam, "Wandering Footloose: Traditional Knowledge and the 'Public Domain' Revisited" (2018) 21 *Journal of World Intellectual Property* 306–325.

80 T Flessas, "Cultural Property Defined and Redefined as Nietzschean Aphorism" (2003) 24 *Cardozo Law Review* 1067–1098, at 1091. See also, T Flessas, "The Ends of the Museum", *Law, Society & Economy Working Papers 14/2013* (London: London School of Economics, 2013); Macmillan, n 54 above, at 354–355; Simpson, n 70 above; P Yu, "Cultural Relics, Intellectual Property and Intangible Heritage" (2008) 81 *Temple Law Review* 433, at 471–473.

81 For a comprehensive examination of this concept in the CICH, see N Akagawa & L Smith (eds), *Safeguarding Intangible Heritage: Practices and Politics* (Oxford & New York: Routledge, 2019).

> contradictory: "intangible value" and "tangible value" … the former is almost inevitably applied to social/cultural and other non-expert heritage values, while the latter is used to describe expert or "scientific" values ascribed to either material or intangible heritage. The development of these terms simultaneously with the implementation of the ICHC [CICH] is no accident; it can be seen as an attempt by those whose heritage practices are framed by the AHD to come to terms with the "intangible" and to attempt to incorporate it into their conceptual repertoire. Nonetheless, these terms work to reassert expert heritage values over community and other non-expert values. Simultaneously they reinforce the position of intangible heritage as being of less legitimacy or stature than tangible (and thus evidential and "real") heritage.[82]

And, of course, in this world of the authorized heritage discourse, it is not just that it is the experts who know all about conservation – and better than the communities of origin – it is also the case that their discourse around conservation has influenced how we understand its apparent opposite, which is the destruction of cultural heritage.

The standard discourse around the destruction of cultural heritage is largely confined to a concern about the physical destruction of monumental, and thus immoveable, objects and is almost exclusively about tangible things. Because conceiving of cultural heritage as being mainly tangible and monumental has a strongly Western flavour, this also means that this discourse is imbricated with an "us and them", West and the rest, flavour. In the current geopolitical situation, understanding the destruction of cultural heritage in these terms focusses upon motivations for destruction that are broadly political and/or indicate the absence of acceptable (Western) values. If, however, we were to refocus our concerns about the destruction of cultural heritage on situations where the inherent nature of something *as heritage* is destroyed, a different picture might emerge. Such a concept might very well include the dynamiting of ancient sites, but my argument is that it is much broader. In order to sustain this argument, it is necessary to focus on the inherent nature of heritage, moveable and immoveable, tangible and intangible, as part of a process of community formation and, therefore, as irretrievably connected to community.[83] In this alternative vision, the destruction of cultural heritage is rooted, not in some epochal clash between the West and the rest, but rather in the geopolitical movements and legal ordering that have emerged in the post-colonial period. There are two dimensions to this argument. One of them is concerned with the destruction of heritage as a result

82 N Akagawa & L Smith, "The Practices and Politics of Safeguarding" in Akagawa & Smith, n 81 above, at 2, citing L Smith & G Campbell, "The Tautology of 'Intangible Values' and the Misrecognition of Intangible Cultural Heritage" (2017) 10 *Heritage & Society* 26–44.

83 This argument is made more fully in ch 3, sections 2.2, 2.3 and 3.2.

of relocation and decontextualization; the other focusses on one of the specific manifestations of decontextualization, which is destruction by commodification.

As is discussed in Chapter 3, the international legal regime has nothing much to say about the problem of decontextualization of cultural stuff in the pre-UNESCO Convention era.[84] Overall, so far as tangibles are concerned, one might even go so far as to say that the regime appears to have been constructed in order to avoid the obligation to return objects and artefacts misappropriated in the colonial period to the communities whose symbolic connection to those objects and artefacts made them into cultural heritage/property in the first place. In this way the regime reduces the possibility of conflicts over the question of to which community this type of cultural heritage/property properly belongs. As already noted, over time artefacts and objects can acquire symbolic significance as cultural heritage/property to different communities. The famous horses of *Piazza San Marco*, one of the symbols of Venice, were looted by Napoleon and subsequently returned to Venice under terms imposed for the return of looted heritage by the Vienna Treaty of 1815. No one much mentions, then or now, that the Venetians had looted them from Corinth several centuries earlier. The reason for this might be that after spending a few centuries in Venice, they acquired a second, but not necessarily secondary, significance as Venetian cultural heritage. Applying the same sort of reasoning, it is necessary to consider the possibility that objects looted in the colonial period, which in many cases have spent well over a human lifetime in the display cases of the former imperial powers, have also become part of the cultural heritage/property of those former imperial powers. Similarly, the confused symbolic claims of colonial settler states, such as Australia, to the tangible and intangible cultural property of its (pre- and still existing) Indigenous Peoples, might be read as a claim to some sort of jointly held cultural heritage/property.[85] Perhaps, however, one of the things that makes these cases different to the horses of *Piazza San Marco* is the very existence of current competing claims, which make a compelling case for the vindication of a prior and continuing connection between the object in question and an existing community. The denial of these claims is a form of destruction of cultural heritage by a refusal to remedy the severing of the link between community and heritage.

The failure of the international law governing cultural heritage to address the severing of the link between artefacts and community in relation to tangibles misappropriated during the colonial period might be understood as a sort of failure by omission. That is, it might be understood as a failure to correct an existing wrong. In some senses, we could say that the system has refused to engage with the assertion to some type of property rights, created at the time of their misappropriation, over those tangibles. Such a failure to engage is a failure after

84 See ch 3, section 4.1.

85 This is particularly noticeable in Australian Government advertising and other publications promoting Australia as a tourist destination.

the event. When, however, we turn to the question of the failure of international heritage law to prevent the severing of the link between intangibles and community, achieved through the process of commodification of those intangibles, we are faced with a more complicated legal landscape. Part of this complication, of course, arises from the questionable distinction between intangible and tangible heritage. Certainly, we could find plenty of examples where the misappropriation of tangible heritage also implicated the misappropriation of intangible heritage. And, it is also clearly the case, that the sort of things that the international legal regime now describes as intangible heritage have been subject to much misappropriation (and not only in the period prior to their recognition by this regime). All this means that, again, the regime sins by omission, that is, by its failure to redress historic and continuing wrongs. However, the questions of the commodification of cultural heritage/property by colonial settler states or by private undertakings as a form of tourist experience, or of the private commodification of intangibles as intellectual property, are current ones.[86] In particular, given the focus of this book, the commodification of intangible cultural heritage/property through the use of intellectual property rights raises unanswered questions about the current relationship between heritage law and intellectual property law.[87] This means that the destruction of cultural heritage/property by commodification raises wider systemic issues because it involves a clash between currently existing legal concepts. This is a clash that the law refuses to see.

In the end, the argument here is a very simple one. It is that cultural heritage/property is destroyed not just when tangible objects are bombed, dynamited or subjected to some other form of physical degradation, but rather when the link between community and its cultural artefacts and practices is severed. Certainly, physical destruction of an object, moveable or immoveable, can have this severing effect. However, this is only one instance of such destruction. There are other ways of severing this link. Decontextualization of tangible or intangible artefacts and the commodification of intangible practices and artefacts, which are largely Western practices in a historic and a legal sense, both operate to sever the link between community and its cultural stuff. Of course, misappropriation and decontextualization can happen anywhere, but so far as tangible and intangible cultural artefacts are concerned, we are currently living with the legacy of systemic misappropriation and decontextualization that occurred in the colonial period. The international legal regime for the protection of cultural heritage, which is rather suspect in any case for its general inability to engage with the concept of community outside nation state

86 On the commodification of intangible cultural heritage for tourism, including the role of the CICH, see L Lixinski, "Intangible Heritage Economies and the Law: Listing Commodification and Market Alienation" in Akagawa & Smith, n 81 above. On the commodification of intangibles by intellectual property generally, see ch 1, section 5.

87 On the relationship between intangible cultural heritage and intellectual property, see ch 3, sections 3.3, 4.2 and 4.3.

formations, may be regarded as tacitly endorsing this state of affairs by its refusal to address it. So far as intangible cultural artefacts and practices are concerned, Western law is perhaps even more deeply implicated. In particular, as was argued in Chapter 3, the concept of private ownership of such artefacts and practices, developed into a system of commodification through the concept of intellectual property, means that their value is expressed only through the market thus severing them from their communities and destroying their character as heritage.[88]

When it comes to the question of the destruction of heritage, the West really has been best at it – and for quite a long time. But why be so strident on this point? The answer to this is also a very simple one. When we talk about the destruction of cultural heritage today, there is a tendency in at least some parts of the discourse to identify this as an East/West, us and them, phenomenon. The famous cases of the *Taliban* dynamiting of the sixth-century Buddhas of Bamiyan, the extensive destruction of archaeological sites in Syria, especially but not only in Palmyra, are often analysed in these terms. By thinking of the destruction of cultural heritage/property in this way, we, of course, betray the Western obsession with monumentality and tangibility, which has been nurtured at the expense of a concept of cultural heritage/property as "a constitutive social process".[89] However, if cultural heritage/property is understood as being such a process – and not just as a collection of static material artefacts – then Western responsibility for its destruction, and not only in the post-colonial world, is breathtaking.

5 Authenticity

The idea of authenticity, as the opposite of the fake, is a foundational concept in both intellectual property and cultural heritage discourse; and it is also a many-headed hydra. The idea that cultural heritage/property should be authentic is implicated in all the previous discussions in this chapter. But understanding what authenticity should mean, when it matters, and according to whom, presents particular challenges in a globalized world. In the Western tradition, there is a premium on a particular version of authenticity. In the world of visual art, authentication through a process to establish provenance is important not just to the market in high end art works, but also to the credibility of the GLAM institutions that exhibit this work as part of "our" cultural heritage. In this context, authenticity focusses on the identity of the artist. Where the artist is one of the famous members of the Western canon, the question of whether they copied the work, or appropriated parts of it from other artists, hardly seems to matter – it might be interesting to know, but it is not relevant to authenticity. Perhaps this is part of the reason why few questions are raised about the authenticity of, for example, the "primitivist" school of art, which freely appropriated works from

88 See ch 3, section 3.3 and ch 4, section 4.

89 L Smith, *The Uses of Heritage* (Oxford: Routledge, 2006), at 82; see ch 3, 3.2.

other cultures.[90] However, that a work is made by the hand of the person claimed to be its maker is not always what authenticity means in the canon of Western art. Sometimes, things that are copied are regarded as fakes, even when it is clear that they were copies and no one is suggesting that they were painted by anyone other than the person who claims to have painted them. How else to explain the allegations of inauthenticity and fakery levelled at carefully hand-painted versions of famous Western works of art produced in, for example, China?[91]

The siren call of authenticity exerts considerable influence over the Western GLAM sector generally. The reluctance of many GLAM sector institutions to return other people's cultural stuff has already been remarked upon a number of times in this chapter. Section 2 discussed the practice of making digital copies of holdings in GLAM institutions as part of a strategy of resistance to, or compensation for, the return of museum holdings. We can understand these digital versions of holdings as being in some sense authentic – both as authentic copies and as new artefacts in their own right. But the concept of authenticity in play here is a self-referential one, at least so far as the question of their status as cultural heritage/property is concerned. Decontextualized cultural stuff held in museums has, as argued in Section 4, already lost its character as cultural heritage/property because its link with its community of origin has been cut. It is, for this reason, no longer authentic as cultural heritage – at least as the cultural heritage of its community of origin. As Slaughter tells us, these objects have been "desanctified in one sign system and resanctified in another".[92] But there is more:

> In addition to the symbolic translations that facilitated the conversion of traditional ethnic artifacts into modern aesthetic objects, their complete transformation usually involved a number of specific material refinements that made them more durable, more portable, and more commodifiable … The process of abstraction that took anthropological items out of the world and into the gallery denuded the traditional object of its ephemera (its "superficial decoration" and symbolic burden), reducing it … to its most basic form.[93]

90 "Picasso made that now-legendary wrong turn into the Trocadéro's Africa room, which eventually detourned African artifacts into modernist fetishes and launched the primitivist revolution in modern European art": J R Slaughter, "'It's Good to Be Primitive': African Allusion and the Modernist Fetish of Authenticity" in P K Saint-Amour (ed), *Modernism & Copyright* (Oxford & New York: Oxford University Press, 2011), at 296, citing A Malraux, *Picasso's Mask* (New York: Da Capo, 1995, trans J Guicharnaud & J Guicharnaud).

91 See the study of this practice in Dafen by Kirsty Robertson in L J Murray, S T Piper & K Robertson, *Putting Intellectual Property in Its Place: Rights Discourses, Creative Labor, and the Everyday* (Oxford & New York: Oxford University Press, 2014), ch 8. See also the discussion in ch 1, section 5.5 and ch 4, section 4.

92 Slaughter, n 90 above, at 298.

93 Slaughter, n 90 above, at 299, citing S Errington, "What Became Authentic Primitive Art?" (1994) 9 *Cultural Anthropology* 201–226; & P Guillaume & T Munro, *Primitive Negro Sculpture* (New York: Harcourt Brace, 1926).

However, neither the symbolic nor physical transformations can ever be evident if the object is to be considered authentic. What the concept of authenticity is really doing in cases like this is erasing the object's interaction with its real history, which is to say with the processes of colonialization and Westernization that have meant that it finished in a glass case instead of being part of a dynamic social process.[94]

If authenticity is understood in this way, then the idea of the authentic copy or the authentic digital representation might become easier to understand. In what has now become the celebrated case of the "Nefertiti Hack", two German artists, Nora Al-Badri and Jan Nikolai Nelles, made an exact three-dimensional copy of the head of Nefertiti, held in Berlin's Neues Museum and subject to claims for its return by the Egyptian government.[95] The artists arranged a ceremony of return at which the copied head was received by the community of origin of the original head with, so the account goes, great joy. How should we understand the role of authenticity here? For the community of origin, the copy was embraced as an authentic piece of their cultural heritage/property even though it was not the original. The Neues Museum, needless to say, took the position that this copy was not legitimate. It raised questions about the way in which the digital data used to make the copy was obtained. It asserted that its intellectual property rights in this data had been breached. The artists, however, claimed to have obtained the data, not by hacking the digital data of the Neues Museum, but rather by using a concealed digital scanner in order to obtain the data from the head of Nefertiti displayed in the museum (which was not, of course, subject to intellectual property protection). The Neues Museum was unable to sustain its allegation that its proprietary data had been used and so was unable to rely on the claim that its intellectual property rights had been infringed. Apart from being an interesting lesson in how GLAM institutions choose to deal with digital copies of artefacts in their possession, the position of the Neues Museum raises a question about the relationship between legitimacy and authenticity in the cultural heritage/property context.[96] If a copy can be authentic, does it matter if its legitimacy is in question? The answer to this question probably depends, as many responses do, on who is being asked. In any case, the question exposes another disjuncture in the relationship between cultural heritage/property and intellectual property because the example of the Nefertiti Hack suggests that a copy could be, at the same time, the authentic cultural heritage/property of a community and the illegitimate and inauthentic offspring of an intellectual

94 Slaughter, n 90 above. See also, e.g., R J Coombe, *The Cultural Life of Intellectual Properties: Authorship, Appropriation and the Law* (Durham, NC: Duke University Press, 1998), ch 5.

95 For the artists' account of the Nefertiti Hack, see N Al-Badri & J N Nelles, "The Other Nefertiti", https://aksioma.org/the.other.nefertiti/, accessed 06/03/2020.

96 On the question of intellectual property rights in digital copies of GLAM institution artefacts, see Section 2.3.

property violation. Although such a violation was not proved in this case, there is no reason to think that it would have changed the game with respect to the question of the authenticity of copy as cultural heritage/property.[97]

This example of the disjuncture between the authenticity of cultural heritage/property and the violation of Western intellectual property rights is part of a much bigger picture that shows multiple examples of mutual incomprehension. One of the most obvious of these is the way in which copyright focusses on a so-called final product that is the work of a specified author (or authors).[98] As is well-recognized, this has the effect of silencing all the other voices and authors and communities that are an inevitable part of the gestation of literary, dramatic, musical, artistic and cinematographic works.[99] It cancels out the chronological layers that make up the copyright work and expunges the cultural and political engagements that give them life. This is true even where copyright manages to engage with some practices of appropriation and re-appropriation. As Murray, Piper and Robertson point out, this engagement has tended to be "on appropriation as an art practice with a single history" that "erases another definition of appropriation as it applies to cultural property".[100] The colonial and post-colonial oppression that is latent in the appropriation by Picasso, and the other primitivists, of African artefacts has been expunged by copyright's discourse on appropriation art.[101] According to this discourse, Picasso is an individual genius and the only author of his famous original and authentic works. Copyright's idea/expression dichotomy has also been fundamental in this context: the appropriation of artistic styles – no matter how distinctive – is legitimized and validated by the claim that style is an idea and therefore not able to be protected by copyright. Left out of this picture is the question of how this arguably inauthentic, and certainly unauthorized, use of other people's cultural heritage/property might damage it or might reflect on the authenticity of the appropriation or of the work in which the appropriation has been used. Another glaring omission is any reflection on the history of political, social and cultural oppression that authorizes Western cultural production to plunder the cultural heritage and property of subjugated colonial and post-colonial communities.

This post-colonial cultural cleansing also works in reverse. As has already been suggested earlier, to be considered authentic products of non-Western culture, such things must be cleansed – at least to some extent – of their associations with colonial and post-colonial occupation and oppression.[102] Slaughter recounts the

97 See also C Voon, "Could the Nefertiti Scan Be a Hoax – And Does that Matter?", *Hyperallergic*, 9March2016,https://hyperallergic.com/281739/could-the-nefertiti-scan-be-a-hoax-and-does-that-matter/, accessed 06/03/2020.

98 See ch 1, section 5.

99 See ch 1, section 5.6.

100 Murray, Piper & Roberston, n 91 above, at 32.

101 Murray, Piper & Robertson, n 91 above, at 32–34; Slaughter, n 90 above.

102 See text acc n 93 above.

startling and emblematic story of the successive translations into English of the 1968 novel of Malian writer Yambo Ouologuem, *Le Devoir de violence*.[103] The novel was twice translated into English, once by Ralph Manheim in 1971 and then again by Christopher Wise in 2008.[104] The first translation resulted in a scandal when it was found to contain a long passage from the French translation of Graham Greene's, *It's a Battlefield*.[105] And this appropriation was far from being the only one: "*Le Devoir de violence* is filled with appropriations from (among many others) Guy de Maupassant, Ian Fleming, Alain Robbe-Grillet, Camara Laye, Georges Bataille, Victor Hugo, Emile Zola, Proust, and Baudelaire".[106] Its opening lines adapt those of Schwarz-Bart's *Les Dernier des justes*, which won the Goncourt Prize in 1959.[107] This literary scandal, as Slaughter says, "offers rich material for examining how the lines between closely related forms of intertextuality – allusion, quotation, translation, parody, and plagiarism (among others) were inflected by the postcolonial politics and dynamics of metropolitan France in the late modernist period".[108] He continues:

> [T]he radical intertextuality of Ouologuem's novel punctures a pair of cultural essentialist (read: racist and racialist) corollaries at the heart of modernism and copyright: metropolitan pretensions about the integrity of French (or, more broadly, Western) literary culture and the equally problematic presumptions about the racial coherence and radical alterity of African literary production.[109]

Ouologuem's practices of intertextuality ran counter, as Slaughter says, to the Western "longing for an authentic African essence that has somehow survived the cultural and intellectual ravages of the slave trade, colonialism, and post-colonial socialization".[110] What, it seems, is authentic "for African writers is very different from the monadic version of existential self-authenticity comprehended by authorial originality".[111]

103 Slaughter, n 90 above.

104 Y Ouologuem, *Bound to Violence* (London: Heinemann, 1971, trans R Manheim); Y Ouologuem, "The Duty of Violence" in C Wise (ed), *The Yambo Ouologuem Reader* (Trento, NJ: Africa World Press, 2008, trans C Wise).

105 G Greene, *C'est un champ de bataille* (Paris: Laffont, 1953, trans M Sibon).

106 Slaughter, n 90 above, at 277n.

107 A Schwarz-Bart, *Le Dernier des justes* (Paris: Les Éditions du Seuil, 1959); A Schwarz-Bart, *The Last of the Just* (New York: Atheneum, 1960, trans S Becker). On the appropriation from Schwarz-Bart, see Slaughter, n 90 above, at 281.

108 Slaughter, n 90 above, at 277.

109 Slaughter, n 90 above, at 279, footnote omitted.

110 Slaughter, n 90 above, at 282.

111 Slaughter, n 90 above, at 282, citing J Clifford, *The Predicament of Culture: Twentieth-century Ethnography, Literature, and Art* (Cambridge, MA: Harvard University Press, 1988), at 235.

And this was just with respect to the original French version of the novel. Things get even more interesting when the attention is paid to the process of translating the *Le Devoir de violence* into English. The first translation into English, in which Ouologuem appears to have participated, is not a faithful translation from the French original. Instead, pieces of well-known English texts make an appearance. Text from T S Eliot and Emily Dickinson appears, as do modified versions of passages from Frank Norris's "classic novel of lust, greed, and murder", *McTeague: A Story of San Francisco.*[112] One might infer from this that Ouologuem wanted to be sure that the reading public in English had the opportunity to appreciate his practices of appropriation, allusion, parody and plagiarism – and perhaps with them the effect of cultural contamination and domination. These practices of intertextuality were certainly noticed, but they were judged to be different from those engaged in by the Western modernists and unacceptable on that account, as if there is also an authorized (Western) form of intertextuality.[113] As Slaughter writes (one last quote from an irresistibly quotable piece):

> Ouologuem was blamed for his recitations because, despite centuries of colonial history, early readers prejudicially assumed that a redlined African author would not (or could not or should not) borrow from the bank of Western literature in an 'authentic African novel'.[114]

In addition to provoking a literary scandal, the first English translation of *Le Devoir de violence* also gave rise to a claim for infringement of the copyright in Graham Greene's *It's a Battlefield.*[115] However, since the books had the same publisher, the matter was settled without the assistance of the courts.[116] Nevertheless, the case shows how the idea of authenticity, or originality, in copyright law is running in tandem with a Western discourse about authenticity in non-Western cultural production. If, as Murray, Piper and Robertson observe, copyright is "inescapably ill-equipped to address all the dimensions of cultural, economic, and political reality that weave through its field of regulation", then this is because it is part of a larger Western discourse about authenticity and

112 F Norris, *McTeague: A Story of San Francisco* (New York: Doubleday Page, 1914): see Slaughter, n 90 above, at 289.

113 Slaughter, n 90 above, at 288.

114 Slaughter, n 90 above, at 291. The 1971 translation was published in the Heinemann African Writers Series, of which Chinua Achebe was the founding editor. Achebe's celebrated *Things Fall Apart* (C Achebe, *Things Fall Apart* (London: Heinemann, 1962, first published 1958) was the first book in the series: https://www.ascleiden.nl/content/library-highlights/heinemann-african-writers-series, accessed 04/03/2020.

115 G Greene, *It's a Battlefield* (London: Heinemann, 1934). Many of the other appropriations were from sources that were out of copyright.

116 Slaughter, n 90 above, at 277n.

originality in cultural production.[117] Altogether, this discourse illuminates another murky post-colonial moment. Western cultural production can glean what it likes from the world, but non-Western cultural production seems to be infected with some obscure requirement of cultural purity, masquerading as authenticity, that limits its field of operation. Picasso and the primitivists can appropriate African art, Disney can make films (mis)appropriating (and distorting) the stories of First Nation Peoples (*Pocohontas*, *Moana*), but cultural contamination working in the opposite direction is somehow inauthentic.[118] As we might expect from this field of complication and contradiction, purity here means what we in the West say it means. Things have to be a bit cleaned up and Westernized before they interest us much. We want them to be a bit Westernized, but only a bit. Artefacts are altered before becoming museum (or privately owned) pieces.[119] Literary works have to be a bit Westernized before we can start judging their non-Western cultural authenticity. Ouologuem's novel, for example, was already a Europeanized post-colonial piece; written in French, it was the 1968 recipient of the *Prix Renaudot* for an outstanding original novel in French, its debt to Homer's *Iliad* undisguised (and partly displaced in the 1971 English translation by a larger debt to T S Eliot's "Wasteland").[120]

This obsession with a constructed idea of authenticity characterizes the framing of the current debates regarding the protection of intangible cultural heritage. This is the case both in the context of the debate about traditional knowledge and traditional cultural expressions, which has been shaped by intellectual property discourses, and in the context of UNESCO's CICH.[121] So far as the question of traditional knowledge and traditional cultural expressions are concerned, the very use of the word "traditional" is the giveaway. If non-Western knowledge and cultural expressions are "traditional", then they are considered authentic and worthy of protection, even if the Western system of intellectual property has trouble accommodating them. In fact, especially if this is so because it reinforces their authentic status as traditional, not modern, not actual, something else altogether. This not only requires non-Western knowledge and cultural production to be authentically pure, and somehow untouched by its long interaction with Western domination and capitalist exploitation, but it also tends to negate the idea that Western communities have traditional knowledge and cultural expressions. Accompanying this idea of traditional authenticity is a

117 Murray, Piper & Robertson, n 91 above, at 34.

118 *Pocohontas* (Walt Disney Feature Animations, 1995, dir M Gabriel & E Goldberg); *Moana* (Walt Disney Animation Studios, 2016, dir R Clements & J Musker). On cultural appropriation in the film industry, see M Sunder, *From Goods to a Good Life: Intellectual Property and Global Justice* (New Haven, NJ: Yale University Press, 2012), ch 6.

119 See text acc n 93 above.

120 Slaughter, n 90 above.

121 On the discursive relationship between intellectual property, traditional knowledge and cultural expressions, see ch 3, sections 3.3 and 4.

way of seeing the world that wants to keep the traditional cultural expressions of non-Western people in a specially delineated area, cleaned up and well-presented, of course, and with only well-controlled interactions with the Western world. According to this worldview, for example, a band like Australia's famous *Yothu Yindi* might be thought of as using a blend of the traditional cultural expressions of the Yolngu people and Western musical tropes.[122] However, another way of describing their music, according to a different worldview, is as a blend of traditional Yolngu cultural expressions and traditional Western cultural expressions (rock music, by the 1990s being an extremely well-established musical form).

This type of engagement between cultural expressions with different origins unsettles ideas about what is authentically traditional especially when, as in the case of *Yothu Yindi*, it has been used to produce explicitly political speech about the post-colonial condition of Indigenous Peoples. Such use transforms those cultural expressions into contemporary (rather than traditional) forms. This transposition also invokes the tensions between the interests of community and private intellectual property rights that are the hallmark of all contemporary cultural works. This is the complex reality that Murray, Piper and Robertson refer to when they say that they "reject the binary view that would presume 'Western' people to be entirely comfortable or hegemonized by IP law, and indigenous or non-Western people to be alienated from it".[123] And it is a complex reality not just for Indigenous Peoples, but for all of us. The obsession of intellectual property scholars – in most cases not Indigenous – with "traditional cultural expressions" as *sui generis* has resulted in the labelling of the cultural practices of Indigenous Peoples as only being authentic if they are not contemporary, even when we know that the political battles around culture and language are extremely contemporary and that Indigenous Peoples have as much right as anyone to be part of, as *Yothu Yindi* put it in one of their most famous songs, the Western "mainstream", or not to be if they so choose.[124] This obsession has been at a very substantial cost to our larger understanding of the relationship between community interests in cultural practices and private interests in intellectual property rights. As Murray, Piper and Robertson argue, we have failed to learn

122 The Australian band, *Yothu Yindi*, was formed from the merger of two bands, one composed of musicians from the Yolngu people from the Arnhem Land in Australia's Northern Territory, and the other a non-Indigenous band called the *Swamp Jockeys*. The band, which was active from 1985 until 2013, enjoying significant chart success in Australia and having been inducted into the Australian Recording Industry Association (ARIA) Hall of Fame, made extensive use of Yolngu songs, instruments and dance, which they blended with the sounds and instruments of mainstream rock music. See also, J Kerr, "Treaty by Yothu Yindi – A Trojan Horse in the Culture Wars", *The Guardian*, 2 March 2015, https://www.theguardian.com/music/2015/mar/03/treaty-by-yothu-yindi-a-trojan-horse-in-the-culture-wars, accessed 10/03/2020.

123 Murray, Piper & Robertson, n 91 above, at 4. See also, ch 4, section 5.

124 Yothu Yindi (B Yunupingu), "Living in the Mainstream", *Homeland Movement* (Melbourne: Mushroom Records, 1989), subsequently re-released on *Tribal Voice* (Melbourne: Mushroom Records, 1991) and *One Blood* (MGM Records, 1999).

from Indigenous Peoples how we might balance these two different interests – casting them and their cultural practices as only "traditional", whatever that means, and thus *sui generis.*

The post-colonial condition of Indigenous Peoples is to be peoples without a state and so lacking political self-determination. This means that they enter into a constant engagement with Western geopolitical power, Western cultural production and Western capitalism. It is this very condition, and their ongoing resistance to cultural suppression, that means that they must find a way to reconcile their own laws on community management of cultural production with intellectual property rights that might belong to community members as a result of the Western legal regimes under which they often live. Instead of paying attention to the management of this complex relationship by Indigenous Peoples, we act as though we in the West have no "traditional culture" or even any contemporary cultural heritage, as though all contemporary cultural production can be effectively mediated through the intellectual property system.[125] We fail to see that systems of cultural property and intellectual property have different ways of measuring value; and that, according to this way of understanding the world, the value of contemporary cultural production inside the intellectual property system can only ever be an artefact of the market measured in terms of the economic value of a property right conferred by law. And what are the results of this failure to learn from the experience of Indigenous Peoples? One particularly important one is that in Western legal systems, we have failed to develop the type of meaningful concept of community rights in cultural property that can resist the creeping privatization of everything through intellectual property rights. Perhaps instead of marginalizing Indigenous Peoples (yet again), by calling their cultural practices "traditional", by insisting that they remain (in)authentically locked in a pre-colonial time-warp, by describing them as *sui generis*, we might be advised to look again at the accommodations the members of such communities have reached in order to balance community rights to culture with individual economic claims to particular parts of that culture.

The idea of authenticity that requires the freezing in time of so-called traditional knowledge and traditional cultural expressions in the tug of war between what belongs in the intellectual property system and what is *"sui generis"* also characterizes UNESCO's CICH regime. As described in Chapter 3, the regime operates by listing intangible heritage on the nomination of states that are members of the CICH.[126] The Convention has no mechanism to allow communities forming less than a state to list intangible cultural heritage to which they wish to make a claim. Although states are obliged to include "communities,

125 See also G Teubner & A Fischer-Lescano, "Cannibalizing Epistemes: Will Modern Law Protect Traditional Cultural Expressions" in C Graber and M Nenova (eds), ***Intellectual Property and Traditional Cultural Expressions in a Digital Environment*** (Cheltenham: Edward Elgar, 2008).

126 See, ch 3, section 3.

groups and relevant non-governmental organizations" (Article 11(b)) in the process of identifying their intangible cultural heritage, all entries to the Convention's lists of intangible cultural heritage are made through state channels. In formal terms, this is as much as an issue for Indigenous communities as it is for other communities forming less than the state as a whole. In reality, however, it particularly affects communities that have an adverse relationship with the states in which they live – a description that often applies with particular force to Indigenous Peoples. Once something is nominated, a decision on its inclusion in one of the UNESCO lists of intangible cultural heritage is made by the UNESCO Intergovernmental Committee for the Safeguarding of the Intangible Cultural Heritage.[127] In addition to (what must by now seem to readers to be) the fairly obvious concern about centralized decisions on the authenticity of a practice as intangible cultural heritage within the meaning of the CICH, reports on its actual operation are not necessarily promising.[128]

Once something is listed, states are obliged to put in place "necessary measures to ensure the safeguarding" of that intangible cultural heritage in their territory (Article 11(a)). According to Article 2.3, safeguarding in this context

> means measures aimed at ensuring the viability of the intangible cultural heritage, including the identification, documentation, research, preservation, protection, promotion, enhancement, transmission, particularly through formal and non-formal education, as well as the revitalization of the various aspects of such heritage.

Leaving aside for a moment the limited scope of these duties, which is considered in Chapter 3, what is striking is the idea that, in order to be authentic for the purposes of the CICH, something intangible can be sufficiently pinned down and frozen in time in order to be included in a list and then lavished with all this "safeguarding" attention. Perhaps what would be more authentic would be to give communities the responsibility of ensuring the ongoing authenticity of their intangible heritage/property, including the questions of how it is accessed and on what terms.[129] (And, frankly, if they don't care about it anymore, then it is more than likely that it is no longer authentic cultural heritage/property.) Admittedly, as already noted in Chapter 3, Article 13(d)(ii) requires states parties to "adopt

127 On the Intergovernmental Committee, see CICH, Arts 5–8; on the Representative List of the Intangible Cultural Heritage of Humanity, see CICH, Art 16; on the List of Intangible Cultural Heritage in Need of Urgent Safeguarding, see CICH, Art 17; and see also the Register of Good Safeguarding Practices, established under CICH, Art 18.

128 See, e.g., K Kuutma, "Inside the UNESCO Apparatus: From Intangible Representations to Tangible Effects" in Akagawa & Smith, n 81 above, which describes the experience of being on a CICH Subsidiary Body.

129 See also J Blake, "Further Reflections on Community Involvement in Safeguarding Intangible Cultural Heritage" in Akagawa & Smith, n 81 above.

appropriate legal, technical, administrative and financial measures aimed at … ensuring access to the intangible cultural heritage while respecting customary practices governing access to specific aspects of such heritage".[130] While it is hard to say what "customary practices" are, and difficult to know what tests of authenticity they will be required to pass, perhaps this is a nod in the right direction. Perhaps it might suggest that states are obliged to limit some types of access, perhaps including appropriation and use. But, even in this context, we are caught in an authenticity bind. Intangible cultural heritage/property, like all cultural/heritage property, must always respond to its environment. Otherwise, it ceases to be cultural heritage/property and just becomes an interesting bit of history (or a bit of dusty old junk). Is intangible cultural heritage that is frozen in a list really authentic? Is intangible cultural heritage that interacts with local commerce, with the machinations of global capitalism, and/or with communities in new geopolitical locations still authentic?[131] It is hard to escape the conclusion that communities of origin might have been best, after all, at knowing how to deal with these types of questions.[132] And this is the case whether we are talking about Indigenous Peoples or other communities of the global North or South.

6 Nature and culture

When it comes to thinking about the intertwined discourses around the protection of cultural property/heritage and the protection of intellectual property, the heavy footprint of the nature/culture distinction is everywhere. And it is everywhere rolled up with the way in which the Western penetration of other cultures has carried with it capitalism and, its handmaiden, occidental law. As Moore comments:

> One can no more extract "nature" from the constitution of capitalism than one could remove law, class struggle, the modern state, science or culture. On the other hand, a binary that is empirically falsifying does not deprive it of real historical force. Here the Cartesian binary is an "abstraction not as mere mask, fantasy, or diversion, but as a force operative in the world." The Cartesian binary is a curious sort of real abstraction, created out of the dialectic of value formation as abstract social labour and abstract social nature. It is an abstraction born of – and immanent to – capitalist development, with deep roots in early modern materialist and scientific revolutions …[133]

130 See ch 3, section 3.3.

131 Cf Lixinski, n 86 above & N Akagawa, "Culinary Heritage and Washoku as Japanese Traditional Dietary Culture under UNESCO's Intangible Heritage" in Akagawa & Smith, n 81 above.

132 See also N Akagawa & L Smith, "The Practice and Politics of Safeguarding" in Akagawa & Smith, n 81 above.

133 J W Moore, *Capitalism in the Web of Life: Ecology and the Accumulation of Capital* (London & New York: Verso, 2015), at 21, quoting A Toscano, "The Open Secret of Real Abstraction" (2008) 20 *Rethinking Marxism* 273–287, at 274.

The distinction between nature and culture is fundamental to the organization of the UNESCO regime for the protection of cultural heritage.[134] It is particularly evident in the WHC, which divides the objects of its projection into "cultural heritage" and "natural heritage", although it should be noted that there is a special hybrid section in the WHC lists for things that are of mixed natural and cultural heritage.[135] Despite this acknowledgement that some things cannot be put into one box or the other, there is an overwhelming Western tendency to make this distinction – and this is a tendency that cannot necessarily be mapped on to non-Western cultures, at least as they were before Western penetration.[136] In post-colonial perspective, the consequences of this can be truly startling, as is demonstrated by the behaviour of some visitors to the UNESCO-listed mixed natural and cultural heritage site of Uluṟu–Kata Tjuṯa National Park in Central Australia.[137] On 26 October 1985, after a long campaign, this sacred site was returned to the custodianship of the traditional owners, the Aṉangu people. After the title deeds were returned to the traditional owners, the land was leased back to the Australian National Parks and Wildlife Service and is jointly managed by the Aṉangu people and what is now Parks Australia. The Aṉangu people have, for many years, asked people to respect the sacredness of Uluṟu by not climbing on it and avoiding certain areas around its base.[138] Nevertheless,

134 See further ch 3, sections 1 and 2.

135 See http://whc.unesco.org/en/list/, accessed 12/03/2020. Mixed natural and cultural heritage sites are contained in both the World Heritage List and the list of World Heritage in Danger: WHC, Art 11.

136 See, e.g., R J Coombe, "The Properties of Culture & the Possession of Identity: Postcolonial Struggle & the Legal Imagination" in B Ziff & P V Rao (eds), *Borrowed Power: Essays on Cultural Appropriation* (New Brunswick, NJ: Rutgers University Press, 1997); M Strathern, *Property, Substance & Effect: Anthropological Essays on Persons & Things* (London: Athlone Press, 1999); I Watson, "Buried Alive" (2002) 13 *Law & Critique* 253–269; M F Brown, *Who Owns Native Culture?* (Cambridge, MA: Harvard University Press, 2003). See also L V Prott & P J O'Keefe, "'Cultural Heritage' or 'Cultural Property'" (1992) 1 *International Journal of Cultural Property* 307, at 310 citing *Milirrpum v Nabalco Pty Ltd* (1971) 17 FLR 141, in which the Federal Court of Australia found that the Yolngu people (the original owners of the Gove Peninsula in Arnhem Land)

> rather than believing that the land belonged to them, ... believed that they belonged to the land: that it had been entrusted to them by their spirit ancestors & that they had certain duties towards it & rituals to perform on it.

(The decision in this case denying native title was subsequently overruled in *Mabo v Queensland (No 2)* (1992) 175 CLR 1, but without disturbing this finding.) On the relationship of Australian Indigenous Peoples to land, see also J Gibson, "Community and the Exhaustion of Culture. Creative Territories in Traditional Cultural Expressions" in F Macmillan & K Bowrey (eds), *New Directions in Copyright Law: Volume 3* (Cheltenham: Edward Elgar, 2006).

137 See "Uluṟu–Kata Tjuṯa National Park", http://whc.unesco.org/en/list/447, accessed 12/03/2020.

138 For an account of the history of this site and its return to the custodianship of the Aṉangu people, see Parks Australia, "Uluṟu–Kata Tjuṯa National Park", https://parksaustralia.gov.

until the closure of Uluṟu to climbers on 26 October 2019, many tourists failed to respect this request. The period immediately before the permanent closure of the pathway on Uluṟu witnessed the unedifying spectacle of people coming from all over Australia and other parts of the world to indulge in their last chance to trample this sacred site.[139] Two explanations for this disturbing and disrespectful behaviour come to mind – neither reflecting a jot of merit on the tourists in question. One explanation is that the fact that this site appears "natural", at least to Westerners, had blinded them to the consequences of their actions; and that, as a result, they had failed to see that Uluṟu has a spiritual significance to the traditional owners that reflects the way in which other communities think about cathedrals, synagogues and mosques. The other explanation is that, even if they understood this, they simply didn't care. Certainly, to the extent that first explanation is correct, it appears to be a consequence of a way of thinking about the world that divides it between nature and culture. The interesting (if that is the correct word) thing about this way of thinking is that it is also manifestly not the way Western society organizes itself in relation to its occupation and use of nature. This is to say that the distinction, while insisted upon in a rhetorical sense, is clearly false in an empirical sense. In the West, and everywhere else that Western law has penetrated, ownership and occupation of nature in the form of land have always determined political, social and cultural orders.[140] Our rapacious use of land and other natural resources in global capitalism's system of production and consumption is at the heart of our current climate crisis.[141] It can hardly be regarded as an exaggeration to say that our treatment of what we regard as nature, or our physical environment, is in danger of extinguishing everything that we think of as culture. Things might have gone very differently for us if we had recognized the indissoluble identity of all our diverse cultures with our natural environment. Perhaps then we might have seen that the planet and its climate is the one thing that is truly the common heritage of humankind.

au/uluru/, accessed 13/03/2020; & see Bowrey & Graham, n 2 above. On requests by the Aṉangu people to refrain from climbing Uluṟu, see Bowrey & Graham, *ibid*. On the closure of the site to climbers, see also L Allam & M Bowers, "New Dawn for Uluru as Climb Closure Ends Decades of Disrespect", *The Guardian*, 26 October 2019, https://www.theguardian.com/australia-news/2019/oct/26/new-dawn-for-uluru-as-climb-closure-ends-decades-of-disrespect, accessed 13/03/2020.

139 See, e.g., C Heaney & S Jonscher, "Uluru Climb Closed Permanently as Hundreds Scale Sacred Site on Final Day", *ABC News*, https://www.abc.net.au/news/2019-10-25/uluru-climb-closed-permanently-by-traditional-owners/11639248, accessed 13/03/2020.

140 See Butler, n 37 above; Section 3.

141 On the relationship between capitalism and nature, see K Polyani, *The Great Transformation: The Political Economic Origins of Our Time* (Boston, MA: Beacon Press, 2001, first published 1944), at 71-80, on land as a fictitious commodity; A Malm, *Fossil Capital: The Rise of Steam Power and the Roots of Global Warming* (London & New York: Verso, 2016); Moore, n 33 above.

So far as intellectual property is concerned, the nature/culture binary has a particular role in determining what is inside the system and what is outside. As discussed in Chapter 2, the metaphorical distinction between nature and culture is frequently called upon to explain the location of the line between intellectual property and the commons or public domain. For these purposes, nature, at least metaphorically, is aligned with raw materials, knowledge (or discoveries) and ideas, and culture with, in respective contrast, manufactured products, innovation and expressions.[142] The distinction between what is in and what is out is, of course, fundamental to the system overall. The functioning of the system also depends on distinctions between different forms of intellectual property, in particular the distinction between patents and copyright. This distinction is frequently understood and referred to as the distinction between science and culture, but it could perhaps also be mapped on to the distinction between nature (the natural sciences) and culture (the social sciences and humanities). The distinction between patents and copyright has important consequences for their respective objects of protection. Patent protection is relatively short but extremely strong in the sense that there are few exceptions or defences to the monopoly rights of the patentee. Copyright protection, on the other hand, is extremely long but relatively weak (compared to patents) in terms of exceptions and defences to its infringement.[143] Where, particularly in non-Western systems of thought, the distinction between what goes where in intellectual property terms is obscure, the intellectual property way of looking at the world completely distorts the thing that it claims to be protecting by subjecting parts of an indivisible whole to different levels of protection.[144] It is for this reason that the intellectual property-led distinction between traditional knowledge and traditional cultural expressions in international policymaking circles is so meaningless.[145]

The CICH perhaps does a better job of understanding the indivisibility of bio-cultural forms. Its inclusive list of "domains" in which intangible cultural heritage is "manifested" lists them separately but in terms of protection treats them the same way.[146] The problem with the CICH, of course, is that it operates in a system that is subject to all the other sorts of Western binary distinctions

142 See ch 2, section 2.
143 See ch 2, section 2.
144 See ch 2, section 4.
145 The division of work in the WIPO Intergovernmental Committee on Intellectual Property and Genetic Resources, Traditional Knowledge and Folklore broadly reflects an equivalence between patents and traditional knowledge, on the one hand, and copyright and traditional cultural expressions, on the other: see F Macmillan, "The Problematic Relationship between Traditional Knowledge and the Commons" in S Pinton & L Zagato (eds), *Cultural Heritage: Scenarios 2015–2017* (Venezia: Edizioni Ca Foscari, 2017); F Macmillan, "Intellectual Property and Cultural Heritage" in I Calboli & M L Montagnani (eds), *Oxford Handbook on Intellectual Property Research* (Oxford: Oxford University Press, 2020). See also, ch 3, section 4.1.
146 See CICH, Art 1.2, which makes reference to: "(a) oral traditions and expressions, including language as a vehicle of the intangible cultural heritage; (b) performing arts; (c) social practices,

that have been considered in this chapter. The imbrication of all these distinctions in the authorized heritage discourse means that UNESCO is at serious odds with critical approaches that seek to challenge this binary thinking. The rejection by critical heritage scholars of the expression "cultural heritage", precisely on the grounds of its embrace of the nature/culture distinction, finds no resonance in the UNESCO worldview. Similarly, it struggles to come to terms with other concepts that seek, in apparently less totalizing ways, to address its embrace of Cartesian dualism. In the context of the nature/culture distinction, its approach to the concept of the cultural landscape is a good example. This concept, at least if it is understood in terms of critical and interdisciplinary theory on law and space, offers some liberatory potential. However, this is largely unrealized in the context of the WHC, where it has been employed since the 1990s.[147]

At the time of writing, 114 "properties" are designated as cultural landscapes in the WHC lists.[148] Of these sites, only 11 are sites of the so-called mixed natural and cultural heritage, including the Uluṟu–Kata Tjuṯa National Park, and none of them are sites of natural heritage. There are three cultural landscapes that are on the list of World Heritage in Danger, including the Bamiyan Valley in Afghanistan, in which the dynamited Buddhas were located.[149] To make sense, in UNESCO terms at least, of the paucity of cultural landscapes that are mixed natural and cultural heritage, it must be noted that "works of man or combined works of nature and man" fall within the definition of a cultural heritage "site" in the WHC, Article 1 (rather than being mixed natural and cultural heritage).[150] For UNESCO, cultural landscapes are either cultural or mixed natural and cultural heritage – otherwise, presumably, they would just be plain old landscapes (without the cultural qualification). The difference between the WHC's concepts of natural and cultural heritage also maps onto its further subdivision of cultural landscapes into three distinct categories: "clearly designed landscape defined and created intentionally by man (*sic.*)", "organically evolved landscape" and "associative cultural landscape".[151] The first category pretty much speaks for itself and so is unambiguously within the WHC defi-

rituals and festive events; (d) knowledge and practices concerning nature and the universe; (e) traditional craftsmanship".

147 For an account of the concept and its use by UNESCO, see G Aplin, "World Heritage Cultural Landscapes" (2007) 13 *International Journal of Heritage Studies* 427–446.

148 See UNESCO, "Cultural Landscapes", http://whc.unesco.org/en/culturallandscape/, accessed 14/03/2020.

149 "Cultural Landscape and Archaeological Remains of the Bamiyan Valley", http://whc.unesco.org/en/list/208, accessed 14/03/2020.

150 See ch 3, section 2.1.

151 See UNESCO, "Annex 3 - Guidelines on the Inscription of Specific Types of Properties on the World Heritage List", *Operational Guidelines for the Implementation of the World Heritage Convention*, http://whc.unesco.org/archive/opguide08-en.pdf#annex3, accessed 15/03/2020.

nition of cultural heritage. The second category is divided into two further sub-categories, as follows:

- a relict (or fossil) landscape is one in which an evolutionary process came to an end at some time in the past, either abruptly or over a period. Its significant distinguishing features are, however, still visible in material form.
- continuing landscape is one which retains an active social role in contemporary society closely associated with the traditional way of life, and in which the evolutionary process is still in progress. At the same time, it exhibits significant material evidence of its evolution over time.[152]

It looks like this category might include things that are either cultural heritage or mixed natural and cultural heritage. The third category seems to focus on mixed natural and cultural heritage, such as the Uluṟu–Kata Tjuṯa National Park. UNESCO regards the inclusion of things in this category on the World Heritage List as "justifiable by virtue of the powerful religious, artistic or cultural associations of the natural element rather than material cultural evidence, which may be insignificant or even absent".[153]

The Uluṟu–Kata Tjuṯa National Park was first inscribed on the UNESCO World Heritage List in 1987, and then subsequently re-nominated as a cultural landscape in 1994. Reviewing the UNESCO texts on the re-nomination of Uluṟu–Kata Tjuṯa as a cultural landscape, Bowrey and Graham comment:

> The criteria suggest an initial boundary between persons/things; legal subjects/objects that, in exceptional heritage cases, can be infilled by "culture", when there is sufficient tangible evidence of living traditions, ideas and beliefs associated with the surrounding geography. The criteria reproduces a concept of place (as landscape) in which "nature" and "culture" remain separate and can at best, interact or co-exist, rather than exist synthetically or holistically. This peculiar framing is entirely contrary to Aṉangu ontology and diminishes the significance of Tjukurpa [law] as a knowledge system.[154]

Things, of course, could hardly be otherwise, given the conceptual ordering of the WHC. The re-nomination of Uluṟu–Kata Tjuṯa re-inscribes it in a post-colonial discourse that organizes space according to the binary distinction between nature and culture. This spatial organization also reifies space within the logic of Western property law.[155] Cultural landscapes, described by UNESCO as "properties", exist in precisely delineated geographical space, the coordinates of which are de-

152 Note 151 above.
153 See n 151 above.
154 Bowrey & Graham, n 2 above, at 145.
155 See also Bowrey & Graham, n 2 above.

fined by the distribution of legal titles to land. This is well-illustrated by the history of the Uluṟu–Kata Tjuṯa National Park recounted earlier – "owned" by the Australian National Parks and Wildlife Service, "returned" to the Aṉangu people, leased back to Parks Australia. The role of Western property law in this context should not come as a surprise given that the whole UNESCO system for the protection of cultural heritage is ordered according to this very same logic.[156] As long as we continue to think about heritage in this way, the currently prevailing political relations of space will always be with us.[157] Cultural heritage laws will always, as Bowrey and Graham say, be "nestled within a dephysicalised property paradigm".[158] This means, in other words, that the place of heritage laws will continue to be inside a paradigm that cuts the physical ties between humans and their environment, disconnecting them from "any exterior reality".[159] This is a state of affairs that is fundamental to a capitalist economy.[160]

UNESCO's failure to realize the promise of the concept of the cultural landscape, the promise to undermine the nature/culture binary, creates another barrier to the achievement of geopolitical justice in the post-colonial world. But this failure is also linked to the failure to understand the interconnections of space and people that might give us, as a global community, our last best hope of saving the environment in which we all live and breathe.[161] Writing this chapter in the wake of the fires that devastated parts of Australia in the summer of 2019/2020, it is worth thinking about the extensive evidence collated by Pascoe on the management of fire by Australian Indigenous Peoples over millennia.[162] How could it be that the lessons of the indivisible connection between people and the space in which they lived, the way in which they understood the indivisibility of nature and culture, have been so spectacularly and disastrously ignored by the colonizers and their post-colonial descendants?

156 With, perhaps, a couple of exceptions: see ch 3, section 1.

157 See further, Section 3.

158 Note 2 above, at 142, drawing on Bentham's concept of "dephysicalised" as cutting the physical tie between humans and their environment, and thus disconnecting them from "any exterior reality": see J Bowring (ed), *The Works of Jeremy Bentham: Volume 1* (Edinburgh: William Tait, 1838), at 308; J Bentham, "A Theory of Legislation" (1864) in C B MacPherson (ed), *Property: Mainstream and Critical Positions* (Toronto, Buffalo, NY & London: University of Toronto Press, 1978, reprinted 2013).

159 Bowrey & Graham, n 2 above, quoting P Fitzpatrick, *The Mythology of Modern Law* (London: Routledge, 1992), at 56.

160 Bowrey & Graham, n 2 above, citing Fitzpatrick, n 159 above.

161 See S M Titchen, "Changing Perceptions and Recognition of the Environment – From Cultural and Natural Heritage to Cultural Landscape" in J Finlayson & A Jackson-Nakanko (eds), *Heritage and Native Title: Anthropological and Legal Perspectives* (Canberra: Native Title Research Unit, AIATSIS, 1996); R Bartel et al, "Legal Geography; An Australian Perspective" (2013) 51 *Geographical Research* 339–353; N Graham, "'This Is Not a Thing': Land, Sustainability and Legal Education" (2014) 26 *Journal of Environmental Law* 395–422.

162 Pascoe, n 40 above, ch 5.

7 Being flattened by the capitalist steamroller

This chapter has argued that the Western discourse of cultural heritage and intellectual property rotates around a collection of binary distinctions – nature/culture, authentic/fake, moveable/immoveable, tangible/intangible – that produce a meaningless mish-mash when faced with the reality of cultural production. The global penetration of Western legal and political-economic forms has created what is, in some cases, an extreme dissonance between how non-Western communities think about their relationship to their cultural heritage/property and the legal techniques available to them to protect that heritage. The unsurprising inability of non-Western cultural heritage/property to fit into Western paradigms has deepened the perception of a fundamental difference between those communities and Western communities. This situation has produced a lose/lose situation for Indigenous Peoples and communities of the global South. The lack of any coherent protection against the appropriation of the cultural heritage/property of these communities has led them to campaign for the extension and adaptation of forms of Western legal technology that might fill the apparent gaps in protection and give them some control over their social processes of identity formation. Since intellectual property law is manifestly unable to achieve these ends, there have been calls to re-design or re-purpose it.[163] These calls have inevitably fallen on political deaf ears. Consequently, intellectual property laws continue to embody a form of commodification and privatization that has meaning only in the context of the market. This means, among other things, that where heritage is absorbed into the intellectual property regime, it loses its character as heritage. At the same time, that which cannot be absorbed in this way appears to be diminished and devalued.[164]

The irony and tragedy in all of this are that, despite perceptions to the contrary, the situation of Western communities is not much better. So much of Western cultural production has been absorbed into the intellectual property, and especially the copyright, system that we understand it as being entirely and only a part of a commodified and privatized system. When we, in the West, think of our cultural heritage/property, we think of the sorts of monumental sites that are listed in the WHC, or of the stuff found on the shelves and in the glass cabinets and other displays of GLAM institutions. As a result of the invasiveness of the copyright system in the process of cultural production, we have lost the idea of heritage as a contemporary constitutive social process. Even if we see that intellectual property has functioned as an imperial legal technology that allows Western corporate interests to appropriate and commodify non-Western culture, we are often blind to the fact that it has also appropriated and commodified Western culture.[165] Having

163 See ch 3, sections 4.1 and 4.2.

164 See also Slaughter, n 6 above.

165 See also ch 3, section 4.3.

no form of cultural defence to a legal technology that has overtaken our cultural production, we have failed to put in place strategies for balancing private interests with community interests in culture. In fact, we have failed to learn these strategies from those communities who have been flattened by the Western capitalist steamroller and have had to learn the hard way how to make accommodations and balance between private and community interests. The next chapter seeks to demonstrate that the constitutive relationship between community and heritage, the idea of cultural heritage/property as a social process, is not just confined to Indigenous Peoples and other communities of the global South. Rather, it is evident in one of the most pervasive and under-studied phenomena of contemporary Western (and non-Western) life.

Chapter 6

Explorations in the cultural landscape – arts festivals

1 Introduction: here, there and everywhere

Arts festivals are a prolific, pervasive and flourishing part of modern life. At certain times of the year, it seems as though one can hardly move anywhere without encountering one. They take place in cities, in small towns, in rural areas, offline, online – in any place where cultural production can rear its head. They serve a wide range of interests and functions, which include stimulating creative interactions, show-casing or developing certain sectors of the arts, providing an alternative method of distribution of so-called cultural products, celebrating forms of solidarity or resistance, consolidating local or regional or sectoral or cultural identity, promoting tourism and providing an opportunity to be together outside the normal patterns of daily life.[1] At one (depressing) end of this spectrum, one could think of arts festivals as being a relict of a former idea of community, which has been captured and subjugated to the logic of capitalist accumulation. Alternatively, and less bleakly, the proliferation of arts festivals could be understood as a response to the loss of community, to the loss of the ethos of the collective, to the loss of being together in a physical sense. Certainly, the function of providing an opportunity to be together is critical to the concept of an arts festival that is considered in this chapter. Proceeding from the claim that as a public site, as a rupture in time and space, and as an exception to the regular conduct of life, arts festivals are a particular and illustrative expression of community, the chapter investigates the way in which arts festivals expose and mediate the relationship between community and cultural production. The chapter argues that the festival is a social process that is constituted by, and constitutive of, community. At the same time, however, the chapter will

1 See, e.g., F Macmillan, "A Taxonomy of Arts Festivals: Mapping Issues in Cultural Property and Human Rights" (Working Paper 2, HERA "Cultivate Project", 2013, http://www.cultivateproject.dk/); F Macmillan, "Testing the Working Taxonomy of Arts Festivals" (Working Paper 3, HERA "Cultivate Project", 2013, http://www.cultivateproject.dk/); L Giorgi, M Sassatelli & G Delanty (eds), *Festivals and the Cultural Public Sphere* (London: Routledge, 2013).

demonstrate the extent to which the relations within this social process are permeated by the copyright system.

2 Definitions: being together in no man's land

In the literature, the concept of the "festival" tends to be defined compositely in both positive and negative terms. In other words, it is defined by both what it is and what it is not. On the positive side of this coin, the overriding and perhaps most general characterization of the festival is that it is, in some sense, a suspension in time and space, during which life – and law and business – does not carry on as normal.[2] Developing this idea of the festival as a period of suspension, the festival has also been described by commentators as a space of openness, de-territorialization and exchange[3]; part of the "public sphere"[4]; a site of democratic debate and transnational identifications[5]; an "interpretation of cosmopolitan community"[6]; and, in the words of Jean Cocteau, an "apolitical no-man's land".[7] As all of these characterizations suggest, the idea of the festival is closely tied in to the notion of being in a particular community, or being together, in a distinct place in time and space. In his description of the Cannes Film Festival, Cocteau also described the festival as "a microcosm of how the world would be if people could have direct contacts and speak the same language".[8] Thus, Sassatelli citing Durkheim's work on festivals describes them as an "intensification of the collective being" and, in Durkheim's words, a "collective effervescence".[9] Along similar lines, Vrettos conceives festivals as a manifestation of the human need to gather, socialize and exchange ideas.[10] Developing this line of thought, O'Grady and Kill argue that in an age of digital and social media with its consequent

2 See (amongst many possible citations for this proposition), e.g., A Falassi, "Festival: Definition and Morphology" in A Falassi (ed), *Time Out of Time: Essays on the Festival* (Albuquerque: University of New Mexico Press, 1987).

3 S Nordmann, "A History of Cultural Festivals in Europe" in J Segal & L Giorgi (eds), *European Arts Festivals from a Historical Perspective* (EURO-FESTIVAL Project: European Arts Festivals and Public Culture, Deliverable 2.1, WP2 Main Report, July 2009), 19–29, at 28.

4 L Giorgi, "Between Tradition, Vision and Imagination: Literature(s) in Search of a Festival" in Segal & Giorgi, n 3 above, 30–52; M Sassatelli, "Public Culture, Cosmopolitanism and Festivals" in M Sassatelli (ed), *European Public Culture & Aesthetic Cosmopolitanism* (EURO-FESTIVAL Project: European Arts Festivals and Public Culture, Deliverable 1.1, WP1 Main Report, October 2008), 15–40.

5 Sassatelli, n 4 above.

6 Sassatelli, n 4 above, at 25.

7 Jean Cocteau quoted in J Segal & C Blumauer, "Cannes: A French International Festival" in Segal & Giorgi, n 3 above, 53–82, at 53.

8 Jean Cocteau (translated from French) quoted in Segal & Blumauer, n 7 above, at 53.

9 Sassatelli, n 5 above, at 18–19, citing E Durkheim, *The Elementary Forms of Religious Life* (1912, republished Glencoe: Free Press, 1954).

10 A Vrettos, "About the Economic Impacts Studies of Arts Festivals" (2009) 3 *Economia della cultura* 341–350.

personal isolation, the festival presents the chance to be with other people, and thus represents an opportunity for "[s]ociability, participation, togetherness and excitement".[11]

Building on the idea of festivals as distinct and sociable places in time and space are conceptions of festivals that refer to their value as social, cultural, economic or political institutions and, thus, as expressing values associated with such institutions.[12] O'Grady and Kill write about the festival as a cultural artefact, while Guerzoni refers to them as a way of filling "il vuoto pneumatico della cultura televisiva" ("the resounding emptiness of television culture").[13] Values such as the promotion of cultural diversity, internationalization or alternative social identities frequently form part and parcel of the festival concept.[14] Festivals may also be understood as a form of asserting identity "in the face of a feeling of cultural dislocation brought about by rapid structural change, social mobility and globalisation processes".[15] Other types of cultural values pave the way for understanding the festival as a type of socio-economic institution. For instance, festivals may play a role in legitimating new artistic forms or new genres within existing artistic forms.[16] At the same time, they function to commodify those new forms or genres.[17] Importantly, they may also offer an alternative avenue for distribution, particularly in highly commodified cultural industries like the film industry, where one effect of commodification has been to suppress independent production and diversity.[18]

11 A O'Grady & R Kill, "Exploring Festival Performance as a State of Encounter" (Unpublished paper, May 2011; on file with author), at 2.

12 While festivals are distinct, they are also semi-permeable (Sassatelli, n 5 above, at 22) and paradoxical (A O'Grady & R Kill, "Environments for Encounter and the Processes of Organizing for Interactivity and Performative Participation within the Festival Space" Conference on *Visuals and Performativity: Researching Beyond Text*, Segovia, Spain, May 2011 (copy on file with author), at 3). See also K Turan, *Sundance to Sarajevo: Film Festivals and the World They Made* (Los Angeles: University of California Press, 2002), who writes about three classes of festivals: *Festivals with Business Agendas*; *Festivals with Geopolitical Agendas* and *Festivals with Aesthetic Agendas*.

13 O'Grady & Kill, n 11 above, at 20; G Guerzoni, "L'impatto economico dei festival: un'annosa prospettiva di ricerca" (2009) 19 *Economia della cultura* 473–486 (my translation).

14 See J Segal, "Film Festivals" in Sassatelli, n 5 above, 111–117, at 115 & 117; L Giorgi, "Literature Festivals: Literature (Festivals) as a Subject of Sociological Inquiry in Search of Cosmopolitanism" in Sassatelli, n 5 above, 95–110, at 107; L Mazdon, "The Cannes Film Festival as Transnational Space" (2006) 25(2) *Post Script* 19–30; M Santoro, J Chalcraft & P Magaudda, "Music Festivals: An Interdisciplinary Literature Review" in Sassatelli, n 5 above, 77–93, at 83.

15 D Picard & M Robinson, *Festivals, Tourism and Social Change: Remaking Worlds* (Clevedon: Channel View Publications, 2006), at 2, quoted in Sassatelli, n 5 above, at 26.

16 Santoro, Chalcraft & Magaudda, n 14 above, at 82.

17 Santoro, Chalcraft & Magaudda, n 14 above, at 83, where it is argued that this observation applies, in particular, to music festivals.

18 See Turan, n 12 above, at 8; C Anderton, *Music Festivals in the UK: Beyond the Carnivalesque* (Oxford & New York: Routledge, 2019). See further F Macmillan, "Copyright and Corporate Power" in R Towse (ed), *Copyright and the Cultural Industries* (Cheltenham: Edward Elgar,

Festivals can be distinguished from the regular programming of concerts, theatre, film and so on that occur in concert halls, auditoriums, theatres, cinemas and other such venues on the bases that first, these are not generally a single cultural event containing a series of connected events; second, the concept of the arts festival seems to imply some degree of audience participation, which might be considered to be linked to the idea, asserted earlier, of the festival as a period of being in community in a physical or virtual sense; third, and perhaps most significantly, regularly programmed arts events might be considered to be part of the ordinary course of life, precisely because they are regularly programmed in venues established for this purpose, and accordingly not occasions of suspension in time and space.[19]

All these observations on the nature of the festival suggest a clear connection with those activities that are usually referred to as the "arts". Once, however, we focus on how the word "arts", as an adjectival qualification to the word "festival", contributes to the definitional process, then we are brought immediately into confrontation with the impact of the copyright system. This is because, as was argued in Chapter 1, one of the open questions pervading the relationship between copyright law and the "arts" is that of constitution and authorization.[20] In other words: is it some generally accepted definition of what amounts to the "arts" that constitutes and authorizes the subject matter of copyright or, inversely, does copyright law constitute and authorize concepts of the "arts"? In either case, it seems clear that there are recognized disciplines within the arts and, at the very least, copyright law has contributed to the compartmentalization of these disciplines. This rigid system of definition leaves very little space for the protection of innovative artistic forms.

3 Saturated by copyright?

The role of copyright in defining what constitutes the arts, and the way in which this impacts on how we understand arts festivals, provides the foundation upon which copyright interests have saturated the arts festival environment. The way in which copyright law defines, controls or affects the meaning of "arts" in the broader social and cultural spheres is evident in the way in which many arts festivals brand themselves as being literary festivals, film festivals, music festivals, theatre festivals, dance festivals and so on – even if in fact empirical research reveals that almost no festivals confine themselves to only one form of "artistic" output.[21] It is also the case that

2002), F Macmillan, "The Cruel ©: Copyright and Film" (2002) *European Intellectual Property Review* 483–492.

19 Falassi, n 2 above, at 2; O'Grady & Kill, n 11 above & n 12 above *supra*.

20 See ch 1, section 2.

21 See Macmillan, "A Taxonomy of Arts Festivals: Mapping Issues in Cultural Property and Human Rights", n 1 above.

a great deal of what happens in the course of the arts festival as an event seems to have copyright implications of one type or another. The following discussion seeks to illustrate this in relation to various types of arts festivals, including film festivals, music festivals and what are described, generically, as culture festivals.[22]

So far as film festivals are concerned, the copyright interests in the films that are shown arise at the time of the making of the film and, depending on the jurisdiction, usually belong either solely to the producer or jointly to the producer and director. There are other creative contributions to films that are recognized by copyright law, such as the copyright in the screenplay and in the sound track, but almost invariably these copyright interests are acquired by the copyright owner of the film. At film festivals, the more interesting copyright questions are posed by the "live" events, such as interviews, workshops and other public encounters with directors and actors. These events, while being apparently supplementary to the main event of showing the films, are, in reality, what makes the festival as an event distinct from daily life. As with all live and unscripted events, there is a question about whether the event has satisfied the copyright requirement of fixation in a material form.[23] Slightly strangely (at least to anyone who is not a copyright lawyer), a recording of the event, whether it is authorized or unauthorized, has the effect of achieving fixation in a material form and conferring copyright on the participants – usually, in the context of film festivals, in their words.[24] Authorized recorders, such as the festival organizers, acquire, subject to the terms of the authorization, a copyright in the recording that they have made.

Despite the high degree of commodification of the relevant cultural product that prevails in both the film and music industries, the copyright aspects of music festivals are different to those of film festivals because music festivals are (usually, if not always) primarily concerned with live musical performances.[25] This adds certain complications to the copyright picture, which means that it is necessary to consider a number of different situations in which music is performed at a festival. From a copyright point of view, the simplest of these situations is where the music performed is no longer protected by copyright, as is generally the case at early music festivals. Recordings of such music, the copyright in which resides in the producer of the recording, may be available to purchase at the festival. While this type of marketing is part of the festival environment, it is not clear that it should be regarded as forming part of the network of copyright relations at the festival itself since it is based on creative relations occurring prior to the festival and has no necessary relationship with the creative relations taking place at the festival as event.

22 For a more detailed account of the role of copyright in the festival environment and its effect on creativity, see Macmillan, "Testing the Working Taxonomy of Arts Festivals", n 1 above, section 5.

23 See, e.g., UK Copyright Designs and Patents Act 1988 (CDPA), s 3(2).

24 See, e.g., CDPA, s 3(3).

25 On commodification by copyright in the film and music industries, see Macmillan, "Copyright and Corporate Power", n 18 above; Macmillan, "The Cruel ©: Copyright and Film", n 18 above.

However, the copyright interests that are clearly implicated in the music festival environment relate to the performances occurring during the festival as event where the works performed are subject to copyright protection. Where the copyright in the music and, in the case of songs, the literary works comprised in the lyrics belong to the festival performers, as often might be the case in rock music festivals, then the copyright situation is relatively straightforward. The interesting questions in this situation relate to variations from the original copyright work made in the course of the festival performance, and to recordings of the performances. Variations in the course of the performance will be protected by copyright where they are reduced to material form. The obvious way of achieving such a reduction to material form is through recording, either authorized or unauthorized. As anyone who has ever spent any time on YouTube knows, the Internet is swamped by unauthorized recordings of performances, usually made on mobile phones. Making such recordings and disseminating them on the Internet is a breach of copyright (and, in some jurisdictions, may also be a breach of performers' rights); however, they do have the advantage of reducing a live performance to material form and thus satisfying this requirement for establishing the subsistence of the copyright interest. As in relation to any other performance or public event, authorized recordings generate a copyright interest in the recording that belongs to its producer.

The final lot of copyright interests that might be relevant in a music festival are those copyright interests in music and lyrics, performed during the festival, which might belong to people other than the performers. The most obvious circumstance where this situation will occur is where the composers/lyricists and the performers are different people. This might be because the composer and/or lyricist never intended to be involved in the performance of the work, or because the performers are covering the copyright work of another performer. The default position in both these cases is that the consent of the copyright owner must be sought in order to avoid infringement. However, it is worth noting that cover versions, which are a particular feature of rock/folk/blues music festivals, are capable of raising questions in what might be considered the grey zone of copyright. Straightforward covers of songs that differ little from their original versions are not particularly problematic from a copyright point of view, but covers that differ substantially from the original copyright work – for example, because they make minimal reference to the original lyrics or music, or because they use a different musical style or genre – raise questions about whether there has been sufficient substantial taking from the original to constitute an infringement and/or whether the use of the material might be justified under the fair use/fair dealing exception in jurisdictions where such defences exist.[26] Covers

26 On substantial taking, see, e.g., CDPA, s 16(3), which requires the taking of a "substantial part" of the protected work in order to constitute an infringement. Fair use/fair dealing exceptions tend to be found in common law copyright jurisdictions, rather than in jurisdictions based on

that incorporate enough of the original to make reference to it, but very little of the actual expression of the work, may not be infringing.[27] If such works are considered to be infringing, they may also be saved by the fair use/fair dealing defences. Similarly, covers that employ a completely different musical style or genre may be considered to fall within the fair use/fair dealing defences in some jurisdictions.[28] Added to these complications are the fact that any new work, whether it is infringing or not, is potentially capable of creating a new copyright interest in the person performing it if it shows sufficient creativity or sufficient investment of skill and labour.[29] Another very grey zone relates to genres of music that depend on a tradition of re-working what has gone before. This applies, for example, to jazz and blues music, where the creative culture of re-working and riffing creates numerous questions relating to who, if anyone, can be considered the owner of the original work, if one can be identified, or of any subsequent re-working; and whether, in the context of the usual traditions applying to this music, such activities can (or should) ever be considered infringing.[30]

Many of these same issues arise in relation to what are here described as culture festivals, which are extremely diverse and might very well comprehend elements of film/video and music amongst their rich diet of cultural activities. These sorts of festivals also tend to encompass – variously – activities such as poetry and prose readings, dance, theatre, story-telling, circus acts, puppetry, busking, blogging, visual art installations, exhibitions of various sorts (photographic, comics, video art, digital art), interviews and public discussions. Four copyright issues that are of particular importance to a number of these types of festivals are first, the relationship of performances, or performative elements, to texts (if any); second, the question of subsistence of copyright in ephemeral performances; third, the impact of interactive works on questions of copyright ownership; and, fourth, the question of what constitutes a copyright work.

---

the civil law tradition of *droit d'auteur/diritto d'autore*. E.g., US Copyright Law 1976, s 10, which contains the fair use defence; and CDPA, ss 30 & 30A, which contain the relevant fair dealing defences.

27 See, e.g., *Joy Music v Sunday Pictorial Newspapers* [1960] 2 WLR 615; *Williamson Music v Pearson Partnership* [1987] FSR 97.

28 See, e.g., *Campbell (2 Live Crew) v Acuff-Rose Music Inc*, 114 S Ct 1164(1994). In the UK, e.g., see also CDPA, s 30A.

29 The question of the degree of input necessary to establish the preconditions for the creation of a copyright interest varies between jurisdictions: see L Bently & B Sherman, *Intellectual Property Law* (Oxford: Oxford University Press, 5th edition, 2018), ch 2, section 4.3.

30 See, K McLeod, *Owning Culture: Authorship, Ownership and Intellectual Property Law* (New York: Peter Lang, 2001); S Vaidhyanathan, *Copyrights and Copywrongs: The Rise of Intellectual Property and How It Threatens Creativity* (New York & London: New York University Press, 2001); J Boyle, *The Public Domain: Enclosing the Commons of the Mind* (New Haven, CT & London: Yale University Press, 2008), ch 6; J Boyle & J Jenkins, *Theft! A History of Music* (Durham, NC: CreateSpace Independent Publishing Platform, 2017).

3.1 Performance and text

The question of the relationship of performance to text, and the copyright issues that consequently arise with respect to ownership and infringement are not, in substance, different from those that arise in relation to performances of existing musical works. Where the performer is not the owner of the copyright interest in any text upon which a performance is based, then there will be questions about whether there has been substantial taking from the text and, if so, whether fair use or fair dealing defences might apply. The law and its practitioners are generally better at understanding these questions in relation to text, where it is clear that the protected subject matter of copyright is the way in which the author of the text has expressed their ideas, and not the ideas themselves.[31] Thus, performances that make reference to a text, as a type of jumping-off point, rather than using the expression from the text itself are generally unproblematic in this respect. Further, it should be noted that a number of the types of performances that take place in the context of culture festivals involving texts are more likely than not to be performances by the author, who is likely to be the copyright owner.[32] For example, it is generally the case at poetry festivals that poets read their own work. Similarly, at literary festivals, authors often read their own prose works. This is obviously, of course, often not the case in relation to theatrical texts unless they are texts written especially for the festival, as frequently happens in relation to interactive theatrical pieces.[33]

Although the same principles apply in theory, the situation can be more complicated in relation to non-textual works. A good example of this, which often arises in the festival context, is dance, which is characterized by a generally problematic relation to copyright law. While dance is technically a protected work under copyright law in most jurisdictions, what Yeoh has described as "the ontological instability" of dance means that questions of the relationship between the work of a choreographer and a dance performance can be fraught with difficulties.[34] The basic problem here is that the material form to which a protected

31 On copyright law's difficulties with non-textual works, see F Macmillan, "Il diritto d'autore nell'era digitale: verso il declino dell'originalità dell'opera?" in G Resta (ed), *L'Armonia del Diritto: Contributi ad una riflessione su diritto e musica* (Rome: Roma TreEpress, 2020), http://romatrepress.uniroma3.it/libro/larmonia-nel-diritto-contributi-a-una-riflessione-su-diritto-e-musica/, accessed 15/04/2020.

32 See, e.g., CDPA, s 11(1), subject to the first owner not having transferred the copyright interest to another person.

33 See, e.g., O'Grady & Kill, n 11 above; O'Grady & Kill, n 12 above.

34 See, e.g., CDPA, which protects dance as a "dramatic work"; the US Copyright Act 1976, which protects dance works as such; and the Canadian Copyright Amendment Act 1988, which protects "any work of choreography, whether or not it has any storyline". See F Yeoh, *Copyright Does Not Adequately Accommodate the Artform of Dance* (PhD Thesis, Birkbeck, University of London, 2012), ch 1 & ff.

dance work is reduced is frequently a form of notation.[35] In the copyright context, understanding the relationship between this notation and a performance is challenging. A dance work tends, even when performed with the involvement of the choreographer, to mutate with each performance, with the result that significant differences between the notation and the dance as performed are likely to develop over time. A dance work, of course, can also be recorded on film. While this might overcome some of the limitations of traditional notation in capturing particular movements of the dancers, it is also subject to the problem that a film of one performance is unable to capture evolutions of the work over time. All this means that the dance community has traditionally tended to operate, in a certain sense, outside the copyright regime and according to its own norms on questions of authorship and ownership of works.[36] However, these norms are increasingly likely to become entangled with copyright law.[37]

3.2 Ephemeral performances

Different problems are posed by works that are ephemeral in the sense that they are not based on a text or are not otherwise reduced to what copyright law considers a material form. This problem might arise in relation to dance works that have not been recorded in some form. Other performances at culture festivals that might raise this type of issue are things like story-telling, circus acts, puppetry and busking. At first blush, it might seem strange to include, for example, story-telling because it might be assumed that a text exists somewhere. However, the point of these festivals is (usually) that there is no strict relation between any text and the performance; rather, the performances are interactive and "free-form". They are, by nature, unstable in the sense that one such performance or work by the performers or artists will not be the same as the next due to differences in the way that the public interacts with the basic structure of the work. Busking is also a classic example of the same style of performance, as are many interactive theatrical performances. Absent, for example, a recording these ephemeral works are not protected by copyright.

3.3 Interactive works

If a recording exists, with the result that the work is reduced to material form and the basis for copyright protection in the work is established, there will still

35 For an excellent account of the various forms of dance notation, see Yeoh, n 34 above, ch 2.

36 Yeoh, n 34 above.

37 See, e.g., the controversy concerning Beyoncé's alleged infringement of De Keersmaeker's *Rosas danst rosas* (1983): R Sulcas, "Has Beyoncé Stepped over the Line?" *The Times*, 26 October 2011, at 11, & the discussion in Yeoh, n 34 above, ch 5. See also F Yeoh, "The Copyright Implications of Beyoncé's 'Borrowings'" (2013) 4(1) *Choreographic Practices* 95–117.

often be questions about who is the author of an interactive work. According to copyright law, the author of a work is its generator or creator.[38] Given that copyright law does not seem to recognize the concept of an interactive work, it is probably not surprising that there is no general principle according to which the authorship of such works is conferred on the person who makes the arrangements, or invests the necessary resources, for its coming into being.[39] Under these circumstances, to resolve the question of who is the author, and thus first owner, of works that are interactively produced by performers and members of the festival-going public, it would seem necessary to fall back on copyright's concept of joint authorship. The UK legislation, for example, describes a work of joint authorship as being "a work produced by the collaboration of two or more authors in which the contribution of each author is not distinct from that of the other author or authors".[40] The room for manoeuvre around the question of whether contributions from the public would be regarded as distinct does nothing to resolve the practical difficulties that could flow from the idea that members of the public were joint authors/first owners of interactive works in circumstances in which the works were commercially exploited outside the festival environment.[41] Inside the essentially participative environment of the festival, however, it is not clear that any particular problems would arise from this legal uncertainty. Questions of authorship also arise in relation to performances that are not typically text-based and involve a degree of interaction, sometimes improvised between the performers.[42] The classic example of this is circus and variety acts, in relation to which problems around the question of authorship are part of a larger issue concerned with the question of whether these types of performances are even copyright works.

3.4 Things that are not copyright works

The great diversity of what have been described here as culture festivals tends to raise some questions about how much of what occurs in such festivals involve copyright works or other works protected by intellectual property rights. In most (if not all) jurisdictions, there are limits on what can be considered a copyright

38 See, e.g., CDPA, s 9(1).

39 Despite the fact that this idea arguably underlies the conferral of the status of author on producers of sound recordings, broadcasters, publishers and film producers (see, e.g., CDPA, s 9(2)) as well on persons who make the arrangements necessary for the creation of computer-generated works (see, e.g., CDPA, 9(3)).

40 CDPA, s 10(1).

41 On the possibilities and limitations of the joint-authorship regime, see Bently & Sherman, n 29 above, ch 5, section 2.3; D Simone, *Copyright and Collective Authorship: Locating the Authors of Collaborative Work* (Cambridge: Cambridge University Press, 2019).

42 See R Arnold, "Are Performers Authors?" (1999) 21 *European Intellectual Property Review* 464–469.

work, even if there is a general lack of clarity at the relevant borders. Things like poetry and prose readings, dance and theatre present less problems in this respect. However, circus acts, general variety acts and puppetry give some pause for thought. There seems to be a lack of consensus on whether circus and general variety acts can be considered to be copyright works.[43] Similar doubts also exist with respect to the protection of things like busking and blogging, as such. With slight variations on the theme, all of these activities essentially raise questions about what amounts to a "dramatic work" in copyright law.[44] In addition to a lack of clarity around the word "dramatic", the use of "work" in conjunction with it imports, as with all copyright works, a concept of something that is able to be separately identified.[45] Consequently, vaguely limited or indeterminate activities, which might be a characterization applicable to things like story-telling, busking and blogging, may not be considered a "work" for copyright purposes – although it is also possible that blogs give rise to continual iterations of new and separate copyright works. This requirement of determinacy, which of course is an aspect of copyright's focus on product rather than process, also manifests itself with respect to visual art. Installations are, for this reason, at a particular risk of falling outside the definition of works of visual art, as might be some types of digital art, particularly those that involve interactivity with the viewer. A point that is worth emphasizing here is that the extensive penetration of copyright into the festival environment is most patchy in relation to things that might be described as creative processes, especially interactive processes. As will be further explored below, this gives some oxygen to the cultural heritage/property dimension of the festival as event. However, it also means that, as always, individual creators working outside the rigid set of copyright categories and/or working on creative processes rather than products are denied copyright protection.

The final point to note when considering the penetration of intellectual property rights into the festival as event is that the conclusion that copyright does

43 In the UK, e.g., there is a line of cases on the questions of protection and authorship of variety acts, which predates the current legislation and which focusses on the question of whether they can be considered "dramatic works": see *Clark v Bishop*, The Law Times, 17 February 1872; *Fuller v The Blackpool Winter Gardens and Pavilion Company, Limited* [1895] 2 QB 429; *Karno v Pathé Frères*, The Law Times, 26 September 1908 & 17 April 1909; *Tate v Fullbrook* [1908] 1 KB 821; *Tate v Thomas* [1921] 1 Ch 503. It seems that the lack of clarity on these questions persists under the current legislation: see *Hadley v Kemp* [1999] EMLR 589.

44 CDPA, s 3(1), defines "dramatic work" as including "a work of dance and mime". At the international level, the Berne Convention for the Protection of Literary & Artistic Works 1886 is not much more helpful. Its Art 2(1) provides:

> The expression 'literary and artistic works' shall include every production in the literary, scientific and artistic domain, whatever may be the mode or form of its expression, such as books, pamphlets and other writings; lectures, addresses, sermons and other works of the same nature; dramatic or dramaticomusical works; choreographic works and entertainments in dumb show ….

45 On copyright's focus on a final product rather than a process, see also ch 1, section 2.

not – or may not – exist does not mean that there are no other relevant intellectual property rights to take into account. The consensus of opinion in the UK, for example, is that "a performance of a variety act or any similar presentation" gives rise to performers' rights irrespective of the existence of an underlying copyright work.[46] That is, in order to gain rights in the performance, it is not necessary for the performer to be performing a copyright work. (Of course, performers performing copyright works – something that happens a lot at festivals, as the foregoing discussion illustrates – would also have performers' rights.) There may also be some types of performances or activities that take place at culture festivals that implicate other types of copyright works. For example, a puppetry festival, which involves the making of traditional puppets from around the world, is likely to involve the production of copyright-protected artistic works.[47]

4 The festival space: cultural production and community

It would be tempting, in the light of their copyright saturation, to treat arts festivals as being just another form for the commercial distribution of copyright-protected works. Turan, for example, argues that film festivals, at least, are an alternative form of distribution for films that have failed to find the usual commercial outlets.[48] This observation might also hold good for music festivals, given that there are particular constraints on commercial distribution in both the film and music industries which, like all constraints, are likely to produce a drive for alternative means of fulfilling desire.[49] However, limiting our understanding of festivals to being merely another means of distribution is really limiting our understanding of the nature of arts festivals and their social, political and economic significance. While it is undoubtedly true that arts festivals, particularly some arts festivals, produce economic value for the entertainment industries, they also encompass a range of other values that are less easily measured but nevertheless present. Thinking back to the definitions of the festival considered in Section 2 – an "intensification of the collective being",

46 CDPA, s 180(2)(d). It appears to be the case, particularly as a consequence of the Rome Convention for the Protection of Performers, Producers of Phonograms and Broadcasting Organisations 1961, Art 9, that circus acts fall within the definition of "variety or any similar presentation" in s 180(2)(d): see the Whitford Committee *Report on the Reform of Copyright Law* (Cmnd 6732) and the UK Government (Department of Trade and Industry), *White Paper on Copyright* (Cmnd 9712, paragraph 14.5).

47 And it is also interesting to note that puppetry makes appearances as a form of intangible cultural heritage on the CICH lists, e.g.: "Puppetry in Slovakia and Czechia" (Slovakia & Czechia, 2016), https://ich.unesco.org/en/RL/puppetry-in-slovakia-and-czechia-01202, accessed 31/03/2020.

48 Turan, n 12 above, at 7–8.

49 See Macmillan, "Copyright and Corporate Power" n 18 above; Macmillan, "The Cruel ©: Copyright and Film", n 18 above.

a "collective effervescence", an opportunity for "[s]ociability, participation, togetherness and excitement" – it is hard to escape the conclusion that there is something more happening in the festival space than just the distribution of commodified cultural products. The long history of the festival, which appears to have its European roots in agrarian or harvest festivals but is surely a feature of human existence everywhere, demonstrates that it is a social process of being together in community.[50]

How should we locate the place of law, including the place of copyright law, within the festival space? One approach would be to regard the festival, and the activities that occur within its spatial and temporal boundaries as being a rupture in legal space that flows from its inherent nature as a rupture in space and time. Scholars have drawn on Turner's distinction between "liminal (obligatory, highly formalized) and liminoid (optional, free flowing) social events" to explain the space of the festival.[51] Lawrence, for example, conceives the festival as a state of "ritual disorder".[52] A similar notion of disorder in relation to festivals is also used by Abrahams, who however contrasts it with ritual:

> While ritual underscores the harmonies and continuities in the expressive resources of a culture, emphasizing the wholeness of the world's fabric, festivals work (at least at their inception) by apparently tearing the fabric to pieces, by displaying it upside-down, inside-out, wearing it as motley rags

50 On the European origins of the festival, see C Hill, *Society and Puritanism in Pre-Revolutionary England* (London: Secker & Warburg, 1964) cited in R Bauman, "The Place of the Festival in the Worldview of Seventeenth-Century Quakers" in Falassi, n 2 above. Festivals are, of course, not just a European or Western thing, as the CICH lists (amongst other things) demonstrate: see, e.g., "Argungu International Fishing and Cultural Festival" (Nigeria, 2016), UNESCO Representative List of the Intangible Cultural Heritage of Humanity, https://ich.unesco.org/en/RL/argungu-international-fishing-and-cultural-festival-00901, accessed 31/03/2020; "Carnival of El Callao, a Festive Representation of a Memory and Cultural Identity" (Bolivarian Republic of Venezuela, 2016), https://ich.unesco.org/en/RL/carnival-of-el-callao-a-festive-representation-of-a-memory-and-cultural-identity-01198, accessed 31/03/2020; "Fichee-Chambalaalla New Year Festival of the Sidama People" (Ethiopia, 2015), https://ich.unesco.org/en/RL/fichee-chambalaalla-new-year-festival-of-the-sidama-people-01054, accessed 31/03/2020; "Festivity of Virgen de la Candelaria of Puno" (Peru, 2014), https://ich.unesco.org/en/RL/festivity-of-virgen-de-la-candelaria-of-puno-00956,accessed 31/03/2020; "Cherry Festival in Sefrou" (Morocco, 2012), https://ich.unesco.org/en/RL/cherry-festival-in-sefrou-00641, accessed 31/03/2020); "Frevo, Performing Arts of the Recife" (Brazil, 2012), https://ich.unesco.org/en/RL/frevo-performing-arts-of-the-carnival-of-recife-00603, accessed 31/03/2020; "Mesir Macunu Festival" (Turkey, 2012), https://ich.unesco.org/en/RL/mesir-macunu-festival-00642, accessed 31/03/2020.

51 See V Turner, "Liminal to Liminoid, in Play, Flow and Ritual: An Essay in Comparative Symbology" (1974) 60 *Rice University Studies* 53–92, cited, e.g., in the introductory notes to R D Abrahams, "An American Vocabulary of Celebrations" in Falassi, n 2 above, at 173.

52 D Lawrence, "Rules of Misrule: Notes on the Doo Dah Parade in Pasadena" in Falassi, n 2 above, at 134.

> and tatters ... Festivals thus draw their own boundaries for the occasion and redraw the boundaries of the host community, ironically establishing themselves in areas that, in the everyday world, have their own boundaries.... [179] Openness, central to our experience of festival, is temporal as well as spatial.[53]

Festivals, on this argument, fit badly within the highly institutionalized and legally regulated world of private intellectual property law.[54] As Abrahams goes on to observe:

> Festivals are ultimately community affairs. Indeed, they provide *the* occasion whereby a community may call attention to itself and, perhaps more important in our time, its willingness to display itself openly. It is the ultimate public activity, given its need for preparation and coordination of effort, and its topsy-turvyness, in which many of the basic notions of community are put to test.[55]

What festivals thus represent is a public (in the sense of not being private), communal and bounded space of openness. This idea of the festival should be reflected in the law's treatment of the creative and synergistic reactions that occur within the rupture or suspension created by the festival space.

5 Law in the festival space

If we were to treat festivals as a rupture in legal space, that would not mean that we should understand them as a legal "no man's land" (to paraphrase Jean Cocteau).[56] Without entering into the long debate about whether such a place exists, it seems clear that the space of the festival is not law free even if, within its boundaries, some of the regular operations of law are suspended.[57] In fact, the place of law here may be to guarantee the suspension of at least some of its own regular operations. This brings us to the question of how to understand the concept of cultural heritage/property within the festival space as a legal counterweight to the copyright saturation described earlier. A simple approach would be to simply suspend copyright relations, or at least some of them, within

53 Abrahams, n 51 above, at 178.

54 This argument might also be regarded as consistent with the observation of Lawrence, n 52 above, that "[i]nstitutionalizing inherently unstable socio-cultural forms, such as ritual disorder [into which category he places festivals] and spontaneity, is theoretically as well as pragmatically problematic".

55 Abrahams, n 51 above, at 181.

56 Note 7 above.

57 Killing people during festivals should not, I think, be countenanced as part of the suspension of normal order.

the festival space. Could this be done by finding a new accommodation between what is heritage and what are private property rights? Such an approach might reflect the types of accommodations that non-Western peoples have found as they seek to respect the social processes and community interests inherent in cultural production and balance them with the private property rights conferred by mainstream Western law.[58] And then, if the law could find a way of producing such an accommodation, could it serve as a wider model for a re-balancing of community rights and market rights in cultural production?

Looking specifically at the festival space, the first challenge in finding such an accommodation is to understand what comprises cultural property/heritage, where it lies on an imaginary festival map and how it relates to the intellectual property rights that also seem to be an obvious part of the festival topography. Would cultural heritage/property be represented as the container or border on the basis that the festival, as an event, is its vehicle? Such a representation might be based on the notion of the "cultural space" provided by the festival. There are nods to this type of approach in the UNESCO Convention for the Safeguarding of the Intangible Cultural Heritage (CICH). The idea of a cultural space is invoked by the definition of intangible cultural heritage in Article 2.1; and Article 2.2(c), which provides an inclusive list of the domains of intangible cultural heritage, makes reference to "social practices, rituals and festive events".[59] Or is the cultural heritage element of the festival more pervasive? Does it appear somewhere between the lines of what is already protected by copyright or other intellectual property interests? Is it already represented by the copyright-free spaces in the festival topography – those spaces of interactive creative processes and those moments of creativity outside copyright's regime scheme of protection? Or does it, in fact, overlap with what is already protected by intellectual property? The last of these alternatives would fit with a focus on the domains of cultural heritage listed in paragraphs (a) and (b) of CICH, Article 2.2, which list (respectively)

58 See ch 5, section 5.

59 Despite the fact that, as noted in ch 3, section 3.2, Western states have made relatively little use of the CICH, as at 01/04/2020, taking into account some blurring at the definitional edges of both figures, of the (approximately) 125 listings by Western states on the UNESCO List of Intangible Cultural Heritage in Urgent Need of Safeguarding and the UNESCO Representative List of the Intangible Cultural Heritage of Humanity, https://ich.unesco.org/en/lists, accessed 01/04/2020, (approximately) 27 are for festivals, as follows: 2019, 12 listings by Western states out of a total of 40, 3 festivals by Western states (Italy, Belgium, Portugal); 2018, 11/38 listings, 0 festivals; 2017, 12 listings/40, 1 festival (Switzerland); 2016, 9/37, 4 festivals (France, Greece, Spain, Switzerland); 2015, 5/28, 2 festivals (Andorra-France-Spain, Bulgaria); 2014, 9/37, 0 festivals; 2013, 6/29, 2 festivals (Italy, France); 2012, 8/30, 4 festivals (France, Spain, Belgium, Austria); 2011, 7/28, 1 festival (Spain); 2010, 13/47, 2 festivals (Belgium); 2009, 20/83, 4 festivals (Croatia(2), Hungary, Belgium); 2008, 13/90, 4 festivals (Estonia-Latvia-Lithuania, Bulgaria, Belgium, Spain). See also A Broccolini, "Italian 'Intangible Communities': Procedures, Tactics and New Key Actors" in S Pinton & L Zagato (eds), *Cultural Heritage Scenarios: 2015–2017* (Venice: Edizioni Ca Foscari, 2017).

oral traditions and expressions, and the performing arts. Similarly, many elements of festivals seem to offer expressions of the sort of cultural diversity with which the Convention on the Protection and Promotion of the Diversity of Cultural Expressions (CCD) is concerned.[60] Of all the UNESCO cultural heritage conventions, the CICH and CCD come closest to understanding heritage as a community-based social process. For this reason, using them as a yardstick to think about the cultural heritage/property credentials of arts festivals has some value. Such a consideration suggests that the space of arts festivals as events is not only saturated by copyright but also with heritage processes that create synergistic and productive interactions within their communities. Where the CICH and the CCD are no real help, however, are in finding an accommodation between this dynamic role of heritage and private intellectual property rights. This is because, as observed in Chapter Three, the operation of both conventions is effectively subject to the enforcement of intellectual property rights.[61]

6 Re-appropriating the space of community

Arts festivals, at least in the Western context, present a messy picture. Reflecting aspects of their forbears, the European agrarian or harvest festivals, they represent a bounded social process that is marked by a suspension of regular life. Since they represent a moment of being together in community, bounded in space (however conceived) and time, in order to celebrate and promote creativity in the various arts, they would seem to fall within the concept of cultural heritage/property as it has been presented in this book.[62] The fact that modern arts festivals are saturated by the legal relations of copyright does not undermine the conclusion that they are the domains of cultural heritage/property. There is no contradiction in the co-existence of community and market. But for community to flourish, the relations of the market – and the private property rights that are part of it – must be embedded in and serve the ends of community. The transformation of Western society by capitalist relations – and, in particular, by the accumulation of capital in the domains of multinational corporations – has inverted this relationship.

The fact that arts festivals have become, to some extent, a means of the distribution of commodified cultural products suggests that they cannot be so easily conceived of as challenging the needs of the capitalist system, as, it has been argued, was the case for the traditional European agrarian festivals that form their historical antecedents.[63] As with the whole of Western society, arts festivals have been captured and transformed by capitalist relations. Perhaps it is no longer the

60 On the CICH and the CCD, see further ch 3, sections 2 and 3.

61 CICH, Art 3(b) & CCD, Art 20.2; see ch 3, section 3.3.

62 See esp ch 3, sections 2.2, 2.3, 3.2; ch 4.

63 Hill, n 50 above, cited in Bauman, n 50 above.

case that the concept of the festival – even with its inherent notion of a departure and suspension from the everyday – does not serve the need for "regular, disciplined labour and the rational accumulation of capital".[64] Perhaps the arts festival is being completely subverted by capitalist relations based, in substantial part, upon the extensive network of copyright interests that it hosts. Nevertheless, one of the startling things about the arts festival is that its form continues to flourish. We continue to seek these bounded moments of being together outside the structures of everyday life. How should we give social meaning to this?

Understanding arts festivals as a form of cultural heritage/property is a way of re-establishing the festival as a site of public culture that can recreate community and play a role in developing what Douzinas has described as the ethos of the collective.[65] Developing this argument, the proliferation of arts festivals could be understood as a response to the loss of community, to the loss of the ethos of the collective, to the loss of being together in a physical sense. Such an explanation might be located within the recent movements to reclaim community and public spaces.[66] These are counter-hegemonic movements. They seek to engage with the use of space as, in Lefebvre's words, "a *political instrument* that facilitates forms of social control" and to act as "a means of human *reappropriation* through the development of *counterspaces* forged through artistic expression and social resistance".[67] They seek to challenge the hierarchical construction of space that is achieved through forms of private property rights over tangibles and intangibles. In this context, it is critical to recall that intellectual property does not just privatize intangibles. As was argued in Chapter 1, it also spreads its net over tangible space, controlling venues and artistic practices within those venues.[68] Reclaiming these venues, these other tangible and intangible spaces of the festival, as public or communal spaces also means forming a site of resistance to the political power of the capitalist system. In this way, the modern arts festival would reclaim its roots as a form of challenge to capitalist accumulation and a site of resistance to the political power of the capitalist system.

Thinking of arts festivals as cultural heritage/property presents us with a cultural and political opportunity, but only if we can find a way to use the liberatory

64 Bauman, n 50 above, at 95.

65 C Douzinas, *Philosophy and Resistance in the Crisis* (Cambridge: Polity Press, 2013), esp ch 11. See Macmillan, "Testing the Working Taxonomy of Arts Festivals", n 1 above, section 5.3.2.

66 E.g., through the concept of the commons or other forms of common property, see, e.g., A Clarke, "Property, Human Rights and Communities" in T Xu &J Allain (eds), *Property and Human Rights in a Global Context* (Oxford & Portland, OR: Hart Publishing, 2015); M De Angelis, *Omnia Sunt Communia: On the Commons and the Transformation to Postcapitalism* (London: Zed Books, 2017).

67 C Butler, "Critical Legal Studies and the Politics of Space" (2009) 18 *Social & Legal Studies* 313–332, at 320, citing H Lefebvre, *The Production of Space* (Oxford: Blackwell, 1991). See also ch 5, section 3.

68 See ch 1, section 5.4.

potential that this offers as a tool to constrain the power of the intellectual property system. In this sense, the bounded space of the arts festival presents us with an interesting laboratory in which to think about and experiment with new ways to balance community rights in cultural heritage/property against intellectual property – or, better still, to find ways to embed private intellectual property rights within a system that privileges and serves the interests of community.[69] The space of the festival gives us a good idea about what cultural heritage/property might look like everywhere – in the West and the rest. It also provides a good example of how such a space can be saturated by intellectual property rights, and how those rights might constrain the social processes, including the creative synergistic interactions that are the heart and soul of the arts festival as event. However, the arts festival as event remains a bounded space. Arguments for the partial or complete suspension of intellectual property rights within the festival space are arguments for suspension inside a bounded space, which is by its nature a suspension of normal life and its focus on what I would describe as the "irrational" accumulation of capital.[70] The big question is whether re-appropriating spaces like the festival space, treating and using them as counterspaces, is something that can also be rolled out on a wider canvas. Can we find ways to make cultural production resistant to the social relations of capitalism, not just in the festival space, but also in the wider space of community?[71] The next and final chapter turns itself to this question.

69 For some thoughts on this, see F Macmillan, "Arts Festivals: Property, Heritage or More" in K Bowrey & M Handler (eds), *Law and Creativity in the Age of the Entertainment Franchise* (Cambridge: Cambridge University Press, 2014); F Macmillan, "Arts Festivals as Cultural Heritage in a Copyright Saturated World" in H Porsdam (ed), *Copyrighting Creativity: Creative Values, Cultural Heritage Institutions and Systems of Intellectual Property* (Farnham: Ashgate, 2014); Macmillan, "A Taxonomy of Arts Festivals: Mapping Issues in Cultural Property and Human Rights", n 1 above, section 7.4.

70 Cf text acc n 64 above.

71 On the production of space by the social relations of capitalism, see Butler, n 67 above, at 321, citing Lefebvre (H Lefebvre, "Space: Social Product & Use Value" in J Freiberg (ed), *Critical Sociology: European Perspectives* [New York: Irvington, 1979]) citing, amongst others, K Marx, *Grundrisse: Foundations of the Critique of Political Economy (Rough Draft)* (London: Penguin, 1973, trans M Nicolaus); D Harvey, *The Limits to Capital* (Oxford: Blackwell, 1982).

Chapter 7

Living between market and community

1 The dynamic duo

There are two dynamically interrelated themes that drive the arguments in this book. The first is capital's occupation of our culture generally. The second is the way in which Western capitalist culture has penetrated and occupied the post-colonial world, controlling, appropriating and reconstituting cultural production; and at the same time perpetuating neo-imperial power relations. Law, rolled out on the global stage, has been the means of this penetration and occupation. Copyright, as a means to promote investment and capital accumulation, has been an essential tool in securing capital's domination over cultural production everywhere. In cases where cultural production cannot be fitted into the copyright system, and where changing the system would imperil its necessary relationship with private property rights and capital accumulation, so-called *sui generis* protection is proposed. In this way, what cannot fit into a Western private property system is cast as anomalous. However, the allegedly *sui generis* nature of some forms of non-Western cultural production has been leveraged in order to obscure a problem that is not just non-Western. This is the problem of the relationship between community rights over cultural production and their obliteration by private property rights. In Western societies, nearly all this territory has been ceded. By distinguishing Western cultural production from what we think of as non-Western cultural production, and categorizing parts of the latter as either outside the intellectual property system or in some hybrid *sui generis* category, the Western world has failed to learn any lessons about how to manage private intellectual property rights within a social process of community-based cultural production. To add insult to injury, at least so far as Indigenous Peoples are concerned, the discourse around *sui generis* protection, and the allegedly generous concession that it represents on the part of the Western intellectual property system, has been used as a sop in order to disguise and ignore the real demands of Indigenous Peoples for political recognition.

While all this has been going on, in another separate part of the Western legal imaginary a towering edifice has been built around cultural production understood as heritage. In this system, cultural production in the form of heritage is not privately owned, but it belongs nevertheless to constellations of people somehow defined. A founding myth of the system is that things that fall within its scope are the common heritage of humanity, but sometimes they also belong to states or to communities or other non-specified groups. Even though this system is separate from that governing private property rights, it replicates its structure dividing up the objects of its regulation in the same way as private property laws: between tangible and intangible, and between tangible immoveables and tangible moveables.[1] Sometimes, the authorized discourse of cultural heritage protection even uses the property word: tangible moveables are described as property, as are tangible immoveables designated as cultural landscapes.[2] Despite these entanglements, there is not much by way of legal mechanisms that hold the two systems, property law and cultural heritage law, together. This state of affairs is particularly marked with respect to the relationship, or lack thereof, between the type of intangible property that constitutes intellectual property and the intangibles that fall within the scope of the cultural heritage protection in the UNESCO system, especially under its 2003 Convention for the Safeguarding of the Intangible Cultural Heritage (CICH).[3]

Conceptually, the systems of intellectual property protection and cultural heritage protection are held together – and held apart – by a series of Cartesian binary distinctions. These distinctions do not hold empirically, but they enable the world to be conceived of in Western terms. Consequently, they have been effective in promoting capital accumulation and Western post-colonial power relations across the globe. While both systems depend upon the distinction between tangibility and intangibility, both are constantly tripped up by the empirical difficulties in drawing this distinction. Nevertheless, the insistence on the dematerialized cultural product in intellectual property law, allied to a conception of authorship that comprehends as one of its forms the investment of economic resources in production and distribution of dematerialized cultural production, has made it a perfect vehicle of investment and capital accumulation.[4] For cultural heritage law, the distinction between tangible and intangible is impossible to draw in reality. As the UNESCO conventions acknowledge, what is tangible heritage – rather than being a pile of junk or a site ready for demolition and redevelopment – depends upon intangible values. Intangible heritage is indissolubly connected to what the CICH describes as "the instruments, objects, artefacts and cultural spaces associated therewith".[5]

1 See ch 3, sections 1 and 2.1.
2 On tangible moveables, see ch 3, section 2.1. On UNESCO-listed cultural landscapes, see ch 5, section 6.
3 See ch 3, section 3.3.
4 See ch 1, section 5.2.
5 CICH, Art 2.1.

The distinction between nature and culture is also everywhere in both systems.[6] It is explicit in relation to the tangible immoveables protected by the UNESCO Convention Concerning the Protection of the World Cultural and Natural Heritage (WHC). It is implicit in the organization of the intellectual property system, where the distinction is subsumed into that between science and culture. The CICH, disturbing the foundations of this distinction to some extent, tells us that "knowledge and practices concerning nature and the universe" are one of the domains of intangible cultural heritage. At the same time, however, intellectual property's system of patent law privatizes the results of scientific research, including research that uses such knowledge and practices. This privatization of scientific knowledge in the exclusive domain of the patent system has functioned well to ensure that, despite the limited efforts of the CICH, we do not think of scientific research as the common heritage of humanity – even when we turn to it in desperation in the face of a global pandemic.[7] The way in which intellectual property divides things up into science or culture means that where it can be applied to non-Western ways of seeing the world, it cannibalizes and dismembers them by chopping them into different parts, or "products", that in no sense represent the sum of the whole. This destroys the authenticity of knowledge systems in real terms, but in another sense makes them conform to a Western understanding of the distinction between authentic and fake, which is also a binary distinction common to both intellectual property law and cultural heritage law.[8] Neither system comprehends cultural production as authentic by virtue of being a community-based process. The intellectual property system focusses on an end product (even where, in the case of patent law, some products are defined as processes). The cultural heritage system, apart from the UNESCO Convention on the Protection and Promotion of the Diversity of Cultural Expressions (CCD), focusses on things that can be specified and included on a list – even if the CICH does a better job than the rest of the system in understanding practices of cultural production. Overall, the use of the distinction between authentic and fake to produce, in varying degrees, an inauthentic version of authenticity has functioned to bolster the organization of Western geopolitical power, and to translate non-Western culture into Western culture and forms of Western capital accumulation.

If all these distinctions hold the two systems together in a conceptual sense, there is also a critical distinction that purports to hold the systems apart conceptually and that functions to separate them in a legal sense. This is the distinction

6 See ch 5, section 6.

7 See, e.g., J Vidal, "'Tip of the Iceberg': Is Our Destruction of Nature Responsible for Covid-19?", *The Guardian*, 18 March 2020, https://www.theguardian.com/environment/2020/mar/18/tip-of-the-iceberg-is-our-destruction-of-nature-responsible-for-covid-19-aoe, accessed 18/03/2020.

8 See ch 5, section 5.

between tradition and modernity. This distinction appears to make it unnecessary to think about how the systems of cultural heritage protection and intellectual property rights relate to each other in a legal sense because they are simply about different things. Tradition, which is the heartland of cultural heritage protection according to the authorized heritage discourse, has been erased from copyright law as a result of the author function in copyright, which cancels out the contribution of everything that has gone before the copyright work vesting all rights in copyright's atomistic author.[9] Tradition may sometimes be about processes (although carefully delineated and frozen in time in the CICH lists), but modernity is about a product. Tradition may look to community, somehow defined, but modernity is about getting your product onto the market. Tradition may buck the processes of capital accumulation, but not modernity. Tradition looks backwards; modernity is not only contemporary, it also looks forward. Why should the West rule the world? Because it is forward-looking and the rest of the world is mired in backward tradition, the answer (if it were ever to be truthfully expressed) would go. Of course, tradition is also interesting, colourful and nice to have around, but it is not the Western capitalist way – better to keep it in museums and galleries and as part of tourist experiences. In fact, much better to keep it like this, isolated from social processes, just in case it slips its moorings and contributes to the types of social and cultural processes that might also unmoor Western dominance and/or Western capitalist accumulation. If, however, it does slip its moorings in this way and become something modern or contemporary, then the fact that there is nothing to protect heritage from being commodified and turned into a form of Western private property is a pretty good back-up to ensure Western capitalist dominance of cultural production.

So what of the conceptual distinction between West and non-West upon which much of the foregoing discussion rests? Is it also open to attack on the grounds of its empirical falsity? Can it hold at all? I think the answer is that, empirically, it holds and it does not hold. It does not hold because there is hardly anything, or anyone, that is non-Western in the sense of being untouched by the impositions of Western law, Western capital and Western cultural production. It holds because there is still a difference between the Western political, economic and social machine that has so ruthlessly sought to dominate that which is other than itself, and those communities, however formed, that in part identify themselves by resistance to Western domination. These strategies of resistance have generated ways of mediating and filtering Western influence that protect social processes, including cultural production, from being entirely overwhelmed by Western culture, politics and law. In particular, in the context of this book, these strategies of resistance have produced ways of accommodating Western intellectual property laws within community processes of cultural production.[10]

9 See ch 1, sections 5.2, 5.3 and 5.5.
10 See ch 5, section 5.

In the West, however, strategies of resistance have been thinner on the ground and of questionable effectiveness, at least in legal terms. Consequently, nearly all our cultural production has been absorbed by the intellectual property, and in particular the copyright, system.

2 Copyright, creativity and the commons

Relying on an excellent and extensive critical literature, one of the premises upon which this book is based is that the copyright has a fundamentally compromised relationship with concepts of authorial creativity in domains such as literature, music, film, and the visual and theatrical arts generally.[11] Its scope of operation, while being extensive, is also rigid. Its concept of the author excludes some types of creative input, while also including investment in production and distribution. It is focussed on products rather than on creative processes. Some of these characteristics, however, also go towards explaining why it has been very effective as an investment right. In this guise its character as a fully transmissible property right, its long duration and its harmonized global reach have also been decisive. In an ugly irony, its very success as an investment right – that is, its success in manipulating processes of cultural production to serve the ends of capital accumulation – has been a significant part of the reason for its failure to operate effectively as a right in relation to creativity.[12] Yet, given its rhetorical insistence on protecting, stimulating and incentivizing at least some types of creativity, it seems worth making some comment on the possibilities for resistance inside – or alongside – the copyright system.

Since scholarly writing is also a process of self-discovery, I admit that I surprised myself when I wrote in Chapter 5 that copyright has a relatively generous range of exceptions and defences.[13] I confess that because this seemed to run against the argument in the book, I tried to think of some other way to make the point. In the end, however, I left the text as it was. I consider that it is accurate to say that the copyright exceptions and defences are generous in comparison to those provided in the patent regime. Whether or not they work well is a different question. Their effective functioning is, in part, a question of their interpretative scope, and in part a question of access to justice and its relationship to political and economic power. However, it is also crucially dependent on the effectiveness of the so-called public domain or commons in offering a site of resistance to power based on the creeping private propertization of cultural production. This is because the effect of successfully establishing a defence or exception to an

11 See ch 1, sections 2, 3 and 5.

12 See ch 1, section 5. For a good account of some of the specifics in this respect, see P K Yu, "How Copyright May Affect Pop Music without Our Knowing It" (2014) 83 *University of Missouri-Kansas City Law Review* 363–401.

13 Ch 5, section 6.

actual or threatened action for breach of copyright is to pull the relevant material into this non-propertized space, at least for a limited period and purpose.

Without wanting to underrate the importance, in at least some contexts of the public domain or commons, I do not think that it is enough on its own to resolve the problems around cultural production that I have tried to present in this book. Certainly, the idea of the public domain and the theoretical positions that have been developed to support, elaborate and nurture it are concerned with the protection of community rights and interests in cultural production.[14] In seeking to maintain the balance between the privately propertized domain of intellectual space and the non-propertized zone, a reinvigorated public domain or commons celebrates the importance of protecting creativity – both by recognizing specific authorial acts of cultural production and by recognizing the need to maintain a space of freedom in order to sustain those acts. However, in the context of cultural production, it also suffers from at least four particular limitations. First, it is a space that is largely created by the intellectual property system itself and by the line it has drawn between what is protected by intellectual property rights and what is unprotected. Certainly, there are occasions when other areas of law pull things out of the protected zone, but its borders are more usually created and policed by the intellectual property system.[15] Secondly, the idea of the public domain or commons only indirectly tilts at capital accumulation inside the intellectual property system. For this reason, it will always be vulnerable. If the line between privately propertized space and non-propertized space is drawn by the intellectual property system and that system is driven by the global interests of the multinational media and entertainment sector, then there will always be a tendency for the propertized zone to expand at the expense of the non-propertized zone.[16] Thirdly, it does not adequately comprehend the point that leaving things in the public domain or commons does not necessarily protect community production. Sometimes, particularly in a world characterized by gross and persistent post-colonial power imbalances, leaving things in the public domain or open commons leaves them open to further predation, including

14 See, e.g., N Mezey, "The Paradoxes of Cultural Property" (2007) 107 *Columbia Law Review* 2004–2046; J Boyle, *The Public Domain: Enclosing the Commons of the Mind* (New Haven, CT & London: Yale University Press, 2008); E Hemmungs Wirtén; *Terms of Use: Negotiating the Jungle of the Intellectual Commons* (Toronto: University of Toronto Press, 2008); J B Holder & T Flessas, "Emerging Commons" (2008) 17 *Social & Legal Studies* 299–311; M Sunder, *From Goods to a Good Life: Intellectual Property and Global Justice* (New Haven, CT: Yale University Press, 2012); M Bruncevic, *Law, Art and the Commons: Space, Materiality and the Normative* (Oxford & New York: Routledge, 2018).

15 See also F Macmillan, "'Speaking Truth to Power': Copyright and the Control of Speech" in M Bassini, O Pollicino & G M Riccio (eds), *Copyright Versus (Other) Fundamental Rights in the Digital Age: A comparative Analysis in Search of a Common Constitutional Ground* (Cheltenham: Edward Elgar, 2020).

16 See also Report of the Special Rapporteur in the field of cultural rights, F Shaheed, *Copyright Policy and the Right to Science and Culture*, UN Doc A/HRC/28/57, 24 December 2014.

the sort of predation that reinforces those very power imbalances.[17] Fourthly, large corporate predators are not confined to the privately propertized domain of intellectual space, they also roam the commons. In particular, those that are most likely to profit and accumulate capital in a space free of intellectual property restrictions are the big technology corporations, which gobble up everything, including the labour of those working or playing (or just living) in the public domain or commons.[18] This, of course, particularly applies to things that are happening online where the discourse of free culture has been effectively leveraged by corporate interests.[19] The commons can produce strategies of resistance to predation. De Angelis points out that what is held in common by a community is not necessarily on open or free access: "a commons is a system, and free access *can* be one of its sub-systems".[20] However, as a consequence of the fact that immaterial common resources cannot be exhausted, he applies this distinction only to material (or "biophysical") resources. Since this seems to overlook the fact that immaterial or intangible resources in the commons can be abused or damaged even if they are not exhausted, we could try to hold on to the idea that even intangible things in the commons should not necessarily be openly or freely accessible. But producing this result relies on an idea of "ownership" of the commons that is not easily recognizable in the legal context of the current tug of war between the privately propertized space of cultural production and its public domain or commons analogue.

The location in intangible or intellectual space of the debate about the relationship between the privately owned domain of cultural production and the public domain or commons is problematic. Cultural production is not just intangible, it does not only take place in intellectual space.[21] The fact that the debate tends in this direction is a consequence of the way in which the focus on intellectual property has shaped the discourse, even when it is often a discourse about ways to liberate ourselves from its effects. Cultural production explodes the boundaries between the tangible and intangible. Its spaces are everywhere; and the communities which identify themselves in relation to its processes are often multilevel and interlocking. Even if the discussion of the spaces of copyright

17 See K Bowrey & J Anderson, "The Politics of Global Information Sharing: Whose Cultural Agendas Are Being Advanced?" (2009) 18 *Social & Legal Studies* 479–504. Cf. Mezey, n 14 above.

18 See ch 1, section 5.3; chapter 2, section 4.

19 See further L J Murray, S T Piper & K Robertson, *Putting Intellectual Property in Its Place: Rights Discourses, Creative Labor, and the Everyday* (Oxford & New York: Oxford University Press, 2014), at 17–21.

20 M De Angelis, *Omnia Sunt Communia: On the Commons and the Transformation to Postcapitalism* (London: Zed Books, 2017), at 146 (my emphasis), & generally at 144–149, deconstructing G Hardin, "The Tragedy of the Commons" (1968) 162 *Science* 1243–1248; & E Ostrom, *Governing the Commons: The Evolution of Institutions or Collective Action* (Cambridge & New York: Cambridge University Press, 1990).

21 As is well recognized by, e.g., Bruncevic, n 14 above.

has a tendency to corral us into the intangible realm, resistance begins by refusing to be corralled in this way. Resistance begins by refusing a vision of the world, and specifically a vision of cultural production, that divides it between the intangible and the tangible. It is exactly this way of looking at the world that has divided up cultural production between the contemporary and the traditional, between digital and analogue, between market and community.[22]

3 Cultural rights

What are the concrete ways in law to resist the domination by intellectual property of the spaces and discourses of cultural production, to resist its commodification of cultural production in the interests of capital accumulation, to resist its potentially destructive effects on community? The authorized discourse of cultural heritage, made into international law by the UNESCO Conventions, puts up very little in the way of resistance. Conceptually hijacked by a system of organization that owes much to the influence of Western property law, mired in the same types of distinctions – between tangible and intangible, moveable and immoveable, authentic and fake, nature and culture – that ground the intellectual property system, it seems to offer little hope. At least in its twenty-first-century manifestations, it is full of florid claims about culture and community, but the one serious legal protection that it could offer to processes of cultural production, protection from privatization, is one of the few things that it says almost nothing about.

Instead of looking for salvation in the unpromising terrain of the UNESCO Conventions, attention has been focussed on cultural rights as a possible counterbalance to, or constraint on, the power of the intellectual property system.[23] The invocation of cultural rights in this context has significant discursive power in drawing attention to the political economy of copyright. Of particular significance in this respect is the 2015 Report of the Special Rapporteur in the field of cultural rights on *Copyright Policy and the Right to Science and Culture.*[24] The Report may have fallen short of a comprehensive critique of the political

22 See also C Butler, "Critical Legal Studies and the Politics of Space" (2009) 18 *Social & Legal Studies* 313–332, at 322: "Both spatial practices and the representations of space which tend to be imposed by law are intersected by representational spaces, embodying spatialized resistances to legal ordering".

23 See F Macmillan, "Development, Cultural Self-Determination and the World Trade Organization" in A Perry-Kessaris, *Law in the Pursuit of Development: Principles into Practice?* (Oxford & New York: Routledge, 2009); F Macmillan, "Copyright Policy and the Right to Science and Culture – Report 2015 (A/HRC/28/57" in L Belder & H Porsdam (eds), *Negotiating Cultural Rights: Issues at Stake, Challenges and Recommendations* (Farnham: Ashgate, 2017); J Käll, "Patent Policy and the Right to Science and Culture – Report 2015 (A/70/279)" in Belder & Porsdam, *ibid.*; H Porsdam, *The Transforming Power of Cultural Rights: A Promising Law and Humanities Approach* (Cambridge: Cambridge University Press, 2019).

24 Note 16 above.

economy of the copyright system, but it contains a good start.[25] (And the fact that it appeared at all in such a resistant international policymaking context makes it a welcome novelty in the international law discourse around copyright.) A particular contribution of the cultural rights approach has been to generate productive lines of thought on how intellectual property rights might be reshaped in order to realize the promise of cultural rights. In the copyright context, this includes proposals for authors' rights that meet the requirement in the International Covenant on Economic, Social and Cultural Rights, Article 15(1)(c), that every person "benefit from the protection of the moral and material interests resulting from any scientific, literary or artistic production of which he is the author", while avoiding making the author a cog in a system of international capital accumulation.[26]

Cultural heritage protection has also been subject to an explicit cultural rights critique that in some respects, as with the cultural rights critique of copyright, mirrors the critique of international cultural heritage law contained in this book. Questions of access to, and enjoyment of, cultural heritage were given critical attention in the 2011 Report of the Special Rapporteur in the field of cultural rights on *Access to Cultural Heritage*.[27] Building on to the right, laid down in Article 15(1)(a) of the International Covenant on Economic, Social and Cultural Rights, to "take part in cultural life", Porsdam argues that:

> [L]inked as it is to the identity and dignity of a person or his or her community, cultural heritage has become a major site for discussions on diversities, power differentials, and historical injustices – but also on how best to promote the idea of living together in harmony. Increasingly, it is through cultural heritage that people express their cultural identity and give meaning and value to their lives.[28]

This resonates, of course, with the arguments made in this book about the functions of cultural heritage/property. Like the cultural rights discourse around copyright, and around other forms of intellectual property, confined to their individual subject matters, there is not all that much with which to disagree.[29] However, it is questionable how far a focus on cultural rights as they are currently

25 See further Macmillan (2017), n 23 above.

26 See, e.g., Porsdam, n 23 above, ch 6.

27 Report of the independent expert in the field of cultural rights, F Shaheed, *Access to Cultural Heritage*, UN Doc A/HRC/17/38, March 2011; see L Belder, "The Right of Access to and Enjoyment of Cultural Heritage – Report 2011 (A/HRC/17/38)" in Belder & Porsdam, n 23 above.

28 Porsdam, n 23 above, at 96; see more generally, *ibid*., ch 4.

29 On patents, see the Report of the Special Rapporteur in the field of cultural rights, F Shaheed, *Patent Policy and the Right to Science and Culture*, UN Doc A/HRC/70/279, 4 August 2015; see J Käll, n 23 above; & Porsdam, n 23 above, ch 6.

located in the international system, and as they are currently triangulated with intellectual property law and cultural heritage law, gets us. Apart from the fact that they are based on many of the binary distinctions that have sustained Western dominance over cultural production generally, the slightly uncomfortable truth is that they have not constrained the copyright-facilitated build-up of corporate power over cultural production.[30] And they have had a limited effect on the shape and content of the international cultural heritage regime. It should be conceded that, with respect to the cultural heritage regime, the UNESCO Conventions of this century show the influence of human rights, and specifically cultural rights, discourse. Even if these Conventions are tacked on to a system where cultural rights concerns have not been a dominant influence, this is a welcome development. It demonstrates that the discourse of cultural rights can open up political opportunities for contestation in at least some parts of the system. The extent, however, to which cultural rights can cross the hard lines in the system of international law that have protected intellectual property from their scrutiny is open to question.[31] (It is conceded that the discourse of cultural rights has made an impact in the intellectual property system, but only in the perverse sense that it has been used in order to bolster the claim that copyright is a fundamental property right.[32])

For liberatory concepts derived from the discourse of cultural rights to be effective, they must be part and parcel of the legal regime that governs cultural production. They cannot easily be understood as being in opposition to copyright, or a counterbalance to it. What sense, for example, would a system of authors' rights, growing out of cultural rights discourse, make if it was only a counterbalance to the system of capital accumulation so effectively managed by copyright? The discourse of cultural rights must enter into the core of copyright and change it from the inside. In order to achieve this, we need to find concepts that enable us to organize and institutionalize the types of approaches that are suggested by cultural rights discourse. In this book, the concept that I propose in order to sustain a regulatory system for cultural production that resists the private propertization of everything, that resists a market mentality that turns cultural production into a site of capital accumulation, that resists the continuing post-colonial dominance of the global North, is that of community. My elaboration of the concept of community, and its importance in this context, is heavily dependent on critical accounts of the fundamental relationship between community and cultural heritage/property.[33] Before, however, turning to the final throes of my argument on the embedding of the market for cultural production

30 See also B Ivey, *Arts, Inc: How Greed and Neglect Have Destroyed Our Cultural Rights* (Berkeley: University of California Press, 2010).

31 On the divided international system, see further ch 1, section 3; ch 3, section 1.

32 See ch 1, section 4.

33 See esp ch 3, sections 2 & 3; ch 4.

in community, something must be said about the expression "cultural heritage/property", which has been employed (with a sort of disclaimer) throughout this book.[34]

4 Heritage or property?

Despite writing in Chapter 1 that I would hedge my bets on whether to call the community-based processes of cultural production with which this book is concerned heritage or property, this section can hardly be regarded as the moment when the mystery is resolved. The title of the book gives the game away before it has really even started. However, it is important to explain why the choice is not an easy one, and what is at stake in making it. The "heritage or property" question, along with the associated question of whether it is important to ask the "heritage or property" question, has been considered by a number of eminent scholars in the field.[35] There is a tendency – albeit not total – amongst legal scholars, at least those from common law backgrounds, to opt for heritage over property.[36] This is largely explicable on the basis of a doctrinal understanding of the limitations of the concept of property. The following argument attempts to shake off these shackles, but it does so advisedly. The analysis of the pros and cons of each concept indicates good reasons why both are problematic and why, at the same time, both offer important critical insights. The final preference for a concept of cultural property is one that is located outside the boundaries of traditional property law and that reflects the political project of this book. The discussion below starts by analysing the reasons for and against the use of heritage, the pre-ordained loser in this competition, before moving on to consider the pitfalls and potential of a property paradigm.

There are a number of reasons that militate against employing a concept of heritage. Significantly, it invokes an association with the authorized heritage discourse and, in particular, its embodiment in the UNESCO regime for the protection of cultural heritage. As the critique of that system in this book should demonstrate, this is not an association that is useful for my argument.[37]

34 See ch 1, section 1.3. & ch 3, section 2.1.

35 See, e.g., L V Prott & P J O'Keefe, "'Cultural Heritage' or 'Cultural Property'" (1992) 1 *International Journal of Cultural Property* 307–320; J Blake, "On Defining Cultural Heritage" (2000) 49 *International & Comparative Law Quarterly* 61–85; M Frigo, "Cultural Property v. Cultural Heritage: A Battle of Concepts in International Law?" (2004) 86 *International Review of the Red Cross* 367–378; R J Coombe, "The Expanding Purview of Cultural Properties and Their Politics" (2009) 5 *Annual Review of Law & Social Science* 393–412; H Geismar, "Anthropology and Heritage Regimes" (2015) 44 *Annual Review of Anthropology* 71–85; V Tr Hafstein & M Skrydstrup, "Heritage Vs Property: Contrasting Regimes and Rationalities in the Patrimonial Field" in J Anderson & H Geismar (eds), *The Routledge Companion to Cultural Property* (Oxford & New York: Routledge, 2017).

36 See Prott & O'Keefe, n 35 above; Blake, n 35 above. Cf. Frigo n 35 above.

37 See esp chs 3 and 5.

Nevertheless, an engagement with the movement from property to heritage in the discourse of the UNESCO system provides important insights. As discussed in Chapter 3, this movement occurs between the 1970 UNESCO Convention on the Means of Prohibiting and Preventing the Illicit Import, Export and Transfer of Cultural Property and UNESCO's iconic World Heritage Convention (WHC) of 1972.[38] Hafstein and Skrydstrup argue that the change in discourse represents a transition from one governmental rationality to another. Specifically, they argue "that cultural property is a technology of sovereignty and cultural heritage is a technology of reformation".[39] So far as the technology of sovereignty that forms the basis of cultural property claims is concerned, they observe:

> The claims that regimes of cultural property recognize and validate are claims to objects which colonialism, capitalism, and science have transported in their common luggage. These claims propose now to reverse their trajectories and return the objects to their countries of origin or to their rightful owners within settler-colonial societies. Claims to cultural property are usually staked in the aftermath of violence: of war or colonial rule, or both. The claims assert sovereign powers and they affirm cultural integrity in the face of foreign invasion and foreign rule, globalized markets and foreign science. Cultural property claims thus help form sovereign subjects, whether independent peoples or semi-autonomous social collectives such as communities and tribes.[40]

In the hands of the UNESCO regime, of course, the concept of sovereignty that is grounded by such a property claim is limited to nation states in the Western system of international law.[41] This "rights"-based system is contrasted by Hafstein and Skrydstrup to the "ethics"-based system that is represented by the UNESCO conventions that have heritage as their object of protection. Instead of focussing on the rights of states, they argue that the system of ethics is concerned with states' "responsibility to current and future generations and to humanity as a whole".[42] The catch-words here are "safeguarding", nicely built into the name of the 2003 CICH, and "participation":

> [P]rojects of safeguarding connect agendas in political centers to those dispersed sites where operations of power connect with the population. The experts, councils, committees, museums, workshops, awareness

38 See ch 3, section 2.1.
39 Hafstein & Skrydstrup, n 35 above, at 39.
40 Hafstein & Skrydstrup, n 35 above, at 40.
41 See ch 3, section 3.2; ch 4, section 1.
42 Hafstein & Skrydstrup, n 35 above, at 43.

> raising, and grassroots organizations that the heritage regime summons into being or summons on site all help to establish lines of communication between the calculations of authorities and the aspirations of free citizens, to mold the ambitions and shape the desires of the latter to safeguard their heritage of their own free accord and initiative. Appealing to their civic duty and moral responsibility for maintaining a particular alignment between the past and the present, in which strong emotions and identities are vested, projects for safeguarding cultural heritage thus are designed to modify behavior, sensitivities, and ideas about preservation and history.[43]

The cosmopolitan claims of this "ethics"-based concept of heritage, the mantra of the "common heritage of mankind" (or of humanity) in the UNESCO conventions, are belied by the reality of the system. This is not only because of the inescapably state-based nature of the international law system.[44] It is also because the systems of listing in both the WHC and CICH work by connecting tangible immoveable heritage and intangible cultural heritage to a particular state or sometimes, in the case of intangible cultural heritage, to more than one state. This can be interpreted, in the ethical mode, as allocating the responsibility of safeguarding that heritage to a particular state or states. However, to understand this as its only significance would be disingenuous, as disputes over the listing of intangible cultural heritage show.[45] With respect to both tangibles and intangibles, listing things – just as much as direct property claims – creates hierarchies of power.[46] As Hafstein and Skrydstrup observe, "[c]ompared with cultural property, we might say that cultural heritage is subtler in both its perpetuation and its disruptions of state hegemony".[47] Perhaps the hierarchical structuring of space by listing regimes is less obvious and transparent than direct state claims to cultural property, but it happens nevertheless. The fact that it is a less obvious and transparent method of reinforcing state sovereignty makes it no less resistant to claims over that heritage by communities formed outside the international law system of sovereign

43 Hafstein & Skrydstrup, n 35 above, at 46. See also T Flessas, "Cultural Property Defined and Redefined as Nietzschean Aphorism" (2003) 24 *Cardozo Law Review* 1067–1098, at 1091, who refers to "the privileging of preservation" that has been at the heart of the Western concept of cultural heritage; see ch 5, section 4.3.

44 See ch 3, section 3.2; ch 4, section 1.

45 See C Antons & L Rogers, "Cultural and Intellectual Property in Cross-Border Disputes over Intangible Cultural Heritage" in C Antons & W Logan (eds), *Intellectual Property, Cultural Property and Intangible Cultural Heritage* (London & New York: Routledge, 2018); see ch 5, section 4.2.

46 See Butler, n 22 above; H Schreiber, "Intangible Cultural Heritage and Soft Power – Exploring the Relationship" (2017) 12 *International Journal of Intangible Heritage* 44–57; ch 5, sections 3 and 4.2.

47 Hafstein & Skrydstrup, n 35 above, at 43.

states. The more subtle nature of the state claim, however, may make it more difficult to identify spaces of resistance, which become occluded and more politically tricky to occupy. This seems to be the case with the CICH, which uses language sensitive to the claims of "indigenous communities, groups and, in some cases, individuals" inside a convention that can only be operated through the state.[48]

For Hafstein and Skrydstrup, the movement in the discourse of the UNESCO conventions from property to heritage is part of the movement in the world order from liberalism to neoliberalism "with its projects of responsibilization, its delegation of tasks of governance from the state, and its cultivation of 'self-governing capabilities'".[49] This is an important insight, which applies with particular force to the most recent UNESCO Conventions. Given the timing of the change in UNESCO discourse, which happens in the arc of a relatively brief period, the likelihood that it marks a move in the direction of a neoliberal rationality should not come as a surprise. The change in UNESCO discourse coincides with the period in which world systems began to change in order to accommodate the political decision by the West's most powerful states to repress calls for a New International Economic Order and to shore up the process of corporate-led economic globalization in the face of exogenous shocks in the world economy.[50]

As long as we stay inside the UNESCO system and as long as the UNESCO system stays inside the system of international law, there will be difficulties in escaping the centrality of the nation state. Nevertheless, in its property paradigm, Hafstein and Skrydstrup see the potential to broaden the base of the technology of sovereignty:

> Regardless even of whether or not they are recognized within legal regimes of cultural property, claims to cultural property help to form sovereign subjects with their own exclusive cultures and autonomous histories: nations, peoples, tribes, etc. Conversely, safeguarding cultural heritage is a technology of reformation, cultivating responsible subjects and entangling them in networks of expertise and management.[51]

48 CICH, Recital 6 & Art 2.1; see ch 3, section 2.3.

49 Hafstein & Skrydstrup, n 35 above, at 48, citing N Rose, "Governing 'Advanced' Liberal Democracies" in A Barry, T Osbourne & N Rose (eds), *Foucault and Political Reason: Liberalism, Neo-Liberalism and Rationalities of Government* (Chicago, IL: Chicago University Press, 1996). See also R J Coombe & L M Weiss, "Neoliberalism, Heritage Regimes, and Cultural Rights" in L Meskell (ed), *Global Heritage: A Reader* (Hoboken, NJ: Wiley-Blackwell, 2015).

50 See further Q Slobodian, *Globalists: The End of Empire and the Birth of Neoliberalism* (Cambridge, MA: Harvard University Press, 2018); F Macmillan, "Critical Law and Development" in E Christodoulidis, R Dukes & M Goldoni (eds), *Research Handbook on Critical Legal Theory* (Cheltenham: Edward Elgar, 2019).

51 Hafstein & Skrydstrup, n 35 above, at 48.

The tainting of the concept of heritage in the UNESCO regime with the transition to neoliberalism certainly counts against it in the context of this book, especially when neoliberalism is understood as being essentially a strategy to lift the market out of the reach of political contestation and regulation.[52] However, it is also the case, as is discussed below, that some considerable work needs to be done with the concept of cultural property before it can achieve the liberatory potential indicated by Hafstein and Skrydstrup.

Given that, whether we opt for property or heritage, the concept will have to undergo some transformation, it is worth thinking about whether – aside from its life inside the UNESCO system – there are other reasons for particular concern about the concept of cultural heritage. One striking consideration in this respect is the fact that heritage tends to invoke the idea of tradition, and the associated distinction between tradition and modernity. This is a distinction that does not hold empirically anywhere in relation to cultural production, which is a contemporary phenomenon that always draws upon, re-imagines and reacts to what has gone before it. In the post-colonial context, the distinction between modernity and tradition has also been used to make further specious distinctions between Western cultural production and cultural production in the rest of the world. This creates a very considerable obstacle to the potential uses of heritage as a conceptual category in the context of my argument. Nevertheless, there are things to be lost by rejecting the use of heritage in this respect. One of them is precisely the danger of obscuring the fact that the past is always present in contemporary cultural production. This is, of course, a consequence of the fact that, as critical heritage scholars insist, cultural production is a constitutive social process rather than being some type of end result or final product.[53] It may be that the concept of heritage, which lacks any precise overarching legal definition and so has not had the misfortune of being captured and exclusively interpreted by the language of law, provides more scope than that of cultural property to recognize cultural production as a process. To these observations, it should also be added that a pitfall in abandoning heritage in favour of property is to put myself outside the discourse of critical heritage scholars, although not necessarily outside the general discourse of critical theorists writing in this field.[54] Still, being outside the discourse of critical heritage scholars is a significant loss in a work that owes so much to their insights.[55] The only thing I can say to redeem myself in this respect is that my final preference for the use of cultural property,

52 Slobodian, n 50 above.

53 See especially, L Smith, *Uses of Heritage* (London & New York: Routledge, 2006), at, e.g., 56; ch 3, section 3.2.

54 As I hope is evident from the discussion of Hafstein and Skrydstrup, n 35 above.

55 Including the critique of the "safeguarding" concept in the CICH in N Akagawa & L Smith, "The Practices and Politics of Safeguarding" in N Akagawa & L Smith (eds), *Safeguarding Intangible Heritage: Practices and Politics* (Oxford & New York: Routledge, 2019): see ch 5, section 4.3.

rather than heritage, does not represent a distancing from their position. Their critique of the authorized discourse of cultural heritage is fundamental to the argument in this book. In particular, it is worth emphasizing the importance of their abandonment of "cultural" as an adjectival qualification to heritage. In this book, which has been written as much in response to the copyright system as to the international law system for the protection of cultural heritage, the use of "cultural" is a useful way of keeping the focus on the objects of the copyright system. However, my argument accepts the rejection of the nature/culture distinction that is implicit in this abandonment of the "cultural" qualifier by critical heritage scholars. I think it may be possible to rethink the concept of culture in order to question this binary distinction.

So, if heritage is a problematic choice, what might it mean to focus instead on a concept of cultural property? The first thing that should be conceded here is that legally, at least in a positivist sense, it does not mean much in common law systems to talk about cultural property, except perhaps in the specific context of the international conventions, and implementing legislation, using this language.[56] Some civil law states recognize a concept that is translatable into English as cultural property, but in general this is a fairly limited legal category that is not broad enough to cover what is currently considered by the UNESCO Conventions to be cultural heritage, let alone any wider concept.[57] However, as should be evident by this point, it is notable that outside positivist legal scholarship, the expression is widely used.[58] Despite this wide use in the literature, the normalization of the concept of heritage by UNESCO clearly dominates international legal discourse and has a significant hold on political and policymaking discourse.[59] In recognition of the attempt in this work to make a political argument that also grounds changes in law, the following discussion is

56 See Prott & O'Keefe, n above, at 312–318.

57 Prott & O'Keefe, n 35 above, at 312, making reference to the French concept of *biens culturels* and the Italian concept of *beni culturali*. The difference between common law and civil law systems is important here and is relevant to Frigo's argument that cultural heritage and cultural property have meanings in law that are not interchangeable: see Frigo, n 35 above.

58 See, e.g., in what could be a very long list: M F Brown, "Heritage Trouble: Recent Work on The Protection of Intangible Cultural Property" (2005) 12 *International Journal of Cultural Property* 40–61; K A Carpenter, S Katyal & A Riley, "In Defense of Property" (2009) 118 *Yale Journal of Law* 1022–1125; Flessas, n 43 above; R Handler, "Who Owns the Past? History, Cultural Property & the Logic of Possessive Individualism" in B Williams (ed), *The Politics of Culture* (Washington, DC: Smithsonian Institution Press, 1991); J R Slaughter, "Form & Informality: An Unliterary Look at World Literature" in R Warhol (ed), *The Work of Genre: Selected Essays from the English Institute* (New York: English Institute in Collaboration with the American Council of Learned Societies, 2011). To which list should be added the influential *International Journal of Cultural Property* itself. Cf. Prott & O'Keefe, n 35 above, at 319, who claim that the expression "cultural heritage" is "well recognized and universally used by historians, archaeologists, anthropologists and other researchers of human life both past and present".

59 See also ch 3, sections 1–3.

concerned with two different questions. First, what is the theoretical and political significance of such a change in discourse? And, second, what is its potential legal significance?

There are a number of good arguments that can be advanced against the use of the expression cultural property. A pervasive argument to this effect is that the use of the word "property" is problematic precisely because it has a clear legal, political and economic significance that is at odds with its use in conjunction with the qualifier "cultural".[60] There are various aspects to this argument that merit further enquiry. First, there is the problem that the legal concept of property is not sufficiently broad to cover everything that is intended to be encompassed in the concept of cultural property.[61] For instance, the property concept does not extend to a wide range of intangibles, such as spiritual beliefs or values that bind together and regulate the relationship between persons, communities and tangibles.[62] This is, of course, also a consequence of the fact that when we talk about property in a legal sense, we, here at the self-declared centre or the world, are generally talking about a Western concept that embodies Western values. Apart from its scope, perhaps the Western value that is most bothersome in the context of cultural property is the concept of rivalrous ownership and possession that is Western property's special bedfellow.[63] Rivalrous ownership and possession are not appropriate concepts in the cultural property context. This is partly because they may not reflect the way that all cultures think about their cultural property.[64] But also because, even in the Western context, they trail in their wake other values and practices that might be thought to be undesirable. Rivalrous property rights are at the centre of a market-based thinking that is capable in the neoliberal period of eclipsing any notion of public (as in non-private) good. This book, written against the current copyright regime, critiques it precisely on the basis that it is centred on a private property right that has facilitated its

60 See, e.g., Prott & O'Keefe, n 35 above, at 309:

> While 'cultural heritage' is a relatively new term & has far less ideological baggage in tow, 'property' has acquired a wide range of emotive & value-laden nuances from the arguments of John Locke to the challenge of Communism in the first two-thirds of this century.

See also Blake, n 35 above, at 65–66.

61 Prott & O'Keefe, n 35 above, at 311–312; Blake, n 35 above, at 66; Flessas, n 43 above, at 1068n.

62 See, e.g., R J Coombe, "The Properties of Culture & the Possession of Identity: Postcolonial Struggle & the Legal Imagination" in B Ziff & P V Rao (eds), *Borrowed Power: Essays on Cultural Appropriation* (New Brunswick, NJ: Rutgers University Press, 1997); Prott & O'Keefe, n 35 above, at 308–309 & 311–312; M Strathern, *Property, Substance & Effect: Anthropological Essays on Persons & Things* (London: Athlone Press, 1999); M Blakeney, "Protecting the Spiritual Beliefs of Indigenous Peoples – Australian Case Studies" (2013) 22 *Pacific Rim Law & Policy Journal* 391–427.

63 See also N Mezey, n 14 above.

64 See, e.g., Coombe, n 62 above; Strathern, n 62 above; M F Brown, *Who Owns Native Culture?* (Cambridge, MA: Harvard University Press, 2003). See also ch 5, section 6, esp note 136.

transformation into an investment right, thus turning cultural production into a site for capital accumulation.[65] Outside the copyright regime, but not outside systems of cultural production, the results of market-based thinking are evident in the thriving private international market for the sale of cultural objects and artefacts.[66] Sitting somewhere in the middle between the market for cultural objects and artefacts and the market for their digital reproductions, the property paradigm is implicated in the practices of museums that claim rivalrous property rights in their exhibits. As is considered in Chapter 5, in this context, the property paradigm has limited or even prevented the return of sensitive cultural objects, conferred control over their second life in digital form, and impeded or prevented engagement with them as part of ongoing cultural practices and processes.[67]

In the face of these arguments, it is clear that to employ a concept of cultural property in the context of an argument that aims at embedding market relations within those of community means divorcing, or at least separating, it from these traditional Western property notions. One way of doing this might be to conceive property in this context, not as a relation of ownership, but rather one of membership.[68] Understood in this way, property is productive of community.[69] This re-conception of property reinforces the idea of cultural production as being intrinsically connected to identity. It also moves us away from a strict division in ownership between public (as in state) and private properties, which both operate to exclude community interests in ways which vary depending upon the community in question.[70] Employing a concept of property reconceived along these lines has other important strategic results. First, the use of the word property has an important political significance retaining – perhaps more clearly than the use of the word heritage – the ideas of "embattled space" and the need to find places

65 See ch 1, sections 5.1 and 5.2.

66 Prott & O'Keefe, n 35 above, at 311; Carpenter, Katyal & Riley, n 58 above, at 1039–1040, critiquing the defence of private property rights and market freedoms in relation to cultural property in E A Posner, "The International Protection of Cultural Property: Some Skeptical Observations" (2007) 8 *Chicago Journal of International Law* 213–233.

67 See ch 5, section 2. See also T Flessas, "The Ends of the Museum" *Law Society & Economy Working Papers* 14/2013 (London: London School of Economics, 2013).

68 S Keenan, *Subversive Property: Law and the Production of Spaces of Belonging* (Abingdon: Routledge, 2014). This idea of property is part of many non-Western systems: see, e.g., J Gibson, "Community and the Exhaustion of Culture. Creative Territories in Traditional Cultural Expressions" in F Macmillan & K Bowrey (eds), New Directions on Copyright Law: Volume 3 (Cheltenham: Edward Elgar, 2006), esp at 32–36, for a discussion of the difference between "This land is mine … This land is me" in the film *One Night the Moon* (Kevin Lucas, Paul Humfress & Aanya Whitehead, 2001, dir R Perkins).

69 Keenan, n 68 above; Gibson, n 68 above.

70 On this point generally, see Keenan, n 68 above. On its specific application in the context of cultural artefacts, see Prott & O'Keefe, n 35 above, at 315ff.

resistance in that space.[71]. Second, using the word property here, instead of heritage, makes the conflict between cultural property and other types of rivalrous property evident and unavoidable, both politically and legally. Arguments that appear to dismiss the importance of the cultural heritage/cultural property debate on the basis that it is merely a semantic question underplay the importance of semantics in bolstering the politics of law.[72] It is hard to avoid the suspicion that the fact that the conflict between rivalrous private property rights, including intellectual property rights, and cultural property is a "category" problem, overlooked or unseen by the eye of law, is connected to what one could describe as semantics. Words have power, especially (but not only, of course) in legal discourse where semantic precision is highly valued. The change in language in the UNESCO system obscures the dimensions of the systemic conflict between cultural property/heritage and other forms of private property, including intellectual property. If, however, we pose property right against property right, the idea that we are talking about different categories starts to flounder. Needless to say, the legal sacralization of rivalrous private property rights and its importance to capitalist relations is not going to go down without a fight.[73] We need to make the fight, however, and obviously semantics can only get us to the starting line. After that, we have to think about whether property concepts themselves, so well-known to the law, can be used to produce a liberatory tool that can be fitted into or recognized by the law.[74]

The particular attraction of the cultural property concept is that by employing the strength of the property construct, it would seem to provide a better bulwark against the creeping private privatization of everything. While it is possible to come up with a list of things that might constitute cultural heritage in certain circumstances, it is much harder to find an overarching concept that defines cultural heritage in legal discourse. Bearing in mind the fairly uniform understanding of the power of private property rights in most legal systems, the fact that there is little consensus on what it means to have cultural heritage rights makes those rights largely impotent when it comes to resisting the privatization of everything. However, the fact that the concept of cultural heritage exists in international law should not be cast too lightly aside. Perhaps, in relation to the unknown quantity that is reflected in the concept of cultural property, there is

71 Flessas, n 43 above, at 1085. See also Butler, n 22 above.

72 Cf. Coombe, n 35 above; Geismar, n 35 above.

73 On the establishment of private property as a basic concept of law at the international level in the imperial period, see D Kennedy, "Three Globalizations of Law and Legal Thought: 1850–2000" in D M Trubek & A Santos (eds), *The New Law and Economic Development: A Critical Appraisal* (Cambridge: Cambridge University Press, 2006).

74 As Prott & O'Keefe, n 35 above, at 312, citing R Crewdson, "Cultural Property – A Fourth Estate?" (1984) 18 *Law Society Gazette* 126, make clear the idea of recognizing cultural property as a further class of common law property (in addition to real property, personal property and intellectual property) has been around for some time.

a political or strategic advantage in the use of the cultural heritage concept. But if this is so, it needs to be radicalized, and the obvious path of radicalization seems to lead towards the idea of cultural property. In the end, re-reading or re-conceptualizing cultural heritage as property compels us to face up to the conflict, to decide when community property rights are more important than private property rights, and to put in place workable legal mechanisms to defend those rights.

5 Embedding the market in community

Starting from their current manifestations in positive law, this book attempts to rethink intellectual property and to radicalize cultural heritage. Focussing on the roles of these two areas of legal regulation of cultural production, the book understands intellectual property, and primarily copyright law, as a market right. Cultural heritage, even in its pre-radicalized state, is located somewhere in the processes of community formation and life. Rethinking copyright and radicalizing cultural heritage should not, however, be understood as demonizing the market or as romanticizing community. So far as the market is concerned, as I argue in Chapter 1, the problem with which this book is concerned is the detachment of the market from its social and political roots and the legal encasement, which is the particular hallmark of the neo-liberal period, that protects it from political interference.[75] The potentially devastating effects on social and material life of this encased market are well recognized. Writing of the relationship between the market and social constitutionalism, Christodoulidis comments on a range of strategies – justiciability, the capabilities approach (made famous by Amartya Sen) and proportionality – that have been proposed to limit or blunt the effects of the encased market by prizing apart or punching holes in its defences to let in the concept of the social. Specifically in the context of Sen's very influential capabilities approach, he observes:[76]

> Attractive as the notion of a *social* market is in theory, it has been shown in practice that the market does not entertain predicates lightly. Instead, the market has the unnerving power to enfold and define for itself what is "social" about it, reflexively, so that any *political* attempt to vary market allocations *must* take a form of external limitation, buttress, and containment.[77]

75 See ch 1, section 5.2.

76 See esp A Sen, *Development as Freedom* (New York: Anchor Books, 1999).

77 E Christodoulidis, "Social Rights Constitutionalism: An Antagonistic Endorsement" (2017) 44 *Journal of Law and Society* 123–149, at 139 (italics as in the original). With respect to the capabilities approach in the specific context of intellectual property, cf. Sunder, n 14 above.

Concepts of balancing will not work to produce some virtuous version of the market. Unless the power of the market is limited and contained exogenously, the market itself will come to define the meaning of the social within its own sphere of operation. In the same way that the public domain or the commons has not acted as a limit on the power of the intellectual property system precisely because it is produced by the system itself, the social cannot be a limit on the power of the market when it is defined and produced by the market. It is for this reason that I argue in this book that the market for cultural production must be embedded in community, not balanced against it. Only in this way can the market find its proper role in community.[78]

And what, then, of community? Chapter 4 of this book considers this concept in depth. As is argued there, embracing a concept of community means running some serious risks. For all the liberatory potential that some see in its reflexivity and solidarity, its shared identity and its shared property, others see only suffocation, repression and the danger of narrow, exclusionary and/or extremist positions.[79] The fact that cultural artefacts are often closely implicated in some of these negative expressions of community is a further reason for caution. However, in the context of cultural production, it is not clear what better choice there is than to think about community.[80] Amongst its attributes is its flexibility, its focus on process and the fact that it can express itself on many different levels, which may (or may not) interact and intersect with the concept of community comprised in law by the nation state. It should be clear from the flexible and multilevel nature of community, especially in the context of cultural production, that it cannot express itself exclusively through the form of the nation state. Understanding that the nation state is one of the more problematic manifestations of community, and the one that is particularly implicated in its most negative expressions, militates against such a simple solution. In a post-colonial world, where not all states are equal and where so many peoples are excluded from even the concession of unequal statehood, we cannot think of cultural property as a domain of state ownership. If all this seems to make community too slippery a concept, it is worth bearing in mind that the difficulties in identifying community share a common ground with the difficulty in identifying the market. Both exist; neither is constituted by law; both can be recognized by law even if they tend constantly to evade its disciplinary eye.

In the context of cultural production, the two approaches investigated here for embedding the market in community – rethinking copyright and radicalizing cultural heritage by developing a concept of cultural property – seek to invert the current relationship between privately and non-privately propertized space. That is, instead of privately propertized space determining the contours of its

78 See also ch 4, section 4.

79 See ch 4, section 2.

80 See ch 4, section 2.

non-privately propertized analogue, the privately propertized space of intellectual property should be created and constituted by non-privately propertized space. This strategy does not, however, leave behind the concept of the public domain or the cultural commons. On the contrary, this concept – this space of freedom – is a critically important environment in which to develop the idea of cultural property subject to certain qualifications. As should be evident from the discussion in Chapter 2 and much of the following chapters, I share the concerns about calls for free culture that locate themselves in some idea of the unregulated commons. In their critique of the "free culture" movement and its predominantly US origins, Murray, Piper and Robertson note "its ability, through emphasis on freedom of expression, to resonate with political positions on both the left and the right".[81] Putting their collective finger exactly on the point, they continue:

> However, it is ultimately limited and limiting in its ability to articulate compelling opposition to neoliberal ideologies and models of cultural life. Individualist in its bones, it is weak in its capacity for theorizing power, ideology, or complex collective action and experience.[82]

As Hemmungs Wirtén writes, in the same vein, "[i]n certain instances culture is perhaps best served by not being free, by not being allowed to be used freely, and by not being subjected to free markets, and by not being free from governmental interventions".[83] Nevertheless, the public domain or commons plays a critical role. Partly because, as suggested by Hemmungs-Wirtén, there are circumstances in which culture is served by being free, but also because it performs an important role in constricting the negative manifestations of community. There are serious dangers in the concept of community. Locating the cultural property of communities within a greater discourse of the cultural commons can have a role in limiting those dangers. It is for this reason that we cannot leave the public domain or the cultural commons out of the strategic equation. Instead, the concept of cultural property must be understood as giving architecture to this space so that it can function in order to control the shape and nature of the privately propertized zone.

81 Murray, Piper & Robertson, n 19 above, at 17.

82 Murray, Piper & Roberston, n 19 above, at 18.

83 E Hemmungs Wirtén, "Out of Sight and Out of Mind: On the Cultural Hegemony of Intellectual Property (Critique)" (2006) 20 *Cultural Studies* 282–291, at 289. See also Murray, Piper & Robertson, n 19 above, at 18, who also quote Hemmungs Wirtén, *ibid.*, commenting on the US-based free culture movement:

> The discourse of 'free' may not even resonate in European settings or other settler colony contexts such as Canada, in which the words 'public', 'social' or 'national' may appear more often than 'free,' indicating a tolerance for, or even expectation of, regulation or negotiation amongst groups or parties.

5.1 Rethinking copyright

The current copyright system, which represents a vehicle for the accumulation of capital globally, is not one that can be subjugated to, or embedded in, a liberatory concept of community cultural production. This is demonstrated by my critique of the political economy of copyright in Chapter 1.[84] To briefly summarize that critique, the legal characterization of copyright as a private property right belonging, at least initially, not only to those who invest immaterial labour in creating copyright works but also to those who invest in their production and distribution has made it into an investment right and, thus, a site of global capital accumulation. The monopoly power of the media and entertainment corporations, within whose domains this capital is accumulated, is self-perpetuating – not only in a socio-economic sense, but also in a political and legal sense.[85] Consequently, this highly concentrated, vertically and horizontally integrated, group of market players uses its power to procure the extension of intellectual property laws in ways that reinforce its global reach and dominance. Extensive social costs are produced by this state of affairs. Immaterial labour is appropriated with, in most cases, minimal returns to those who have created works of cultural and economic values. Cultural production becomes an object of consumption rather than a process of dialogic engagement.[86] Cultural diversity shrinks and withers. The power of Western capital over Western and non-Western cultural production distorts that cultural production, while at the same time expanding Western law and political power globally. The very thing that copyright claims to be in some way about – cultural creativity in the arts – turns out to be little more than verbiage to sustain a system of global capitalist dominance.

If this sounds like a damning account of the copyright system, then its objective has been achieved. What might be the building blocks of a radical rethinking of this system? I suggest that there are three of them. The first is that system must be based on the proposition that cultural production and the use of cultural goods, services and other intangible resources are a part of the same process. This means that every moment of cultural production implies the use in some form of cultural products or resources that already exist. So, in this sense, cultural production is always a collective undertaking. However, acknowledging

84 See ch 1, section 5.

85 See also J E Stiglitz, "Economic Foundations of Intellectual Property Rights" (2008) 57 *Duke Law Journal* 1693–1724, at 1705.

86 I cannot resist here quoting the always eloquent Frederic Jameson, writing in a different context, who observes in "Time and the Sea", (16 April 2020) 42(8) *London Review of Books* 29–30, at 30:

> Marxian debates about value and immaterial labour are scarcely exotic or superfluous when they concern a system in which universal consumerism tends to conceal production in favour of distribution, a category that includes not only circulation and exchange as such, but also the full-blown ideology of communication and information that has become our dominant mode of understanding in a media society.

that cultural production is a collective process does not mean that individuals should be required to abandon their rights with respect to specific instances of that process for which they are responsible. So the second building block of a new system is that creators should have the right to be recognized and remunerated for their work.[87] This moves things in the direction of authors' rights systems, subject to the qualification that the authors can only be the human persons whose immaterial labour produces cultural value. There is no place here for the *ersatz* (usually corporate) author of the existing copyright system that attains this status by the expenditure of capital in production and distribution. Third, an accommodation must be found between the importance of securing this outcome and the recognition that, by its nature, cultural creativity in the arts is a common good. What is needed, therefore, is a balance inside the re-thought copyright system between individual (private) rights and the collective interest in stimulating cultural production and a dialogical relationship with that production. This means the reinvigoration of a system of defences and exceptions to the exercise of authors' rights. As mentioned earlier, the existing copyright system already has a potentially robust collection of exceptions and defences, which have been subject to contraction under the pressure of capitalist power expressed through inequalities in bargaining positions, vastly unequal access to the judicial system, and extensive political lobbying with the object of changing the law in order to protect what are argued to be fundamental property rights.[88]

This brings us to the question of whether authors' rights in a re-thought system should retain the character of private property rights. Private property rights can, of course, have a place in community, provided that they are subject to the mutual obligations of community. As Chapter 4 seeks to demonstrate – with the aid of the series case studies by Murray, Piper and Robertson – creative communities often find their own equilibrium between community obligations and norms, on the one hand, and the market access offered by copyright, on the other.[89] The problem is that the higher the stakes in economic terms, the more likely it is that the property right will dictate the terms of cultural and creative production, lifting it out of the mutual obligations of community and into the market for investment rights. This is why copyright's character as a private property right is at the heart of the critique of the political economy of copyright in this book.[90] It is for this reason that it has become an investment right; and it is for this reason that it has acquired the power to shape tangible and intangible spaces, defining hierarchical relations within that space.[91] As the discussion of

87 On the fate of immaterial labour in the current system, see ch 1, section 5.3.

88 On the potential of this system, see, e.g., R J Coombe, D Wershler & M Zeilinger (eds), *Dynamic Fair Dealing: Creating Canadian Culture Online* (Toronto: University of Toronto Press, 2014).

89 See further ch 4, section 4.

90 See ch 1, section 5.1.

91 See ch 1, sections 5.1 and 5.4; ch 4, section 4; ch 6, sections 3–5.

the so-called copyright wars in Chapter 1 shows, not all justifications or theoretical elaborations of copyright rely on its characterization as a property right.[92] In fact, it is only in the copyright maximalist position that this claim is made with fervour, mainly by representatives of the media and entertainment corporate sector. Neither the claim that copyright is a fundamental speech right nor that it is instrumental to stimulating cultural production depends on a property model. Removing its character as a property right is not to deprive it of a life in the market place; and this is important because it is this life that will allow the real authors of protected works to make a living off them without the present compromising effects on the social processes of community. The risk here is, of course, to the systems of production of costly creative works – in particular, film in its various manifestations (feature films, television series, documentaries) – and more generally to the distribution of the results of cultural production. Specifically, the concern is that without investors in production and distribution channels, the ability of the creators of copyright works to live by them in a material sense will be compromised. If these producers and distributors can no longer acquire a property right upon which to generate surplus profits, will they desert the field leaving us instead with a surplus of unmade ideas and undistributed cultural products? In a world where technology has democratized production and distribution, it is hard to take this concern seriously.[93] It may be, of course, that the global media and entertainment giants that currently make up a large part of the production and distribution sector lose interest in it. However, the idea of a world comprised by a plethora of small independent producers and distributors is not an unwelcome one.

I have argued earlier that a concept of cultural property, rather than one of heritage, has the strategic advantage of making direct reference to the clash of concepts with which this book has been concerned. Further, in substantive terms, a more fully articulated idea of cultural property has a better chance of standing up to the might of the private property concept and thus to offer a bulwark against its continual expansion into the domains of cultural production. Of course, if copyright – while remaining a private right – were no longer to be a property right, this would change the relative balance between the two forms. A cultural property right would have more space to flower and develop its role as an artefact of community. But even outside such a radical change in the copyright system, the concept of cultural property, for which the following and final section seeks to lay down a blueprint, is designed to advance the process of embedding the market for cultural products in the reciprocal obligations and social processes of community. In this second and slower version, where cultural property must still contend with the private rights of intellectual property, it might be helpful

92 See ch 1, section 4.

93 Although it does raise the question of the regulation of the power of the communications technology sector.

to think of the process of embedding as arising from a "slow pedagogy" turning "on the potential release of learning processes that dovetail with the embeddedness, and re-embedding, of practices".[94]

5.2 Radicalizing cultural (heritage/)property

To employ the concept of cultural property is, as argued in Section 4, in some respects to return to a concept that previously enjoyed prominence in the UNESCO system. However, radical alterations must be made to it in order to endow it with the capacity to operationalize the embedding of the market for cultural products in the social processes of community. In making these alterations, the contradictions between the legally well-worn concept of rivalrous private property, the collective concept of cultural property and the cultural commons (or public domain) must be embraced as consequences of lived experiences for which no categorizations in (Western) legal or political thought seem to exist. It is the contradictions that carry the radical potential. As Christodoulidis argues of contradictions (in the context of social rights constitutionalism):

> They point ... to a shortfall of the categories available to us to make sense of the processes of value production and social reproduction, the mismatch between the categories of thought and the modes of social being. Their emergence as contradictions marks the crisis points of articulation, of expressibility, and of intelligibility: of meaninglessness that is experienced as such. It is important to emphasize this experiential dimension, the lived incomprehensibility (the "Dasein" of the contradiction, as it were) that emerges in particular experiential contexts and that carries its potential energies. It is the lived dimension that is the potential site of disruption of the economy of representation that would otherwise organize meaning, seal it over and, in this state of self-immunization, place it out of reach.[95]

Much is asked here of the concept of cultural property – contradictory in its own right – which must be strong enough to provide a bulwark against private property rights without replicating their intrinsically rivalrous character. It needs to transcend outdated thinking that divides property rights between public (as in state) and private rights holders. It needs to provide safeguards against the unauthorized interference with, appropriation of, or damage to, processes of community formation expressed through cultural production. It needs to be flexible enough to exist in the interlocking community relations that make up the

94 Christodoulids, n 77 above, at 143–144, citing F Atria, "Social Rights, Social Contract, and Socialism" (2015) 24 *Social and Legal Studies* 598–613.

95 Christodoulidis, n 77 above, at 144–145.

cultural commons. As I have argued earlier, its location in the cultural commons gives it some immunity from the dangers of the type of exclusivity or essentialism that constrains cultural interchange and finds its expression in oppressive political formations. In this way, the concept of cultural property can find ways of co-existing with some of the promises of a cosmopolitan vision of the world without that vision itself becoming a manifestation of Western global homogenization. Accordingly, what is proposed in the present account is a type of architecture of the cultural commons that is based on a radicalization of the concept of property itself, while also re-engaging with the idea of the regulated commons.[96] The discussion below investigates three possible strategies for realizing a concept of community cultural property as part of the architecture of a regulated cultural commons. These are a stewardship model, the idea of cultural property as *res universitatis*, and the potential uses of the existing legal concept of geographical indications.

Stewardship model

The proposal of Carpenter, Katyal and Riley for a stewardship model of cultural property, which specifically aims to vindicate the cultural property claims of Indigenous Peoples, seeks to find a liberatory use of the property paradigm that transcends its current narrow legal focus on private rights, and on the distinction between private property and some form of publicly held property.[97] Effectively, this stewardship model uses the property paradigm without replicating those aspects of traditional property law that have already been identified as problematic in the context of cultural production. Theoretically, the model is located in Radin's work on the constitutive relationship between property and personhood, in which she argues that some forms of property are constitutive of identity in ways that take them out of the normal processes of the market place:[98]

> Radin's account of personhood captures precisely the meaning that cultural property may carry for indigenous people: that some properties are so constitutive of one's identity that they demand treatment that transcends – and surpasses – that of an ordinary market transaction. It is quite legitimate in Radin's view, to make exceptions to the prevailing 'universal commodification' standard for property that is nonfungible, incommensurable, and inalienable, as some indigenous cultural properties surely are.[99]

96 As Hemmungs Wirtén, n 14 above, shows, the real property commons was always regulated.

97 Carpenter, Katyal & Riley, n 58 above.

98 M J Radin, "Property & Personhood" (1982) 34 *Stanford Law Review* 957; M J Radin, *Contested Commodities* (Cambridge, MA: Harvard University Press, 1996).

99 Carpenter, Katyal & Riley, n 58 above at 1022, referring to and quoting Radin (1996), n 98 above, at 8–15.

To use Radin's work in this way, however, requires a transition from her emphasis on the relationship between individual personhood and property to a concern with the relationship between peoplehood and property that is implicated in the idea of a group claim. In laying the groundwork for this development of the argument, Carpenter, Katyal and Riley do not neglect the possibility that some Indigenous claims to property maybe located in personhood rather than peoplehood.[100] However, their emphasis is on community rights. They are fully aware that arguments about community rights often appear to be teetering on the edge of the type of essentialism that suggests cultural (and political) closure.[101] For this reason, their model builds in a notion of community rights that is capable of resting on more than one level of identity, thus moving away from an essentialist position. In relation to Indigenous Peoples, this type of multilevel identity is often present and is increasingly legally embedded in national regimes.[102]

Whether the elegant and persuasive use of the property concept embedded in the stewardship model, which is intended to address the situation of Indigenous Peoples, can function as well outside the context of Indigenous cultural property claims is open to question. The fact, as Carpenter, Katyal and Riley note, that the identity and claims of Indigenous Peoples as a community are already recognizable within the legal environment of many states in which Indigenous communities live is, ironically, a reaction to the dispossession and loss of political autonomy visited upon them in the colonial and post-colonial periods. At the same time, it is this very environment of legally recognized identity, in the context of multi-layered identities, that may make the stewardship model functional for Indigenous Peoples. Further, their suggestion that the use of the property paradigm in their stewardship model is an appropriate response to the massive land dispossession suffered by Indigenous Peoples everywhere militates against the use of the model as a paradigm of cultural property outside the context of the cultural property of Indigenous Peoples.

While recognizing that the treatment of Indigenous Peoples in the colonial and post-colonial period, especially the denial of political autonomy, makes their case particular, I have argued at some length in this book that *sui generis* solutions for the protection of the cultural property of Indigenous Peoples are problematic.[103] They are problematic for Indigenous Peoples for two reasons.

100 Carpenter, Katyal & Riley, n 58 above, at 1022–1023:

> Following Radin, we observe that some indigenous cultural property claims may well fall into these categories of property that are critical for personal development, either because the property forms the context for human individuation or because individual rights are exercised in a collective setting.
>
> (Footnotes omitted)

101 See also ch 4, section 2 & 3; & ch 5, section 4.1.

102 See, in relation to the US, Carpenter, Katyal & Riley, n 58 above, at 1056–1059.

103 See ch 2, section 4; ch 3, section 4; ch 4, section 5; ch 5, esp section 5.

First, they are used to obfuscate, ignore and deny claims for political sovereignty. Secondly, they do not represent the lived experience of Indigenous Peoples and other peoples of the global South, which is the experience of being both Indigenous/non-Western and, at the same time, living within Western capitalist mainstream. *Sui generis* solutions are also damaging to the rest of us. They suggest that the only interests that we have in cultural production are those recognized and institutionalized by intellectual property rights; and they deny us the possibility of learning from the experience of Indigenous Peoples how to reconcile community processes of cultural production with rivalrous private rights to cultural products. While the stewardship model of Carpenter, Katyal and Riley takes into account, and even operationalizes, the different identities of Indigenous Peoples – as Indigenous Peoples, citizens of nation states and also as participants in the mechanisms of global capitalism – the fact that it appears to be (and to the extent that it is) a *sui generis* solution means that it falls outside the concept of cultural property proposed in this book.

5.2.1 *Res universitatis*

In seeking to develop the concept of a regulated cultural commons, we do not have to re-invent the wheel even if we might need to add a few modern adaptations to it. As Chapter 2 shows, Roman law contained a complex architecture of non-privately owned tangible space.[104] Contrary to the modern tendency to make a sharp division between the closure of private property and the openness of the commons, Roman law admitted shades of meaning and complications of form. Even though the cultural commons is a space that crosses the putative boundaries between tangible and intangible, some of the concepts that make up the architecture of openness in Roman law might be fruitfully adapted for its purposes. The difference between what is subject to public or collective ownership, what cannot by its nature be owned and what is unowned is reflected in the interactions of the concepts of *res publicae*, *res communes* and *res nullius*. The associated recognition that some things should never be owned privately because of their cultural significance can be developed and adapted from the concept of *res divini juris*, which prevented the ownership of sacred or religious things because it would confer too much power on the owner. The development of the concept of group and communal rights, belonging to less than the public as a whole, bounded by property on the outside, but inside promoting freedom and space for creativity, innovation, invention and cultural conservation is embodied in the concept of *res universitatis*.

Translated into modern terms, *res univeritatis* refers to a type of property that surrounds the productive activities of a group. From the outside, those activities are protected by a shell or shield of property rights, but inside activities are not

104 See ch 2, esp section 5.

constrained by property relations.[105] The result is that inside the shell, there is freedom from property restraints: freedom of speech, freedom to innovate and create, freedom to produce knowledge, freedom of use, freedom to exchange ideas, freedom to develop the ideas of others. This form can be understood as a possible corrective to the concern, often used to justify the grant of private intellectual property rights, that without them there would be no incentive to create or innovate.[106] This is because it preserves productive synergies within the relevant group or community while maintaining the incentive to produce such synergies through the exercise of rights against outsiders. I am, however, not particularly concerned about its credentials in this respect. As I have argued in Chapters 1 and 2, the idea that property rights are needed to stimulate creativity or innovation misunderstands the nature of those two concepts.[107] In any case, the nature of community rights in cultural property cannot be understood in the intellectual property frame of reference with its focus on the rivalrous individual owner. The concept of cultural property in play here is one that is held up by membership of a community.[108] What is interesting about the form of *res universitatis* is its reflection of the social processes of community cultural production and its capacity to confer defensive rights on the community in respect of them. Further, it contains no necessary contradiction to the idea of individual rights over particular manifestations of creativity, subject to the practices and determinations of the community.

5.2.2 Cultural property as a geographical indication?

That all invocations of the idea of the cultural property of communities run up against the problem of identifying community must be regarded as a given.[109] Legal accounts of community, of course, exist. Despite the paucity (both quantitative and qualitative) of references to the concept of community in international law instruments, it is clear that there is a substantial engagement with this concept in national legal systems. Given the reflexive relationship between community and cultural heritage, which is acknowledged at least in the CICH, it is not surprising to discover that this engagement sometimes takes place in the context of the regulation of cultural heritage. National laws recognizing the cultural heritage of Indigenous Peoples or of ethnic or linguistic minorities are examples of this. To some extent, these types of rights reflect obligations (actual or hortatory) in international law even though their origins might not be directly

105 For a description of *res universitatis*, see C M Rose, "Romans, Roads and Romantic Creators: Traditions of Public Property in the Information Age" (2003) 66 *Law & Contemporary Problems* 89–110, at 105–108.

106 See ch 1, section 4; ch 2, section 2.

107 See ch 1, section 5.6; ch 2, section 2.

108 See Keenan, n 68 above.

109 See ch 4, section 3.

attributable to such obligations. However, there are also other well-known examples in national law of the recognition of community and associated community right. It is common, for example, for legal systems to recognize community rights in property based on customary use.[110] An interesting variation on this is the recognition, nationally and internationally, of certain rights associated with the marking of products made in a certain geographical location.[111] With this in mind, this section considers whether the concept of geographical indications might offer a model for the protection of cultural property. The very idea marks the turning of an ironic full circle: to embrace it would mean finding that national and international intellectual property law already contains the germ of a cultural property model.[112] This casts an interesting light on the strenuous resistance of common law countries, under pressure from their corporate sectors, to the inclusion of geographical indications in the WTO TRIPs Agreement.[113]

The concept of protected geographical indications, exceptionally for an intellectual property right, grants a collective right rather than a private individual right. Specifically, a recognized geographical indication gives a right to every person that sells products coming from a certain geographical region and having particular qualities on account of that provenance to apply the indication to their products. Cultural property often has a geographical dimension in the sense that it is formed around communities in a particular place and that place is part of the dynamic that holds the community together.[114] There are, however, two fairly obvious problems with seeing this as a solution for recognizing community cultural property generally. One of them is that common geographical location is not necessarily a characteristic of all

110 A Clarke, "Property, Human Rights and Communities", in T Xu & J Allain (eds), *Property and Human Rights in a Global Context* (Oxford & Portland: Hart, 2015).

111 N Aylwin & R Coombe, "Marks Indicating Conditions of Origin in Rights-Based Sustainable Development" in R Buchanan & P Zumbansen (eds), *Human Rights, Development and Restorative Justice: An Osgoode Reader* (Oxford: Hart, 2013).

112 At the level of international law, see the TRIPs Agreement, Arts 22–24.

113 On the role of corporate sector in the TRIPs Agreement negotiations, see S Sell, *Private Power, Public Law: The Globalization of Intellectual Property Rights* (Cambridge & New York: Cambridge University Press, 2003). On the contestations around the system of geographical indications, see G E Evans & M Blakeney, "The Protection of Geographical Indications after Doha: Quo Vadis?" (2006) 9 *Journal of International Economic Law* 575–614.

114 Cf.

> Culture is knowledge and skills that flow *socially* from individual to individual and generation to generation. It's not in genes. Socially learned skills, traditions and dialects that answer the question of 'how we live here' are crucial to helping many populations survive – or recover. Crucially, culturally learned skills vary from place to place.

C Safina, "The Secret Call of the Wild: How Animals Teach Each Other to Survive", *The Guardian*, 9 April 2020, https://www.theguardian.com/environment/2020/apr/09/the-secret-call-of-the-wild-how-animals-teach-each-other-to-survive-aoe, accessed 09/04/2020.

communities. The other is that geographical indications are market rights (to sell products using particular marks). The first of these objections begs the question of whether it would be feasible to adopt instead a concept of "community indications", where common geographical location is one significant, but not a determinative, indicium. The second objection is not such a serious challenge to the idea of community cultural property as it may sound at first blush. I have already argued that there is nothing incongruous about the idea of market relations existing in the context of community. The market that is embedded in community is one that is subject to the mutual obligations that constitute community.[115] The question would be whether the construction of this market right can be made coherent with the idea that community cultural production is process, rather than product, based; and, if it could, there might be a further question about the progressive effects of subsuming those processes in a product.

Perhaps, then, the already existing concept of geographical indications made over into a system of "community indications" can be used to protect at least some types of cultural property in the context of market relations. If it seems anomalous to make use of a device currently recognized as a part of intellectual property law for this purpose, then perhaps it is worth reflecting that the real anomaly is the concept of geographical indications, located in the intellectual property camp, but in reality a collective right. What militates in favour of its use is that such a right would seem to be capable of responding to many of the needs of cultural property identified in this book. It could contribute to controlling the unauthorized appropriation and use of a community's cultural property; by recognizing communities that are not co-terminus with the nation state form, it is capable of transcending the problematic and antiquated idea that property must be either public (in the sense of belonging to the state) or private; it may allow for distinctions between free and open access to community property, and between access and use, depending on the choices and processes of the community; and if correctly conceived, it could provide safeguards against the dangers of a type of exclusivity that is oppressive and limits cultural interchange and development. Given, however, its life as a market right focussed on the sale of a final product, it may be more appropriately (re)conceived as one aspect of a larger cultural property right. For this larger right, the model provided by *res universitatis* seems a promising starting point.

6 A last (short) word on heritage as a cosmopolitan ideal

In this book, I have argued for a political project that invokes law's political register and its capacity for transformation – both of itself and of its subjects. I

115 See ch 4, section 4.

have argued for the winding back of the intellectual property, and specifically the copyright, regime; and I have argued for the development of new models of cultural property. Despite prevaricating for most of the book, I have opted for a concept of cultural property as being better equipped for the job of embedding the market in community than that of cultural heritage. But I wonder if we can dispense entirely with the idea of heritage understood as a cosmopolitan concept – that is, with the idea of the common heritage of humanity? The argument that, in the end, it is not necessary to choose between heritage and cultural property has value in this respect.[116] In the thicket of the regulated commons and its many sites of community cultural property, is there a place for things that belong to everybody just by virtue of being human (or even just being a sentient being)? These might include things like our natural environment, and the life and health-preserving benefits of research and knowledge production wherever it takes place and by whomever it takes place. Does the heritage of humanity also lie in the intersections and connections of communities, and their cultural processes and products? Certainly, to lose the focus on the importance of these things in favour of a more particular notion of the cultural property of communities would be to cut off our collective human nose in spite of our face.

Prevaricating, then, to The End.

116 Cf. Frigo, n 35 above; see Section 4.

Index

Abrahams, R. D. 171, 172
aesthetic theory 8–11
African Digital Cultural Heritage 117
Akagawa, N. 136
Al-Badri, Nora 142
Anangu people 151, 152, 156
Anderson, B. 95, 96, 101
anti-copyright crew 21
anti-copyright position 21
arts festivals: concept of 4, 8, 159, 160; copyright interests 162; copyright law and creativity 9; copyright works 168–170; cultural heritage/property 174, 175; definitions 160–162; ephemeral performances 167; interactive works 167–168; modern copyright protection of 8–9; performance and text 166–167; proliferation of 159
"associative cultural landscape" 154
Australian Indigenous Peoples 124, 125, 156
Australian National Parks and Wildlife Service 151, 156
authentic digital representation 142
authenticity 140–150, 141, 142, 145, 148
authorial creativity, concepts of 181
authorized heritage discourse 63, 64, 83, 91, 92, 123
authors/authorship 4, 7, 11; author/owner distinction 27–28; civil law concept of 13; conception of 178; copyright's concept of 20, 27; creative input 181; interactive works 167–168; of misappropriation 123; ownership function 119

The Background (Saki) 1–4
Bataille, Georges 144
Berlin's Neues Museum 142
Berne Convention for the Protection of Literary and Artistic Works (1886) 13, 15
Blake, J. 90
Bowrey, K. 155, 156
Braudel, F. 24
Bretton Woods diplomatic conference 62
British Museum 131, 133, 136
Buddhas of Bamijan 119, 120, 140
Butler, C. 123

Canada's National Research Council 107
Cannes Film Festival 160
capabilities approach 196
capital accumulation process 180, 184
capitalism 34, 150, 152, 176, 205
capitalist steamroller 157–158
capital, mechanisms of 126
Carpenter, K. A. 203–205
Cartesian binary distinctions 150, 178
Cartesian dualisms 3, 5, 63, 91, 92, 154
Christodoulidis, E. 101, 196, 202
Cocteau, Jean 160
colonialization 132, 142
commodification 24, 27, 37, 54, 83, 90, 110, 126, 138, 139, 140, 157, 161, 163, 184
common heritage of humanity 83, 84, 90, 116, 125, 133, 134, 178, 179, 209
common language and religion 103
common political identity 93, 103
commons/cultural commons 30, 35, 38, 40, 46, 55, 57, 59, 198, 202, 205
communal intellectual property rights 55
community 128; artists and tattooists 105; community rights 103; complex reality 108–111; concept of 128; consequences of 104; constitutive relationship 75; constitutive social

process 92; and copyright law 104–108; cultural heritage/property 70–71, 93, 202–208; cultural practices 114; cultural production 170–172; and cultural stuff 139; etymological reading 97; fascism and totalitarianism 97; fundamental relationship 186; identification of 102; immune tolerance concept 98; intangible cultural heritage 75–79; and intangibles 139; international legal regime 102–104; liberatory concept of 199; mutual relationship, heritage 75; nothingness – no-thingness 98; philosophies of 94; political theory 93; post-colonial world 197; recognizing community 94–102; reflexivity and solidarity 197; rethinking copyright 199–202; selective narrative of 97; temporal aspect of 96
community-based social process 174
community of origin 122, 132, 137, 141
community rights 182
community space, re-appropriating 174–176
Congress of Aix-la-Chapelle of 1818 62
conservation 3, 5, 57, 58, 116, 128, 136–140, 137, 206
contemporary art market 106
copyright: aesthetic theory 8–11; and consequences 7–11; creativity and innovation 10, 35–37; cultural production, property rights 37–39; economic benefit from 11; geo-political impact of 34; geo-political projection of 36; history of 7–11; idea/expression dichotomy 10; intellectual property rights 31; in international law 11–16; investment rights 24–26; labour 27–31; market paradigm 24–26; market regulation 8–11; in market regulation 11; political economy of 13, 22; politics of 16–21; printers' privileges 8–11; property paradigm 22–24; regulation of creativity 7–8; romantic discourse of 13, 14; state and geo-politics 31–34; subject matter of 8
copyright law 9, 167–168; authorship/ownership function 119; "dramatic work" in 169; idea/expression dichotomy 10; incentive-based justification 12; legal framework of 15; multi-party conflicts 17; natural rights theory 12; political economy of 23; primary creative works 11; primary function of 11; property right 12; rhetorical aesthetic theory 10, 11; romantic conception 14; three-step test 15
Copyright Policy and the Right to Science and Culture 184
copyright protection: commercial distribution 170; copyright's scheme of 9; copyright works 168–170; ephemeral performances 167; interactive works 167–168; modern systems of 8; performance and text 166–167
"copyright wars" 16, 17, 200–201
copyright works 9, 33, 168–170
cosmopolitanism 99, 209
cosmopolitan position 99
cosmopolitan vision 134
Council of Europe's 2005 Framework Convention on the Value of Cultural Heritage for Society (Faro Convention) 77
counterspaces, development of 175, 176
creative industries 22, 108
creativity 35–37; authorial creativity concept 181; conditions of 12; and copyright law 9; and cultural innovation 35; cultural redefinition of 36; idea/type of 9; intellectual space 41; "necessity of industry" 37; regulation of 7–8; rhetorical paradigm of 8; Western concepts of 35, 36
critical heritage studies 5, 92, 96
cultural artefacts 51, 52, 60, 62, 72, 122, 139, 140, 197
"cultural colonization" 135
cultural diversity 63–67, 120, 135, 161, 174, 199
cultural hegemony 34
cultural heritage/property 3, 51–57, 112, 154; authentic piece of 142, 143; authorized heritage discourse 92; Buddhas of Bamijan in Afghanistan 119, 120; central foundational concepts 95; commercialization of 110; commodification 139; community management of 148; community, property 70–71; community role and rights 95; concept of 52; concepts of 7; consistent and coherent policy 118; and cultural heritage 52; democratization

of 120; features of 53; geographical indication 206–208; groups of buildings 68; humanity and cultural diversity 120–121; identification and enjoyment of 100; individual and community rights 56; "inherent contradiction" 90–91; intellectual property rights 53; international law concept of 66; mankind/humanity 64; monuments 68; national identity 70–71; neo-imperialist misappropriation 122; non-propertized domain 57; non-Western knowledge 56; overarching concept 69–70; philosophical and legal concept of 60; post-colonial discourse of 112; private intellectual property 116; privatization of 87–88, 122; protection of 112; public *vs.* private claims 88–90; *res universitatis* 205–206; social and political process 121; stewardship model 203–205; tangibility and intangibility 114; UNESCO regime 66–69
cultural landscape 154, 156
cultural production 159; authorial acts of 182; capital accumulation 181; commodification of 184; community-based processes of 187; fundamental role of 14; legal regulation in 196; non-propertized space of 38; oligopolistic global market for 21
"cultural re-transmission" 135
cultural rights 184–186; "category" problem 195; contribution of 185; copyright, critique of 185; cosmopolitan ideal 209; liberatory concepts 186
cultural self-determination 63
"cultural space" 173
cultural value 35; copyright's system of 36; natural and cultural heritage 114; socio-economic institution 161
"customary practices" 80

dance community 167
Danish cultural heritage 129–130
Danish People's Party 129–130
De Angelis. M. 183
decolonization: and cultural property 83–84; developing countries, claims of 84–87; Indigenous Peoples 84–87; privatization, cultural heritage 87–88; public *vs.* private claims 88–90; tangibility and intangibility 87–88
decontextualization 113, 132–136
dematerialization 118
democratization 120
designs and symbols 55
destruction 136–140
Dickinson, Emily 145
digital art 165, 169
digital artefacts 118, 121, 122
digitization 114–123; access and use 120–121; co-constitution 118–119; of cultural artefacts 122; dematerialization 118; intellectual property 121–123; re-representation 118–119
Disney 146
Douzinas, C. 175
"dramatic work" in copyright law 169
Drassinower, A. 19
Dumbarton Oaks diplomatic conference 62
Durkheim, E. 160

Edelman, B. 23, 26, 29, 30, 36
"Elgin" Marbles 131, 136
Eliot, T. S. 145, 146
encyclopaedic collection 132, 133
"encyclopaedic museum" 120, 134
Enns, D. 97, 98
entrepreneurial copyright work 11
ephemeral performances 167
Esposito, R. 94, 95, 97, 98, 101, 129
"ethics"-based system 188, 189
European agrarian festivals 174
European colonization 127
European cultural artefacts 60

fair use/fair dealing 164, 165, 166
fascism and totalitarianism 97
festival concept 161
festival space: audience participation 162; and community 170–172; cultural production 170–172; law in 172–174
film festivals 162, 163
First Nation Peoples 146
Fisher, W. 38
Fleming, Ian 144
Fraysse, O. 30
"free culture" movement 198
free trade 62, 65
fundamental speech right 201

geographical indication 206–208
geo-political concept 6–7

geo-political movements 60–66
geopolitical power 99
Ghetto, Drohobycz 127
GLAM sector 116, 121–123, 136, 141
global north 33, 34, 83, 89, 116, 150, 186
global south 5, 6, 16, 33, 157, 205
Goonetilake. S. 135
Graham, B. 102
Graham, N. 155, 156
Greene, Graham 144, 145
"groups of buildings" 124
Guerzoni, G. 161

Hafstein, V. Tr. 188–191
Hague Convention (1954) 66
Halbert, D. J. 34
Harrison, R. 74
"hierarchisation" of geographical space 124
"high culture" bias 35–36
Hobbesian anti-community claim 99
Howard, P. 102
Hugo, Victor 144
humanity 52, 54, 71, 78, 83, 84, 90, 99, 120–121, 125, 179, 209
human rights 17, 50, 62, 66, 186
human rights law 63

Icelandic identity 131
idea/expression dichotomy 8, 10, 143
Iliad (Homer) 146
imagining intellectual space 40–42, 53
immoveability 123–127
immoveable cultural stuff 113, 127
immune tolerance 98
imperialism 89, 116, 133
Indigenous Peoples 34, 52, 84, 86, 111, 115, 122, 136, 138, 147; cultural property 203; post-colonial condition of 148; *sui generis* protection 177
individual and community rights 56
innovation 35–37
intangibility 114–123
intangible cultural artefacts 140
intellectual property rights 3, 4, 13, 31; cultural rights 185; international law-makers 32; political economy of 22; private and public spaces 33; tangibility and intangibility 115; "trade-related" aspects of 14; TRIPs Agreement 13–15
intellectual public domain 41
intellectual space: concept of 42; cultural property/heritage 51–57; definition of 40; exclusive rights 48; free speech 51; hyperreal space 40; imaginary domain of 40, 42; modern notion of 43; non-propertized zone 45, 48; non-rivalrous 42; non-wasteable 42; ownership concept 44, 45; property power 48–51; property rights in 48; public domain 41, 43; symbiotic relationship 49; traditional cultural property 55
interactive works 167–168
international copyright landscape 15, 16
International Covenant on Economic, Social and Cultural Rights: Article 15(1)(a) 185; Article 15(1)(c) 185
investment rights 24–27, 181, 200
It's a Battlefield (Greene) 144, 145

jazz and blues music 165
Johns. A. 33
Joint Anti-Piracy Intelligence Group 34
JyskeLov (Jutlandic Law) 130, 131

Katyal, S. 203–205
Kill, R. 161

Landau, Felix 127
Lawrence, D. 171, 172
Laye, Camara 144
Le Devoir de violence (Ouologuem) 144, 145
Lefebvre, H. 175
Liang, L. 38
liberalism 190
literary festivals 166
Locke, J. 27, 28
Lowenthal, D. 91

Mabo case 125
Manheim, Ralph 144
market: capabilities approach 196; and community 99; in community 196–198; for cultural objects and artefacts 194; for cultural production 186–187; cultural (heritage/) property 202–208; investment rights 200; rethinking copyright 199–202; and social constitutionalism 196
market-based thinking 194
market economy 24, 46

market paradigm 24–26
market regulation 8–11
de Maupassant, Guy 144
Mausoleum of Halicarnassus 131
McTeague: A Story of San Francisco (Norris) 145
modernity 74, 180
monological corporate culture 14
monumentality 123–127
monumental occidental tragedy: authenticity 140–150; capitalist steamroller 157–158; conservation and destruction 136–140; decontextualization 132–136; digitization stuff 114–123; immovability and monumentality 123–127; moving targets 127–128; nature and culture 150–156; origin and community 128–132; physical destruction of 137; tangible/intangible distinction 112–123
Moore, J. W. 150
moral rights 27
moveable cultural property 64
moveable cultural stuff 113, 123
Murray, L. J. 26, 31, 56, 106, 107, 143, 145, 147
Museum for the United Nations: UN Live 134
museums: digitization 117; "encyclopaedic" museum 134
music festivals 162–164
Music production companies 25
mutual obligation 6, 105, 108, 109, 200, 208

Nancy, J. -L. 104, 129
Napoleon 138
Napoleonic Wars 60, 62
natural rights theory 12, 18
nature/culture distinction 150, 154
"Nefertiti Hack" 142
Nelles, Jan Nikolai 142
neo-imperialist misappropriation 122
neoliberalism 33, 190, 191
Neues Museum 142
New International Economic Order 190
nihilism, polar opposite of 97
non-propertized zone 45–46, 48, 50, 182
non-Western cultural production 146, 177
non-Western knowledge and culture 55–56
non-Western Peoples 115, 173
Norris, Frank 145

O'Grady, R. 161
O'Neill, M. 30
OpenGLAM Principles 120
Ouologuem, Yambo 144, 145
"outstanding universal value" 68, 69, 72
ownership 44, 45, 83, 91, 127, 128, 135, 183

Parthenon Marbles 136
Pascoe, B. 124–126
Patent law 34, 44, 55
Patent protection 153
Pavis, M. 117, 120
peoplehood and property relationship 204
physical space: concept of 42; limitations of 42; in Roman law principles 43
Piazza San Marco 138
Pincini, Andreas 1
Piper, S. T. 26, 31, 56, 106, 107, 143, 145, 147
poetry festivals 166
Polanyi, K. 24
Porsdam, H. 130
post-colonial cultural appropriation 79
post-colonial discourse 130
post-Westphalian international law 60
"primitivist" school of art 140
printers' privileges 8–11
private-property-free zone 32
pro-copyright positions 20
property paradigm 22–24
"prosumers" 30
pseudo-cosmopolitanism 100
public domain/commons 40, 41, 43, 57, 181, 182
public international law 65

Radin, M. J. 203
regulation of creativity 7–8
res publicae, concept of 47
res universitatis 58, 59, 203, 205–206, 208
rethinking copyright 199–202
rhetorical aesthetic theory 8, 10, 11
"rights"-based system 188
Riley, A. 203–205
Robbe-Grillet, Alain 144
Robertson, K. 26, 29, 31, 56, 106, 107, 143, 145, 147
rock/folk/blues music festivals 164

Roman law concepts 43, 45, 57–59; private property rights 59; *res communes* 57, 58; *res divini juris* 58; *res publicae* 57, 58; *res universitatis* 58, 59
Rome Convention for the Protection of Performers, Producers of Phonograms and Broadcasting Organizations (1961) 13
Rose, N. 47

Saki (H H Munro) 1–4
Sarr-Savoy Report 2018 117
Schulz, Bruno 127–129
Second Treatise (Locke) 17
Second World War 61, 62, 83, 107, 127
self-determination 85
Sen, A. 196
Settlement of Vienna of 1815 62
"sharing economy" 30
"sites," protection of 68
Skrydstrup, M. 188–191
Slaughter, J. R. 83, 115, 141
Slobodian, Q. 24
Smith, L. 63, 75, 105, 109, 136
social constitutionalism 196
socialmarket 196
solidarity 96, 105
sovereignty 83, 127, 132, 188
state and geo-politics 31–34
stewardship model 203–205
subject matter of copyright 166
sui generis protection 177
sui generis solution/s 205

tangibility 114–123
tangible and intangible stuff 112; community cultural practices 114; cultural heritage/property 114; cultural re-transmission 135; decontextualization of 134, 139; intellectual property 115; moveable *vs.* immoveable 113
tangible immoveable cultural heritage 125, 178, 179
tangible/intangible distinction 73, 112, 113
tangible moveables 178
tangible objects 22, 53, 57, 119
tattoos 1, 3, 105
taxonomic model 67
terminology, note on 6–7
"total market thinking" 6, 24, 26, 108, 109
tourism 126
trademarks 55
Trade-Related Aspects of Intellectual Property Rights (TRIPs Agreement) 13–16, 62, 66
tradition 180
traditional cultural expressions 55, 147, 148
traditional cultural property 55, 148
traditional knowledge 81, 148
"trans-boundary" works 9
transplanted law 125
trans-statal heritage community 79
Treaty of Westphalia of 1649 62
Turner, V. 171

Uluru–Kata Tjuta National Park in Central Australia 151–152
UN Charter on Economic Social and Cultural Rights (Article 15(1)(c)) 17, 18
underwater cultural heritage 64, 67
UNESCO Convention Concerning the Protection of the World Cultural and Natural Heritage (WHC) 66, 69, 72, 113, 124, 151, 179
UNESCO Convention for the Protection and Promotion of the Diversity of Cultural Expressions (CCD) 65, 66, 73, 87, 88, 135, 174, 179
UNESCO Convention for the Safeguarding of the Intangible Cultural Heritage (CICH) 65, 66, 68, 69, 71, 73, 74, 76–83, 86–88, 93, 114, 135, 136, 146, 148, 149, 153, 173, 174, 178, 179, 180, 188, 189, 190, 206
UNESCO Convention on the Means of Prohibiting and Preventing the Illicit, Import, Export and Transfer of Ownership of Cultural Property (1970) 65, 66, 69, 72, 89–90
UNESCO Conventions 62; commodification and privatization 126; community concept 70; "cultural diversity" concept 64; cultural landscape 154, 156; cultural property protection 64; expression "cultural heritage" 67–68; humanity operates, common heritage of 125; human rights 186; identity and continuity 69; immoveable cultural heritage 64; immoveable heritage, listing of 125; intangible cultural

heritage 64; international human rights law 63; international law by 184; moveable cultural property 64; pseudo-cosmopolitanism 100; trajectory and content of 64
UNESCO Intergovernmental Committee for the Safeguarding of the Intangible Cultural Heritage 149
UNESCO regime: "common heritage of mankind" 189; cultural heritage protection 187; cultural property/heritage 195; cultural self-determination 63; free trade ideology, dominance of 65; geo-political context 60–66; "innocent" purchasers 65; international policymaking 64; nature/culture distinction 151; neoliberalism 191; sovereignty, concept of 188; taxonomic model 67
UNIDROIT Convention on Stolen or Illegally Exported Cultural Objects (1995) 85, 93
United Nations Declaration on the Rights of Indigenous Peoples (DRIPs) 65, 86, 88
United Nations Guidelines for the Protection of the Heritage of Indigenous Peoples (1995) 115
Universal Declaration on Human Rights (Article 27(2)) 18

Verrines of Cicero 60
Vienna Convention on the Succession of States in Respect of State Property 61
Vienna Treaty of 1815 60, 138
Vrettos, A. 160

Waldron, J. 19
Wallace, A. 117, 120
Western capitalism 148; Western capitalist accumulation 34; Western capitalist culture 177; Western capitalist steamroller 157–158
Wirtén, Hemmungs 198
Wise, Christopher 144
World Intellectual Property Organization (WIPO) 13, 86
World Intellectual Property Organization's Intergovernmental Committee on Intellectual Property and Genetic Resources, Traditional Knowledge and Folklore (WIPO IGC) 86, 87
World Trade Organization (WTO) 13, 14, 62, 65

Yad Vashem Museum 128
Yolngu people 147
Yothu Yindi (musical band) 147

Zagato, L. 77
Zola, E. 144

For Product Safety Concerns and Information please contact our EU representative GPSR@taylorandfrancis.com
Taylor & Francis Verlag GmbH, Kaufingerstraße 24, 80331 München, Germany

www.ingramcontent.com/pod-product-compliance
Ingram Content Group UK Ltd.
Pitfield, Milton Keynes, MK11 3LW, UK
UKHW011006180926
475701UK00004B/601
* 9 7 8 0 3 6 7 6 2 0 8 7 5 *